National Geographic

Essential
Visual History
of the Bible

National Geographic

Essential
Visual History
of the Bible

☐ NATIONAL GEOGRAPHIC
Washington, D.C.

Table of Contents

Cherubim, see Angels, p. 42

The Serpent, see the Fall of Man and Original Sin, p. 40

The Pharaoh, see Moses, p. 114

Jephtha's daughter, p. 178

David and Jonathan, see Saul, p. 212

Hanukkah candlesticks, see the Maccabees, p. 290

Prophet Amos, see the Minor Prophets, p. 332

Mary with her mother Anne and the baby Jesus, p. 386

The three wise men with Jesus, Mary, and Joseph in Bethlehem, p. 395

The Pope, the Leader of the Catholic Church, p. 454

The Execution of Paul, p. 491

Elements of the Book

The bold text refers to the Testaments.

Colored tabs indicate the biblical epoch and chapter.

A **scripture quotation** gives a vivid impression of the given person.

The **main text** features the given person and identifies he or she within the proper historical and theological context.

Key facts summarize the significant chracteristics of the given person.

A **biographical sidebar** lists the most important events of the given person while indicating where to find **scripture references**.

Cross references to related topics in the book are given at the bottom of the page.

36 The Old Testament | FROM CREATION TO ENTERING THE PROMISED LAND

So God created humankind in his image, in the image of God he created them; male and female he created them. Genesis 1:27

■ Adam and Eve were the first people

■ There are two different versions of the creation of humanity

■ The Fall of humanity, the disobedience of Adam and Eve against the laws of God, is the start of the troublesome human existence

Adam and Eve

According to the first biblical account of creation, man and woman were created simultaneously. The second account tells a different story. First God created a garden, the "Garden of Eden." Then he formed a man out of dust before blowing the breath of life into his nostrils. This man was called Adam (**1**), as he was crafted, according to the biblical description, from earth—or "Adama" in Hebrew. This first man was lonely; something that even the introduction of animals could not change. Thus God decided to give him a "helper as a partner," as it is described in the Hebrew text. God made Adam fall asleep and he created Eve from Adam's rib. Adam and Eve were naked without feeling ashamed and knew nothing of good and evil.

A fruit doomed Adam and Eve

Genesis 1:26–28 God creates humans as main and woman

Genesis 2:7 God creates the first human from dust

Genesis 2:8–14 God plants the Garden of Eden

Genesis 2:21–22 God forms Eve from Adam's rib

Genesis 3:1–6 The serpent entices Eve to eat from the Tree of Knowledge

Genesis 3:14–15 God punishes the serpent for his role in the Fall of Man

Genesis 3:16–19 God punishes Adam and Eve

Genesis 3:23–24 God banishes Adam and Eve from paradise

Genesis 4:1–2 Eve gives birth to Cain and Abel

Figures and Stories Relevant to Adam and Eve

God, Creator of Adam and Eve, see pp. 28–33

Serpent, see the Fall of Man and Original Sin, pp. 40–41

Animals in the Bible, see Balaam and his Donkey, pp. 140–141

Adam and Eve's Offspring, see pp. 24–25

Cain and Abel, Sons of Adam and Eve, see pp. 44–45

✦)) God as Creator: p. 29

Framed boxes refer to stories and figures surrounding the given person.

Picture related text provide detailed information regarding selected events.

Each chapter starts with a **timeline** that povides a chronological overview.

From the Conquest of Canaan to the Judges

The Era of Conquest
Joshua
pp. 156–159

The 12 Tribes of Israel

Israel's Neighbors
The Canaanites
pp. 160–161

The Neighboring Peoples of Israel
pp. 160–161

From the Judges to the Kings
Samuel
pp. 196–197

Adam and Eve 37

...uction by the Serpent
...gave Adam and Eve the ...of cultivating the Garden ...en. They could eat from ...tree, except from the tree ...nowledge of good and evil. ...serpent [2] promised them

that by consuming the tree's fruit, they would become like God and know of good and evil. Eve wanted to obtain this knowledge so she ate from the tree and gave some of the fruit to Adam. Their eyes were

opened and they realized that they were naked. Adam and Eve felt ashamed so they used fig leaves as clothing. God discovered this misdeed when he found Adam hiding out of shame at being naked.

The Garden of Eden—Paradise

The second account of creation details the Garden of Eden, which is called a "paradise" in the Greek translation. This garden was watered by a river with four branches and had mineral-rich soil. The names of the river's branches cannot be traced to any existing river. The attempt to locate this region within the fertile land of Mesopotamia between the Euphrates and the Tigris is not likely to find any success, as it is a mythological location. Judaism, Christianity, and Islam all hold a conception of this paradise; however, each of these religions has its own take on its description and meaning.

Numbered picture references within the text match each image with its context.

Colored boxes summarize specific religious and cultural aspects.

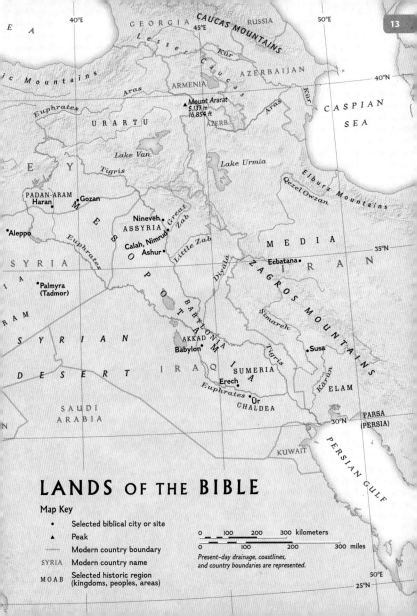

LANDS OF THE BIBLE

Map Key

- • Selected biblical city or site
- ▲ Peak
- — Modern country boundary
- SYRIA Modern country name
- MOAB Selected historic region (kingdoms, peoples, areas)

0 100 200 300 kilometers
0 100 200 300 miles

Present-day drainage, coastlines, and country boundaries are represented.

The Old Testament

The Old Testament forms the Jewish Bible, as well as the first part of the Christian Bible. In Latin, the word "testament" means both "legacy" and "alliance." Thus, the Hebrew Bible—as the Old Testament is often called today—is foremost the story of God's alliance with his people, the Israelites. In Judaism, the Bible is also known as the Tanach, based on the Hebrew acronym for its sections: Torah, prophets, and writings. The Hebrew Bible contains 39 books. The canon of the Catholic Church includes additional texts, such as the books of Judith and the Maccabees, which were passed down in Greek translation.

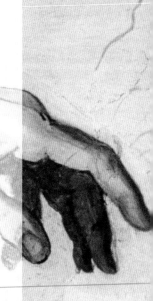

The Old Testament tells of God's special relationship with humanity.

From Creation to Entering the Promised Land

God with the first humans, Adam and Eve, in the Garden of Eden

From Creation to Entering

p. 29

p. 36

1800 *   1700

* The Bible is predominantly a theological, not historical, work. Most scholars doubt whether events such as the migration of Abraham or the flight out of Egypt happened precisely as they are depicted in the Bible. Attempts to date events or identify bibilical people with historical people remain speculation. Only from the time of the later kingdoms of Israel and Judah is it possible to attest some Bible stories through archaeological discoveries, non-biblical sources, or other findings. The dating of events before these kingdoms is dependent upon, for example, a comparison and analysis of archaeological finds that suggests changes in settlement structures.

p. 49

the Promised Land

p. 132

The Exodus From Egypt

p. 120

1600   1500   1400   1300   1200

The Patriarchs and Matriarchs

p. 60

p. 89

From Creation to Entering the Promised Land

The Torah, the first five books of Holy Scripture (Greek: "Pentateuch") (**2**), forms the foundation of the Hebrew Bible. It is repeatedly referred to in other parts of the Bible, including the New Testament. The Torah begins with God's creation of the world (**1**) in the Book of Genesis. The creation is the beginning of history, with its focus on all of humanity. The freedom granted to humans by God enabled Adam and Eve to disobey their creator's commands, resulting in their banishment from paradise. Afterward, chaotic conditions reigned on Earth, and the people became so corrupt that God planned to kill them all in a Great Flood. He stopped short of annihilation by saving Noah and his family. After the Flood, God formed a covenant with humans, promising to not kill them.

With Abraham, individual figures took on greater importance in the chronicles of God's actions: Abraham, his son Isaac, his grandson Jacob, and their wives Sarah, Rebekah, Leah, and Rachel became the patriarchs and matriarchs of Israel. Jacob, father of 12 sons, became ① the ancestor of the 12 Tribes of Israel. His son Joseph reached Egypt, later bringing his family to join him there.

The Book of Exodus began in Egypt, where the Israelites were forced into slavery under the pharaoh. God liberated them, and they traveled through the desert under Moses' leadership toward the Promised Land. God's intentional deliverance of the Israelites from slavery formed the foundation for the special relationship between God and Israel. On Mount Sinai, God gave Moses the Ten Commandments, the basic laws for his covenant with the people. The Israelites accepted them unanimously, sealing their position as "God's people."

The Ten Commandments include religious, ethical, and legal instructions. In addition, detailed directions for worship services and religious sacrifices are contained in the Book of Leviticus. The Book of Numbers presents additional commandments and describes the Israelites' 40 years of wandering through the desert. Finally, the fifth book of the Old Testament, Deuteronomy, again summarizes the instructions for life in God's Promised Land, in the form of a final address by Moses before his death, after which the Israelites moved into the land of Canaan under Joshua's leadership.

3

The Torah, which describes Israel's experiences, is history interpreted through the lens of theology. Thus, its statements does not necessarily coincide with the findings of historians. For example, scholars disagree about whether—and in what manner—a group of Israelites fled from Egypt (**3**). The circumstances surrounding the occupation of Canaan are also unclear.

The word Torah means "teaching"—God's instructions for a successful life. It has been compared to a "tree of life" and to milk and honey. Psalm 119 describes the joy associated with studying the Torah and following God's laws.

"The laws take their meaning from history. Only those who remember the flight out of Egypt know that the law means freedom and are in a position to obey it," explains cultural and religious historian Jan Assmann.

Until the 17th century, the Torah (**4**, illustrated page from a medieval Torah) was considered the work of Moses and a direct revelation from God. However, viewed literally, the Pentateuch is not a consistently unified work; in fact, it contains numerous contradictions. Increasingly, doubts arose about Moses' authorship. For example, how can Moses describe his own death? In addition, the scriptures contain two creation stories, each with different points of emphasis. In the story of the Great Flood, repetitions and contradictions can also be found. There are also noticeable differences in language within individual texts, as well as among the various books. Scholars are now convinced that the Torah is not the work of a single author, but was assembled from a number of different sources. Various models have been developed to explain this process, including the "basic text" hypothesis (other texts were added to a basic text); the "source" hypothesis (a number of sources were joined together), the "narrative circle" hypothesis (assorted narratives related to a theme or person were combined); and Wellhausen's theory, which hypothesizes four sources, designated by the letters Y, E, D, and P. The source Y (referring to the use of YHWH as the name for God) stands for Yahwist, created around 950 B.C.E.; E is for Elohite (using Elohim as a name for God), from around 800 B.C.E.; D is the Deuteronomist and the Deuteronomist revision, in 622 B.C.E.; and P is the "priestly" text or the priests' additions during the Babylonian exile, around 550 B.C.E. None of these models have been fully accepted. It appears that the process took place over a period of time and involved numerous text versions. The Torah took on its final form at a relatively late date, probably around 400 B.C.E.

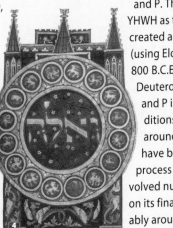

The Family Tree

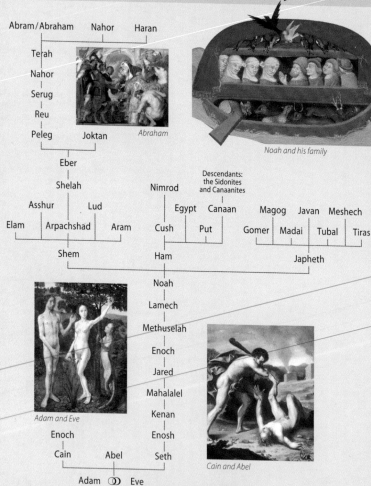

Abram/Abraham — Nahor — Haran
Terah
Nahor
Serug
Reu
Peleg — Joktan
Eber
Shelah
Asshur — Lud
Elam — Arpachshad — Aram
Shem

Abraham

Noah and his family

Nimrod

Descendants:
the Sidonites
and Canaanites

Egypt — Canaan
Cush — Put
Ham

Magog — Javan — Meshech
Gomer — Madai — Tubal — Tiras
Japheth

Noah
Lamech
Methuselah
Enoch
Jared
Mahalalel
Kenan
Enosh

Adam and Eve

Enoch
Cain — Abel — Seth
Adam ⚭ Eve

Cain and Abel

The family trees are abbreviated and refer to only the most important people.

From Adam to David

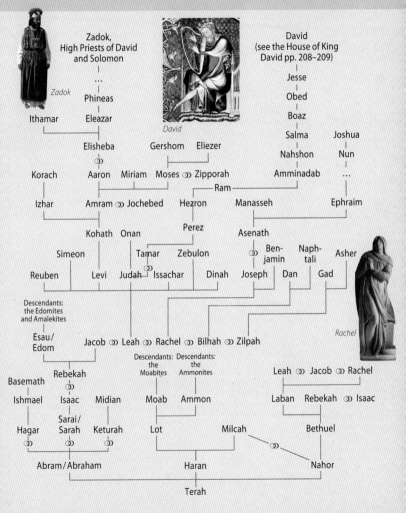

Zadok,
High Priests of David
and Solomon

Zadok

...

Phineas

Ithamar — Eleazar

Elisheba

Korach — Aaron — Miriam — Moses ⚭ Zipporah

Izhar — Amram ⚭ Jochebed

Kohath — Onan

Simeon — Tamar — Zebulon

Reuben — Levi — Judah — Issachar — Dinah

Descendants:
the Edomites
and Amalekites

Esau/
Edom — Jacob ⚭ Leah ⚭ Rachel ⚭ Bilhah ⚭ Zilpah

Descendants: Descendants:
the the
Moabites Ammonites

Basemath — Rebekah
⚭

Ishmael — Isaac — Midian — Moab — Ammon

Hagar — Sarai/ — Keturah
Sarah

Lot — Milcah

Abram/Abraham — Haran — Nahor

Terah

David

Gershom — Eliezer

Ram

Hezron — Manasseh

Perez — Asenath

Benjamin — Naphtali — Asher

Joseph — Dan — Gad

David
(see the House of King
David pp. 208–209)

Jesse

Obed

Boaz

Salma — Joshua

Nahshon — Nun

Amminadab — ...

Ephraim

Rachel

Leah ⚭ Jacob ⚭ Rachel

Laban — Rebekah ⚭ Isaac

Bethuel

Nahor

Creation—The First Day and the Origin of Humanity

Genesis 1:1–5, 26–28

¹ *In the beginning when God created the heavens and the earth,*

² *the earth was a formless void and darkness covered the face of the deep, while a wind from God swept over the face of the waters.*

³ *Then God said, "Let there be light"; and there was light.*

⁴ *And God saw that the light was good; and God separated the light from the darkness.*

⁵ *God called the light Day, and the darkness he called Night. And there was evening and there was morning, the first day.*

... ²⁶ Then God said, "Let us make humankind in our image, according to our likeness; and let them have dominion over the fish of the sea, and over the birds of the air, and over the cattle, and over all the wild animals of the earth, and over every creeping thing that creeps upon the earth."

²⁷ *So God created humankind in his image, in*

the image of God he created them;
male and female he created them.
28 God blessed them, and God said to
them, "Be fruitful and
multiply, and

fill the earth and subdue it; and have
dominion over the fish of the sea and
over the birds of the air and over
every living thing that moves upon
the earth."

■ According to the Bible, God is the creator of the Earth and all beings

■ God is conceived of as a personal figure

■ For most Christians, God is the unity of Father, Son, and Holy Spirit

Genesis 1:1–2; 2:4–5 God creates the world

Genesis 9:1–17 God makes a covenant with Noah

Genesis 15:1–21 God makes a covenant with Abraham

Exodus 3:2 God appears to Moses in a burning thorn bush

Exodus 32:7–10 God is angry with the people for praying to an idol of a golden bull

Exodus 33:11 God speaks with Moses as a friend

Exodus 40:1–33 God tells Moses to keep the Ten Commandments safe within the Tabernacle of the ark

Matthew 28:19 Believers are baptized in the name of the Father, Son, and Holy Spirit

Luke 15:11–32 Parable of the prodigal son shows God's love

O Lord, how manifold are your works! In wisdom you have made them all; the earth is full of your creatures. Psalm 104:24

God

The concept of a single God is deeply rooted in the consciousness of practicing Jews and Christians. According to some historians of religion, the development of the concept of God in Israel's past can be traced from polytheism, through monolatrism, to monotheism. At first, faith resided in many gods (polytheism). Then many people converted to worshiping only one god without actually denying the existence of others (monolatrism). In the end, there was faith in only one God (monotheism).

In the Hebrew Bible there is a great diversity in the conceptions of God. He is described as a shepherd, a king, a warrior, a father (**1**), but also as a mother and as the husband of the people of Israel. Their God is the God of all humankind, but he holds a special bond with the Israelites. ▷▷

▷▷ **The Cult of Baal:** pp. 168–169

God as Creator God created the world and he preserves it. Everything that exists was brought to pass by God and is "very good." In the first two chapters of the Bible, two different stories of creation stand side by side. In the first, there is an elaborate description of the various stages of creation. First God created the heavens and the earth, and then ordered the elements so that day and night along with the seas and continents came into being (**2**). After this came the creation of plants, animals, and finally humans. God spoke and through his words came life. The second creation myth places the creation of humankind as its focus. God formed Adam out of dust and blew life into his nostrils. Later God created Eve from one of Adam's ribs (**3**). God's function as a creator is also emphasized in the Psalms, where he is praised and thanked for the wonders he brought into being.

Figures and Stories Relevant to God

Adam, see pp. 36–39

Eve, see pp. 36–39

Angels, God's Messengers, see pp. 42–43

Noah, see pp. 46–49

Abraham, see pp. 60–63

Judaism, Christianity, and Islam, see Abrahamic Religions, pp. 66–67

Moses, see pp. 110–115 and 120–125

The Ten Commandments, see pp. 126–127

God's Covenant With Israel, see pp. 142–143

Job, see pp. 346–349

Jesus of Nazareth, see pp. 402–409; 414–419

Sabbath

After the creation of the world, God rested. In remembrance of this day of rest, Jews to this day celebrate Sabbath, or Shabbat as it is called in Hebrew. To celebrate the importance of this day, Jews are not allowed to work, but rather to celebrate, pray, and study. The Sabbath begins at sundown on Friday night when the woman of the household lights two candles. It ends on Saturday evening with a special ceremony.

According to biblical conceptions, God is a living God, who shows himself to humanity and takes care of it. An assortment of stories in the Bible depict various encounters and experiences of humanity with God. The bond between God and humanity is shown in the many covenants (pp. 142–143), the first of which was made between God and Noah (p. 48), and followed by the covenant with Abraham (p. 62) and then with Moses and the people of Israel at Sinai. There, the Israelites received the Ten Commandments from God, which were kept safe in the ark, a transportable vessel (**4**). Later, the ark was installed at the Temple of Solomon. ⟫⟫

4

Theodicy—Is God Just?

The concept of justice plays a great role in the Hebrew Bible. God does not only show his justice by judging, but also in the formulation of laws, with which he shows humankind the holy order. However the impression left by human suffering leads people to question the justification of God, which is known as theodicy (p. 503). If God is omnipotent, why does he allow so much suffering? One can observe in the Psalms that the question of "why?" is changed into "how much longer, God?" Even Job (pp. 346–349) asked this question in the face of his torments and God refused to give him answers.

Appearances of God God shows himself to people in various ways, such as a burning bush (**5**) with Moses. When asked who he was, God replied: "I am who I am." In this phrase God implied his elusiveness but also his reliability. Later, God spoke with Moses face to face, "like a man with his friend"; on another occasion, however, he said that no man would be able to see his countenance. On Mount Sinai, God showed himself to the Israelites in the form of thunder and earthquakes.

The Tetragrammaton The name of God consists of four consonants: YHWH, which is known as the tetragrammaton (**6**). Historians assume that the name "Yahweh" was vocalized. When this name appears in the Hebrew Bible it is read out as "Adonai" (Hebrew: "Lord"). Numerous Christian translations follow this tradition by using the word "Lord" at these points. The inability to say the name of God out loud is an expression of his elusiveness. This is also expressed in the commandment banning the making of images of God. In the story of the golden bull, the people of Israel break this law (**7**) (pp. 121, 136).

The conceptions of God in the New Testament were built from the traditional depictions in the Hebrew Bible. In the Gospels, there are a range of parables, many of which emblematize God's works. One of these is the parable of the Prodigal Son (p. 408) (**8**). This parable expresses God's joy when people who have strayed return and accept his love. This caring devotion of God toward humanity has been particularly emphasized in the second half of the 20th century. A separation of the qualities of God between the two testaments is not possible, as God acts in both as a simultaneously punishing and loving God.

The Trinity In the Christian conception of the Trinity, God appears in three different persons: as Father (creator), Son (savior), and Holy Spirit (**9**,**10**). Teachings on the Trinity are not explicitly stated in the Bible. Rather, this idea was developed by a long process of theological and political confrontations. It was not until the Councils of Nicaea and Constantinople that the Trinity was made a standard part of church doctrine. From the Jewish and Muslim perspectives the question has been and is still being posed as to whether the concept of the Trinity can be made to fit with the idea of a singular God.

Where Is God Present? The presence of God, according to biblical conceptions, can be experienced in a variety of ways, even in everyday life. Since the destruction of the Temple in 70 C.E. (pp. 372–373) there has been no specific sanctum for Judaism. Humanity has been able to congregate anywhere to call upon God. Among Christians, it is debated whether there is a presence of God in church buildings (**12**).

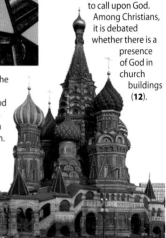

The Qualities of God A range of properties is attributed to God in the Bible. First and foremost God is a savior, as he rescued the people of Israel from Egyptian slavery (p. 112). He is holy, merciful, omniscient (**11**), graceful, and patient, but also reprimanding and jealous. God punishes when he wants to regulate human righteousness by having them experience the consequences of their sin. He is jealous because he is a living God, who has a covenant with humankind. As he is the God of his people, he should be the only God of his people. This is a God who takes part in the fate of his creation. He is not an abstract principle, but is instead described in a variety of images that are oriented toward human experiences and characteristics.

Pantheism and Conceptions of God

Alongside the biblical images of God there are also many other variant conceptions of a deity. Some of the modern conceptions of such deities, which have predominantly developed within the field of philosophy, are pantheism, panentheism, and deism. Pantheism sees God in all things. In this way God is not thought of as distinct from the world, but rather as being identical with the cosmos as a whole. In panentheism, the whole world exists in God, as God exists in the whole world and is not transcendent to it. Deism, on the other hand, views God as the world's creator but has no further influence over what transpires.

⏩ **Temples and Synagogues:** p. 368

The Creation of the First Man and Woman

Genesis 2:21–25

21 *So the Lord God caused a deep sleep to fall upon the man, and he slept; then he took one of his ribs and closed up its place with flesh.*
22 *And the rib that the Lord God had taken from the man he made into a woman and brought her to the man.*
23 *Then the man said, "This at last is bone of my bones and flesh of my flesh; this one shall be called Woman, for out of Man this one was taken."*
24 *Therefore a man leaves his father and his mother and clings to his wife, and they become one flesh.*
25 *And the man and his wife were both naked, and were not ashamed.*

■ Adam and Eve were the first people

■ There are two different versions of the creation of humanity

■ The Fall of humanity, the disobedience of Adam and Eve against the laws of God, is the start of the troublesome human existence

Genesis 1:26–28 God creates humans as man and woman

Genesis 2:7 God creates the first human from dust

Genesis 2:8–14 God plants the Garden of Eden

Genesis 2:21–22 God forms Eve from Adam's rib

Genesis 3:1–6 The serpent entices Eve to eat from the Tree of Knowledge

Genesis 3:14–15 God punishes the serpent for his role in the Fall of Man

Genesis 3:16–19 God punishes Adam and Eve

Genesis 3:23–24 God banishes Adam and Eve from paradise

Genesis 4:1–2 Eve gives birth to Cain and Abel

Genesis 4:25 Adam and Eve conceive Seth

Genesis 5:1–32 The list of descendants from Adam to Noah

So God created humankind in his image, in the image of God he created them; male and female he created them. Genesis 1:27

Adam and Eve

A fruit doomed Adam and Eve

According to the first biblical account of creation, man and woman were created simultaneously. The second account tells a different story. First God created a garden, the "Garden of Eden." Then he formed a man out of dust before blowing the breath of life into his nostrils. This man was called Adam (**1**), as he was crafted, according to the biblical description, from earth—or "Adama" in Hebrew. This first man was lonely; something that even the introduction of animals could not change. Thus God decided to give him a "helper as a partner," as it is described in the Hebrew text. God made Adam fall asleep and he created Eve from Adam's rib. Adam and Eve were naked without feeling ashamed and knew nothing of good and evil.

①

» **God as Creator:** p. 29

Seduction by the Serpent

God gave Adam and Eve the task of cultivating the Garden of Eden. They could eat from any tree, except from the tree of knowledge of good and evil. The serpent (**2**) promised them that by consuming the tree's fruit, they would become like God and know of good and evil. Eve wanted to obtain this knowledge so she ate from the tree and gave some of the fruit to Adam. Their eyes were opened and they realized that they were naked. Adam and Eve felt ashamed so they used fig leaves as clothing. God discovered this misdeed when he found Adam hiding out of shame at being naked.

The Garden of Eden—Paradise

The second account of creation details the Garden of Eden, which is called a "paradise" in the Greek translation. This garden was watered by a river with four branches and had mineral-rich soil. The names of the river's branches cannot be traced to any existing river. The attempt to locate this region within the fertile land of Mesopotamia between the Euphrates and the Tigris is not likely to find any success, as it is a mythological location. Judaism, Christianity, and Islam all hold a conception of this paradise; however, each of these religions has its own take on its description and meaning.

Exile From Paradise When God discovered that Adam and Eve had disobeyed him by eating from the Tree of Knowledge, they—as well as the serpent—had to bear the consequences of their actions. God took away the serpent's legs, forcing it to crawl from that point on. Both Adam and Eve were banished from the garden. Eve would have to bear children under great pain and Adam would be her master. Adam would have to work hard for his life's sustenance. The time of a carefree life spent in close proximity to God was over. He positioned an angel with a flaming sword (**3**) in front of the garden so that no one could break back in. In spite of the banishment, God still cared for Adam and Eve, and made garments to clothe them.

Adam and Eve Living in Exile With Cain and Abel

After their banishment from their carefree lives in the Garden of Eden, Adam and Even slept with one another and Eve became pregnant. She had Cain first, then his brother Abel (**4**). Adam and Eve's insubordination against God's laws made them become mortal. They were created from the earth and after their deaths would become earth once more. Yet the loss of their immortal life in God's garden did grant Adam and Eve knowledge of good and evil, which was previously reserved only for God himself. The story of the Fall of Man into sin and of exile from paradise serves to explain why humans are mortal and why humanity must earn its sustenance under such adverse conditions. In this regard it is less a justification for current circumstances, than an attempt to explain how they came to be that way.

Figures and Stories Relevant to Adam and Eve

God, Creator of Adam and Eve, see pp. 28–33

Serpent, see the Fall of Man and Original Sin, pp. 40–41

Animals in the Bible, see Balaam and His Donkey, pp. 140–141

Adam and Eve's Offspring, see pp. 24–25

Cain and Abel, Sons of Adam and Eve, see pp. 44–45

Noah, Descendant of Adam and Eve, see pp. 46–49

The Offspring of Adam

According to the Bible, Adam and Eve are the progenitors of humanity (**5**, Adam and his offspring up to Methuselah). Abel was beaten to death by his brother Cain. Soon after Abel's death, Eve became pregnant again and bore Seth. Cain sired a single son, Enoch. The first people of the Bible had unusually long lifespans, the greatest of which was Methuselah, Noah's grandfather, who died at the very old age of 969 years.

The Fall of Man and Original Sin

The phrases "Fall of Man and "original sin" are Christian concepts. Both are not found within the Hebrew texts. In Genesis 3 there is, of course, an account of Adam and Eve's (**2**) defiance of God's laws and their exile from the Garden of Eden. However, it is only in the Christian tradition that the idea is put forward that this act of disobedience caused original sin to be passed from one generation to the next through the very act of procreation. Before the Fall of Man, people were free to do as they wished, including to sin or not to sin. This freedom was lost through the Fall. Through the grace of God, which Christians experience at their baptism, they regain—

Saint Augustine has himself baptized. Augustine of Hippo (died 430 C.E.) is regarded as one of the most significant Christian church leaders and, among other things, preached about original sin.

according to the church father Augustine—the freedom to choose to sin or not to sin. The Jewish tradition interprets the banishment of humankind in a different way. Humankind was indeed made mortal due to the disobedience of Adam and Eve, but this did not rob people of their freedom to act according to the will of God. The nature of man did not, therefore, undergo a fundamental change.

The Significance of the Serpent The serpent or snake (**1**) is described in the Bible as the "craftiest of all the animals that God had made." In the Jewish tradition they are linked with slander. Passages from Psalm 140:3 speak of men who have forked tongues like snakes and viper poison under their lips. In the Christian tradition, serpents represent evil, for example, when the reformer Martin Luther saw Satan speaking from out of the snakes' mouths.

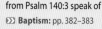

⟫ **Baptism:** pp. 382–383

(**1**)

Genesis 3:24 The cherubim guard paradise

Genesis 19:1–3 Two angels find Lot in Sodom

Genesis 22:11–12 An angel stops Abraham from sacrificing his son Isaac

Genesis 32:22–30 Jacob fights an angel by the Zarqa River

Exodus 3:1–4 An angel appears to Moses on Mount Horeb

Numbers 22:22–35 An angel appears to Balaam and his donkey

II Samuel 24:16–18 An angel enforces David's

I Kings 19:5–8 An angel appears to Elijah on Mount Horeb

Daniel 6:17–24 An angel protects Daniel in the lions' den

Daniel 10–12 Daniel and the archangel Michael

Luke 1:26–38 Gabriel announces the birth of Jesus to Mary

John 20:11–13 Two angels appear to Mary Magdalene by the tomb of Jesus

He placed the cherubim, and a sword flaming and turning to guard the way to the tree of life. Genesis 3:24

Angels

Angels are the messengers of God and are able to appear to people in various ways. They are also referred to in the Bible as "God," "the children of God," or "holy beings." The secretive being that wrestles with Jacob by the river Jabbok is interpreted as being an angel (p. 90), but is first identified in the text as a man, then later as God.

The Bible mentions cherubim (**1**) and seraphim—angelic beings—which hold a variety of offices. According to Isaiah 6:3, seraphim belong to God's household and sing a song of praise, the "holy, holy, holy," which is a part of Christian and Jewish liturgy. The prophet Ezekiel describes God as sitting on a throne, being transported by four cherubim.

Angels in Islam

The Qur'an mentions the angels Michael and Gabriel, who also appear in the Bible. The Muslim tradition also recognizes Raphael and Azrael, the angel of death. These four angels play a significant role in Islam. Those who do not believe in angels belong to the "strayed," according to Surah 4.

The Three Archangels and Lucifer In the Catholic tradition, Michael, Gabriel, and Raphael are known as the archangels (**3**). Often wielding a flaming sword, Michael is depicted in the Book of Revelation throwing the dragon out of heaven. Michael is the master of the cherubim and seraphim; his symbol is the lily. Raphael, who stands by the faithful, is often painted as a pilgrim with a rod, flask, and fish. The Christian conception of Lucifer is as an angel who sets himself up against God and is consequently banished.

Fallen Angels Genesis 6, which describes prehistory, speaks of the sons of God, heavenly beings, who find pleasure in the daughters of humans. According to mythological conceptions, such unions produced giants. In the Hebrew Bible, Satan is named as an angel who, in the service of God, judged the righteousness of humanity and punished accordingly, but he does not represent the devil. The idea of fallen angels (**2**) first appeared in post-biblical literature.

■ Cain murders his brother Abel out of jealousy

Genesis 4:1–2 Adam and Eve conceive their sons Cain and Abel

Genesis 4:3–5 Cain and Abel make sacrifices to God

Genesis 4:8 Cain kills his brother Abel

Genesis 4:9–12 Cain is cursed by God

Genesis 4:15 God places a mark upon Cain

And when they were in the field, Cain rose up against his brother Abel and killed him. Genesis 4:8

Cain and Abel

Biblical human history outside of the Garden of Eden begins with a case of fratricide. Cain and Abel were the sons of Adam and Eve; Cain was a farmer, Abel a shepherd. When both of them brought a sacrifice to God, Abel's was to God's satisfaction whereas Cain's was not (**1**). Angered, Cain murdered his brother in a field. When God asked Cain where his brother was, he answered: "I do not know; am I my brother's keeper?"

Since the Fall (p. 40–41), humankind has had an awareness of good and evil and thus has been in a position to act morally. Because humans constantly committed evil deeds, God took action. He punished Cain for murdering his brother by ending the close relationship they shared. However, even the punishment of murder had its limits: God forbade the arbitrary punishment of murder by humans. For the success of communal life, God made rules for human behavior.

Figures and Stories Relevant to Cain and Abel

God, see pp. 28–33

Adam and Eve, see pp. 36–39

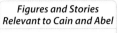

God's Punishment God punished Cain for Abel's murder (**2**) in two ways: Cain would always remain a wanderer and no field would yield a crop for him; secondly Cain had to depart and move to the Land of Nod, where his wife brought Enoch into the world. As Cain was afraid of being killed by other men (**3**), God gave him a sign, the mark of Cain. This warned that if anyone were to attack Cain, God would punish them sevenfold for it.

Sacrifice

The Israelites developed a sacrificial cult, the center of which was the Temple of Jerusalem (p. 368). The first seven chapters of Leviticus are dedicated to this topic. There was a range of different types of sacrifice, such as sacrifices of thanks and sacrifices of atonement, which were supposed to make amends for transgressions of God's laws. On Yom Kippur, the Day of Atonement, the entire people would make sacrifices for their wrongdoing. The destruction of the Temple in 70 C.E. ended the sacrificial cult.

▶▶ **Yom Kippur:** pp. 138–139

■ Noah, his family, and various species of animals survive the Great Flood

Genesis 6:13–22 Noah builds the ark

Genesis 7:10–24 God's Flood exterminates all life on the Earth

Genesis 8:8–12 Noah lets a dove loose

Genesis 8:20–22 Noah's sacrifice and God's promise

Genesis 9:1–17 God's pact with Noah

Genesis 9:20–22 Ham sees the nakedness of his father Noah

These are the descendants of Noah. Noah was a righteous man, blameless in his generation; Noah walked with God. Genesis 6:9

Noah

Beginning with Cain killing his brother (p. 44), the freedom that God had given to humankind was continuously abused. Noah's contemporaries were violent and depraved, so God decided to wipe out everyone and everything. Noah was the only one worthy of clemency in God's eyes because he was "righteous and blameless." God gave him the task of building an ark (**1**) so that he, his family, and all species of animals would survive the coming Flood planned by God. Shortly afterward, this formidable Flood destroyed all human life on the Earth, leaving only Noah and his family alive.

When the waters subsided, Noah and his family left the ark. Noah built an altar and made a sacrifice to God. This prompted God to make a promise that he would never again make an attempt to exterminate humanity. In the Jewish tradition, the seven Noachian Laws developed from this first covenant between God and humanity.

①

Noah Collects the Animals

The biblical texts about the Flood are not consistent. According to Genesis 6, God's mission for Noah was to take a pair of each animal with him in the ark (**2**), but then it says in Genesis 7 that he was to take seven pairs of the clean animals and only one pair of those deemed unclean. In one account, the name YHWH is used for God and the Flood lasts 40 nights. In the other account, the name Elohim is used, the ark is described in detail, and the Flood continues for 300 days. Historical-critical (p. 501) interpretations of the Bible assume that two different stories about Noah were blended into one in this case. The Bible—in particular the five books of Moses—developed over a long time in which various traditions were assembled together in written form.

Humanity Drowns in the Rains of the Flood

After the completion of the ark, God sent out a Flood that covered the Earth. The waters reached so high that even the mountains were covered. All life forms, other than those that were brought onto the ark by Noah, were drowned (**3**).

⯈⯈ The Name of God: p. 31

The worship of false gods, blasphemy, the spilling of blood, thievery, sexual offenses, and cruelty to animals were all prohibited by this code. It was ordered that legal practices be put in place. Compliance with these rules would make it possible for gentiles (non-Jews) to be a part of the "world to come," the Jewish conception of the afterlife.

God realized that man's capability to do evil was an integral part of being human. In order to stem violence, laws would have to be put in place that held one accountable for his actions. As a sign of his promise to never again destroy humanity, God placed a rainbow (**4**) in the sky (pp. 142–143).

Dove With an Olive Branch

After the Flood, the waters receded and Noah's ark was planted upon the summit of Mount Ararat. To check if it was safe to leave, Noah sent out a raven that came back because it could not find a place to land.

Next, he sent out a dove (**5**), which returned with an olive branch. On the third attempt, it did not return. Doves hold significance, especially in the Christian tradition, as they represent the spirit of God. For example, when Jesus was baptized by John the Baptist in the River Jordan, the Holy Spirit descended upon him "like a dove" (p. 404).

Noah's Sons See the Naked Body of Their Drunken Father
Noah planted a vineyard and enjoyed its wine so much that one day he fell asleep drunk and naked. His son Ham hap-pened upon him and informed his brothers Shem and Japheth. The two brothers covered up Noah's body without looking at him (**6**). When Noah discovered that his son Ham had seen him naked, he cursed Ham's son, Canaan (p. 55) while he praised and blessed his sons Shem and Japheth. Noah lived long after the Flood and died at the "bib-lical" age of 950.

Figures and Stories Relevant to Noah

God, see pp. 28–33

Cain and Abel, pp. 44–45

Noah's Sons, see Shem, Ham, and Japheth, pp. 54–55

The Tower of Babel, see pp. 58–59

The Ten Commandments, see pp. 120–121

Animals in the Bible, see Balaam and His Donkey, pp. 140–141

God's Covenant With Israel, see pp. 142–143

The Holy Spirit, see pp. 466–467

Prehistory

The first 11 chapters of the Bible form a single unit that de-scribes creation, which was considered by God himself to be "very good"; but also the behavior of humankind, which cannot be described positively. They begin with a violation of the laws of God (pp. 36–37), and then continue with fratricide (pp. 44–45) and further acts of violence. Instead of wiping out all life, God formed a covenant with humanity. The building of the Tower of Babel (pp. 58–59) and the dis-persal of humanity, as well as the explanation for the variety of languages in the world, bring the Bible's description of prehistory to a close in the 11th chapter of Genesis.

⏩ **The Curse:** p. 55 **Stories of the Patriarchs:** p. 88

The Great Flood

Mythological tales of floods are widespread in the Middle East. The structures of the stories have many similarities. The respective gods decide to annihilate the sinful elements of humanity through a worldwide flood (**3**). However, a righteous man, standing in the favor of the specific god(s), is spared. In the Sumerian tale, the survivor's name is Ziusudra, in the Assyrian variant it is Atra-Hasis, and in the Sumerian Epic of Gilgamesh it is Utnapishtim.

Academics attest that a literary dependence exists between the biblical texts and the lore of the Fertile Crescent, but there are also stories about floods that do not share such a literary dependence while still exhibiting similar motifs. An example of this is the Deucalion flood from Greek mythology.

Deucalion Flood The Greek tale of the Deucalion flood (**2**) describes the plot of the god Zeus to destroy humanity. The Titan, Prometheus, told his son, Deucalion, to build a ship so that he and his wife Pyrrha could survive. The flood lasted for nine days and nine nights. To repopulate the world, Deucalion and Pyrrha threw stones, which turned into people.

Gilgamesh The Epic of Gilgamesh is an anonymously composed Babylonian poem from the second century B.C.E. The tale centers around Gilgamesh (**1**), the son of a king. Utnapishtim, a forefather of Gilgamesh, was the only one who knew about the gods' plan to wipe out humanity. Along with animals, he took his property, all of his relatives, and all of his workmen with him on the "ark," which he built at the behest of one of the gods. After the end of the flood, Utnapishtim let a dove, a swallow, and a raven fly away to investigate whether they could leave the ark. In contrast to the Bible's rendition, the dove took on the first attempt at flight and the raven the last.

The Great Flood—
God Destroys Sinful Humanity

Genesis 7:10–15, 17, 19, 23

10 And after seven days the waters of the flood came on the earth. **11** All the fountains of the great deep burst forth, and the windows of the heavens were opened. **12** The rain fell on the earth for forty days and forty nights. **13** On the very same day Noah with his sons, Shem and Ham and Japheth, and Noah's wife and the three wives of his sons, entered the ark, **14** they and

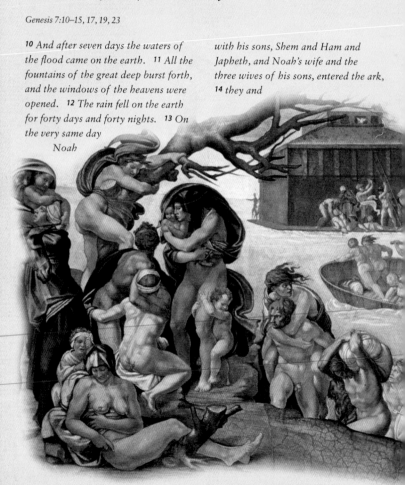

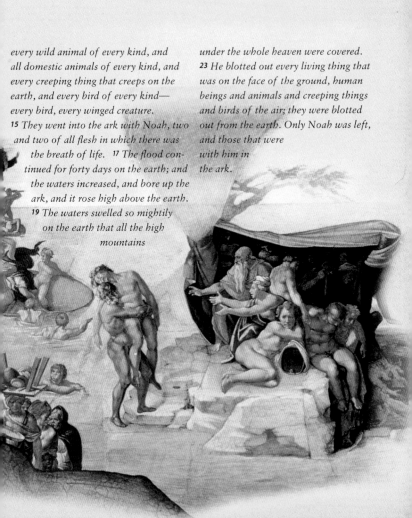

every wild animal of every kind, and all domestic animals of every kind, and every creeping thing that creeps on the earth, and every bird of every kind— every bird, every winged creature. 15 They went into the ark with Noah, two and two of all flesh in which there was the breath of life. 17 The flood continued for forty days on the earth; and the waters increased, and bore up the ark, and it rose high above the earth. 19 The waters swelled so mightily on the earth that all the high mountains under the whole heaven were covered. 23 He blotted out every living thing that was on the face of the ground, human beings and animals and creeping things and birds of the air; they were blotted out from the earth. Only Noah was left, and those that were with him in the ark.

■ Noah's sons are the forefathers of all the world

Genesis 7:13 Shem, Ham, and Japheth survive the Flood on the ark with their father Noah

Genesis 9:24–27 Noah curses Ham's son Canaan

Genesis 10 The Table of Nations

Ezekiel 38; Revelation 20:7–10 Gog and Magog fight in the final battle

God blessed Noah and his sons, and said to them, "Be fruitful and multiply, and fill the earth." Genesis 9:1

Shem, Ham, and Japheth

Shem, Ham, and Japheth were the three sons of Noah, who survived the Flood along with their parents and spouses. Genesis 10 describes the Table of Nations (pp. 24–25), the descendants of the sons of Noah, their children, their children's children, and the nations that derived from their lineage. These nations settled around Israel from the Caucasus to Ethiopia and from the Aegean to Iran.

The Israelites—descendents of Shem—seem to have not existed as a people from the outset, but rather appear first as individuals such as Abraham. Initially, God only made an alliance with the patriarchs. It was not until later, on Mount Sinai, that he held a covenant (pp. 142–143) with Israel. An assembly of tribes emerged (**1**) and increasingly distinguished itself through its religion.

Noah Curses Canaan One day, Ham discovered his father naked and drunk in a tent and informed his brothers (p. 49). When Noah awoke he was angry at Ham's disrespect and cursed Ham's son Canaan (**2**), saying that he would be a slave to Shem and Japheth. The story served to justify the Israelites' claim of supremacy over Ham's descendants, the Canaanites. These people were the neighbors and competitors of the Israelites, who were said to originate from Shem.

2

Gog and Magog In the Table of Nations, Magog is mentioned as one of Japheth's sons. The visions of Ezekiel and the Revelation to John both state that Magog will enter into a final battle together with Gog. They will fight until God destroys them, demonstrating his might. In the Middle Ages, Gog and Magog were considered wild peoples from the north (**3**).

The Curse

A curse is the opposite of a blessing. As a blessing holds a restorative power within it, so a curse wields a power that brings about a disaster. The power to curse or to bless other humans is as much a power of God as it is of humanity: God cursed Cain for killing his brother; Noah cursed Ham. Cursing and blessing do not belong exclusively to the world of religion, but rather are part of everyday life.

3

▶▶ **Blessing:** p. 79

■ The Bible identifies Nimrod as the first sovereign

■ The figure of Nimrod embodies humanity's struggle for power

Genesis 10:8; I Chronicles 1:10 Nimrod is the first sovereign

Genesis 10:9 Nimrod is a great hunter

Genesis 10:10–12 Nimrod rules over Babylon, Akkad, and Assyria and founds cities

Genesis 11:1–9 Tower of Babel

Nimrod ... was the first on earth to become a mighty warrior. He was a mighty hunter before the Lord. Genesis 10:8–9

Nimrod

Nimrod was the son of Cush and the grandson of Ham, who, along with his descendants, was cursed by Noah. The Bible mentions Nimrod only briefly in the Table of Nations of Genesis 10 and I Chronicles 1. Nimrod, whose passion for hunting has become proverbial, was described as the first man to ever win power on Earth and as the first sovereign figure in human history. The Bible attributes to him the rule of Babylon, Akkad, and Assyria, which were three large powers in the ancient Middle East.

The Jewish tradition views Nimrod as a rebel against God. To this end his name is construed as "he who instigates all humankind against God." According to this tradition, Nimrod was also the original erector of the Tower of Babel (**1**) (pp. 58–59), which is referred to in rabbinic lore as "the house of Nimrod."

Nimrod and the Hunt

Nimrod's attributes typified a monarch of the ancient Middle East. Along with construction projects and the founding of cities, hunting (**2**) also displayed the prowess of a leader. In war, a ruler would have to prove himself as a warrior, but during peace, hunting was sufficient to show strength and courage.

Nimrod and Abraham

The Qur'an details the story of a ruler who wanted to throw Abraham into a fire oven because he refused to worship foreign gods. Both the Muslim and Jewish traditions believe that Nimrod was this ruler. According to Jewish lore, Nimrod will be called up after the coming of the Messiah to prove that Abraham never prayed to false idols.

The Tower of Babel

At the beginning of Genesis 11, humankind spoke the same language. Worried that their community could fall apart, they planned to build a tower (**2**) that would be so high that its summit would reach heaven. This not only displeased God, but he also feared they could actually achieve this task if they worked together. Therefore he obliterated the tower and saw to it that people were spread out and spoke different languages.

Model of a Babylonian ziggurat

In the Christian tradition, the story of the tower is interpreted as a sign of human arrogance, which God brought to an end. In contrast, the British Chief Rabbi, Sir Jonathan Sacks, sees this biblical narration as a challenge for humanity to avoid the "clash of civilizations," a concept first postulated by Samuel Huntington, which predicts an inevitable conflict between the cultures of East and West. Sacks requires a view of theology that can handle cultural divergences. According to the interpretation in his book *Dignity of Difference*, the biblical story of the Tower of Babel shows that God did not want the cultures, languages, and religions of the world to be uniform. Humanity's challenge is to learn to live with such differences.

The Ziggurat Within the Israelite sphere of influence, Babylon was the third power base after Assyria and Egypt. According to the Babylonian language, the name of the city of Babel meant "gateway to God." Within the biblical narrative, this name was given a different meaning. It was a place where God confused language. The Hebrew word for "confuse" sounds similar to the name of the city of Babel. Scholars believe that there is a link between the tiered temples, the ziggurats (**1**), which were a constituent part of ancient Middle Eastern temple architecture, and the tower described in Genesis 11.

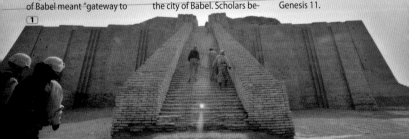

The Babylonians: pp. 268–269

■ Abraham was the first patriarch, one of the founding fathers of Israel

■ God created a covenant with Abraham: He promised him innumerable descendants and the land of Canaan as his new home

Genesis 12:1 God tells Abram to travel to Canaan

Genesis 14:17–20 King Melchisedech blesses Abram

Genesis 16:1–15 Hagar has Abram's first son: Ishmael

Genesis 17:1–16 Abram and Sarai received new names from God: Abraham and Sarah

Genesis 18:1–15 Three angels promise Abraham and Sarah a child

Genesis 21:1–7 Abraham and Sarah have a son: Isaac

Genesis 22:1–19 Abraham has to sacrifice his son Isaac

Genesis 23:1–20 For Sarah's burial Abraham selects a cave in Machpelah in Hebron as a family tomb

Genesis 25:1–2 Abraham has six more sons with Keturah

Genesis 25:7–11 Abraham is buried in Machpelah

In you all the families of the earth shall be blessed.

Genesis 12:3

Abraham

Abraham was the first of the biblical patriarchs to form a covenant with God. God asked Abram—his original name—to leave his home in Mesopotamia and to move to Canaan (**1**) under the promise of land and a long line of descendants. Abram trusted God and traveled with his wife Sarai and his nephew Lot to Canaan.

Abram and Sarai remained childless and so Abram had a child with Sarai's handmaid Hagar: Ishmael. After a while, God announced to Abram that Sarai would bear a child. Then, God changed their names: Abram to Abraham ("father of many nations") and Sarai to Sarah. Afterward, Sarah actually did become pregnant and gave birth to Isaac. As a sign of this covenant with God, Abraham had the males circumcised. When Isaac grew up, God seemed to go against his own promises. In order to test Abraham, God ordered him to give his son Isaac as a burnt offering. Abraham followed these instructions, but was stopped by an angel ▶▶

▶▶ **The Descendants of Adam and Eve to David:** pp. 24–25   **The Promised Land:** p. 122

Abraham and the Three Angels One day, three men appeared before Abraham. He asked them to be his guests and slaughtered a calf for them. Then, the men declared that they were the messengers of God (**2**) and promised Abraham, who had already had a child with the handmaid Hagar, that a son would be born to Sarah. Hearing this, she laughed because she was too old to conceive. God, however, confirmed that nothing was impossible through his intervention, not even the pregnancy of a 90-year-old woman.

Abraham and King Melchisedech Returning from where he freed his imprisoned nephew Lot, who was a prisoner of war, Abraham encountered King Melchisedech (**3**). Also a "priest of God on high," Melchisedech, whose name means "my king is justice," blessed Abraham and praised his God as the creator of heaven and earth. In the Jewish tradition, Melchisedech counts as one of the righteous gentiles, and in the Epistle to the Hebrews, Jesus is named as the "high priest according to the order of Melchisedech."

just before carrying out the sacrifice (**4**). Seeing the proof of Abraham's faith, God renewed their covenant, and promised Abraham of a number of descendants as great as the number of stars in the sky (**5**).

Abraham's faith in the promises of God was tested many times. Ultimately, the stories of Abraham demonstrate God's fulfilled promises and emphasize Abraham's closeness to God, as was acknowledged by foreigners like King Melchisedech.

Figures and Stories Relevant to Abraham

(**4**)

» **Sacrifices:** p. 45

The Tomb at Machpelah
When Sarah died, Abraham chose a burial site for his family in Machpelah, current-day Hebron (**6**). Sarah, Abraham, Isaac, Rebekah, Jacob, and Leah were all buried here. Only Rachel, of all the patriarchs and matriarchs, has her own burial site in Bethlehem (p. 95). This fixed burial site has great significance, as it was the first place in the Promised Land of Canaan that actually belonged to the half-nomadic tribe of Abraham.

Circumcision

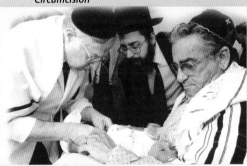

To this day, circumcision acts as a sign of the covenant between God and his people within Judaism. A man specially trained for the task, a mohel, performs a circumcision during a ritual ceremony on the eighth day following the boy's birth. Moreover, a celebratory meal with special blessings is part of the circumcision ceremony.

Matriarchs and Patriarchs: p. 69

The Sacrifice / Binding of Isaac—Abraham Is Ready to Sacrifice His Son for God

Genesis: 22:9–13

⁹ *When they came to the place that God had shown him, Abraham built an altar there and laid the wood in order. He bound his son Isaac, and laid him on the altar, on top of the wood.* ¹⁰ *Then Abraham reached out his hand and took the knife to kill his son.* ¹¹ *But the angel of the Lord called to him from heaven, and said, "Abraham, Abraham!" And he said, "Here I am."* ¹² *He said, "Do not lay your hand on the boy or do anything to him; for now I know that you fear God, since you have not withheld your son, your only son, from me."*

¹³ *And Abraham looked up and saw a ram, caught in a thicket by its horns. Abraham went and took the ram and offered it up as a burnt-offering instead of his son.*

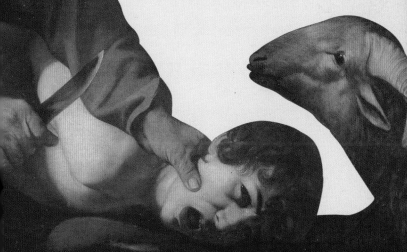

Abrahamic Religions

Judaism, Christianity, and Islam are sometimes referred to as the "Abrahamic religions." Each of these religions views Abraham as its progenitor. The term "Abrahamic religions" is mainly used to highlight what Judaism, Christianity, and Islam have in common. Reference to Abraham does not only unite Jews, Christians, and Muslims, but also differentiates them, as each one of these religions interprets this figure in its own way and these interpretations contain beliefs that may exclude one another. The various evaluations of Abraham's sons act as examples of this. Ishmael, who has great significance in Islam, is also a blessed son of Abraham in the Hebrew Bible, but it is to his brother Isaac and his offspring that the Promised Land is granted. After times of separation, Jews, Christians, and Muslims have the challenge of finding the common ground in this religious heritage, without denying their differences (**2**).

The Kaaba in Mecca In many ways the Kaaba in Mecca is the central point of the Islamic world, as Muslims look to it during prayer. During pilgrimages to Mecca—one of the Five Pillars of Islam—the participants ritually walk around the Kaaba (**1**). According to the Qur'an, it was originally made by Adam and later rebuilt by Abraham and Ishmael. When Prophet Muhammad conquered Mecca, he destroyed 360 false idols at the Kaaba.

Abraham's Tomb in Hebron The tombs of the patriarchs and matriarchs in Hebron (**3**) are holy to Jews, Christians, and Muslims. Access to the tombs for Jews and Muslims is regulated so as to avoid a repeat of past conflicts (p. 63).

⏵⏵ Matriarchs and Patriarchs: p. 69 **Ishmael:** pp. 70–73 **Isaac:** pp. 78–79

3

■ Sarah was the first matriarch, a mother of the tribe of Israel

■ Sarah's new name meant "woman of high rank"

■ Sarah gave birth to her son Isaac at an old age

Genesis 12:10–20 The Egyptian pharaoh shows interest in Sarai, whom Abram introduces as his sister

Genesis 16:1–15 Sarai asks her husband to have a son with her handmaid Hagar

Genesis 17:1–16 Sarai and Abram are given new names: Sarah and Abraham

Genesis 18:9–15 Sarah laughs in disbelief as an angel promises her a son

Genesis 21:1–7 Sarah conceives and bears Isaac

Genesis 21:8–14 Sarah puts pressure on Abraham to cast away Hagar and Ishmael

Genesis 23:1–20 Sarah dies and is buried in Hebron

So Sarah laughed to herself, saying, "After I have grown old, and my husband is old, shall I have pleasure?" Genesis 18:12

Sarah

Abraham's wife Sarah is one of the matriarchs, the female progenitors of Israel. She is described as a very beautiful woman. When she had given up hope of conceiving a child of her own, she asked her husband to sire a child with her handmaid Hagar (**1**). Later on, however, she conceived her own son, Isaac. Out of jealousy she demanded that her husband cast out Hagar. The strong position of the matriarchs is demonstrated by Sarah placing demands upon her husband. She was supported by God and she saw that her will was heeded.

Abraham's choosing of a burial site for her (p. 63) underscores her importance, as burials for women are hardly mentioned elsewhere in the Bible.

Announcement of a Birth

When an angel told Sarai about her pregnancy (**2**), she laughed at the prospect as she had not expected to get pregnant at her age. Because of this, her son was given the name Isaac, meaning "he will laugh." Like her husband, Sarai was given a new name by God: Sarah, which means "a woman of high rank." God blessed Abraham and Sarah and promised them both a great progeny and rich lands.

2

Matriarchs and Patriarchs

The patriarchs are identified as Abraham, Isaac, and Jacob while the matriarchs are their respective wives: Sarah, Rebekah, as well as the sisters Leah and Rachel. They were the progenitors of the people of Israel. In the Bible the matriarchs appear as confident and influential women who know how to get their way by exerting their influence over their offspring.

■ Judaism and Islam consider Ishmael to be the forefather of the Arabs

■ At the request of Sarah, Hagar gave birth to Abraham's first son Ishmael

Genesis 16:1–4 Sarah prompts Abraham to have a child with Hagar

Genesis 16:4–8 When Sarah wants to punish her, the arrogant, pregnant Hagar flees into the desert

Genesis 16:7–14 An angel comforts Hagar in the desert

Genesis 21:8–14 Hagar and Ishmael are thrown out of Abraham's family

Genesis 21:15–19 An angel saves Hagar and Ishmael from dying of thirst and promises Ishmael numerous offspring

Genesis 21:21 Ishmael marries an Egyptian woman

Genesis 25:9 Ishmael and Isaac entomb Abraham

Genesis 25:12–18 Ishmael's offspring and his death

The angel of the Lord also said to her, "I will so greatly multiply your offspring that they cannot be counted for multitude." Genesis 16:10

Hagar and Ishmael

As Sarah could not get pregnant, she asked Abraham to have a child with Hagar, her Egyptian handmaid. However, once Hagar became pregnant, she began to act boastfully in front of Sarah. When Sarah wanted to punish her, she fled into the desert. There she encountered an angel who comforted her by promising that her son's offspring would be so numerous that a whole nation would arise from them. Thus comforted, Hagar returned and gave birth to her son. His name was Ishmael, meaning "God is listening," because God heard the plight of Hagar and did not leave her and her son alone. When Sarah had her own child, Abraham finally sent Hagar and Ishmael away (**1**). Yet God stuck to his promise and stood by both of them.

(2)

Hagar in the Desert As she did not want her own son to have to share his inheritance with his half-brother, Sarah demanded that Abraham send Ishmael and Hagar away. While he disapproved, Abraham gave in and cast them out. They wandered around in the desert helplessly until their water supply ran out. In despair, Hagar laid Ishmael under a bush and left, as she could not bear to watch her son die. Then an angel appeared (**2**) and showed Hagar a fountain. The angel renewed God's promise to Ishmael that he would remain with him and that an entire nation would derive from his offspring. Hagar and Ishmael settled in the desert of Paran, and Ishmael became a military archer. He married an Egyptian woman, with whom he had 12 children. Ishmael later entombed his father Abraham with his half-brother Isaac.

Hagar in Islam

The story of Hagar and Ishmael's recovery in the desert is also known in Islamic lore. However, it takes place in Arabia rather than Canaan, and the lifesaving watering hole—shown to them by an angel—is identified as the well of Zamzam, which is found in the great mosque of Mecca. A tradition springs from this tale, which is practiced by Muslims during pilgrimages to Mecca: Like Hagar in her search for water, the pilgrims have to walk seven times backward and forward between the Al-Safa and Al-Marwah hills, between which the Zamzam well is found. Furthermore, healing powers are attributed to the waters of this well.

Eid Ul-Adha– The Festival of Sacrifice

Eid Ul-Adha is a Muslim religious festival celebrated to remind Muslims of Abraham's readiness to give one of his sons as a sacrifice to God. While recognizing this tradition, the Qur'an does not mention which one of the sons was to be sacrificed. In early Islamic theology there was a great altercation over which son was meant. Finally, the view prevailed that it was Ishmael (Ismail in Arabic) (**1**). Later, the tradition held that Abraham covered his eyes while preparing to sacrifice Isaac, and it was not until afterward that he saw God had replaced his son with a sacrificial animal.

In both the Jewish and Islamic traditions, Ishmael is considered to be the progenitor of the Arabs. In the Qur'an, Ishmael is described as a prophet and along with Abraham, Isaac, and Jacob counts as one of the worshipers of Allah. As with Isaac, Ishmael also received a promise from God that he would become the father of a great people. On the first day of Eid Ul-Adha, which takes place on the tenth day of the month of pilgrimage, a special prayer is said in the mosques and the farewell sermon of Muhammad is read out loud to the practitioners. The ritual slaughter of a sacrificial animal is added to this (**2**), which is traditionally the task of the eldest son in the family.

» The Sacrifice / Binding of Isaac: pp. 64–65

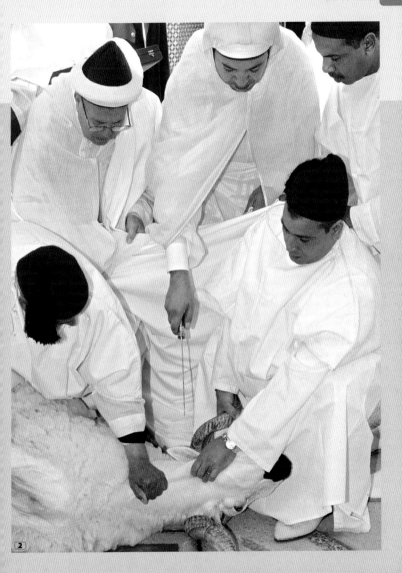

2

■ Lot was Abraham's nephew
■ Lot was the ancestor of the Moabites and the Ammonites

Genesis 13:1–13 Abram and his nephew Lot divide up their land and herds and part from each other's company

Genesis 14:1–16 Lot is saved from imprisonment by Abram

Genesis 19:1–14 Two angels visit Lot and blind the inhabitants of Sodom

Genesis 19:12–25 God wants to bring about the downfall of Sodom. Lot leaves the city beforehand

Genesis 19:26 Lot's wife looks back to Sodom and turns into a pillar of salt

Genesis 19:30–38 Lot's daughters get themselves impregnated by their drunken father

» **Sexuality in the Bible:** p. 106

They said, "Flee for your life; do not look back or stop anywhere in the Plain; flee to the hills, or else you will be consumed." Genesis 19:17

Lot

Lot, Abraham's nephew, lived in Sodom. One night, two strangers arrived in the city and were invited by Lot to be his guest. Before they could even lie down to sleep, the inhabitants of Sodom surrounded Lot's house, wanting to rape his guests. Lot, however, refused to deliver his guests into their hands. Instead, he offered them his virginal daughters, but the Sodomites had no interest in them and they decided to storm Lot's house. Lot's guests, who revealed themselves as angels (1), struck them with blindness so that they could not find the door.

This singular stone formation on the eastern bank of the Dead Sea is commonly known as Lot's wife.

Lot and His Family Leave Sodom Due to the sinful ways of its inhabitants, God planned to destroy the city of Sodom. When the angels told Lot and his family to leave the city, Lot asked his daughters' fiancés to join them, but they did not take his warning seriously. He urged his family to hurry and even took them by the hand to lead them out of the city (**2**). As they evacuated the city, they were instructed neither to stand still nor to look back. Despite these warnings, Lot's wife looked back and she turned immediately into a pillar of salt (**3**). At dawn, God had fire and brimstone rain from the heavens, and thus destroyed all life around the cities of Sodom and Gomorrah.

Figures and Stories Relevant to Lot

God, see pp. 28–33

Angels, see pp. 42–43

Abraham, Lot's Uncle, see pp. 60–63

Sodom and Gomorrah, see pp. 76–77

Moabites, Lot's Offspring, see the Neighboring Peoples of Israel, pp. 166–167

Ammonites, Lot's Offspring, see the Neighboring Peoples of Israel, pp. 166–167

Lot's Daughters Commit Incest As no men survived, Lot's daughters feared that they would remain without children. The elder of the two proposed that they get their father drunk so that they could sleep with him (**4**). Their plan worked and they both had sons. The elder daughter called her son Moab and, according to the biblical tradition, the nation of the Moabites descended from him. The younger daughter called her son Ben-ammi; he is seen as the patriarch of the Ammonites.

Sodom and Gomorrah

The cities of Sodom and Gomorrah probably lay on the southern side of the Dead Sea. In the Bible, it states that God wanted to destroy both cities because of their sinful ways. In a superb dialogue in Genesis 18:16–33, Abraham tried to prevent the downfall of Sodom by asking God not to destroy it on account of the righteous people who live there. He struck a bargain: If at least 50 righteous people could be found in the city, God should not destroy it. God was in agreement; however, Abraham haggled the number ever lower. Finally, God agreed to spare Sodom if ten righteous people could be found there. In the end, none could be found in either city.

The sins of Sodom's inhabitants are erroneously understood by the Christian interpretation to be sexual intercourse between men. The Bible speaks of their wish to rape Lot's guests, the two angels (**1**).

By the Dead Sea There are various theories as to whether a historical event could lie behind the story of the downfall of Sodom and Gomorrah (**3**). For instance, the cities could have sunk due to an earthquake, and a subsequent landslide could have occurred in the boggy shore areas around the Dead Sea (**2**).

Abraham: pp. 60–63

■ Isaac was the second patriarch after his father Abraham

■ As a sign of the covenant between God and Israel, Isaac was circumcised

Genesis 17:9–14 God demands Isaac's circumcision as a sign of the covenant

Genesis 22:1–19 Isaac narrowly escapes being sacrificed by his father Abraham

Genesis 24:1–67 Isaac marries Rebekah

Genesis 26:1–5 God renews the covenant with Isaac

Genesis 27:1–40 Isaac is tricked into blessing Jacob

Isaac sowed seed in that land, and in the same year reaped a hundredfold. Genesis 26:12

Isaac

Along with Abraham and Jacob, Isaac was one of the three patriarchs of Israel. He was the son promised to Sarah and Abraham by God and the inheritor of the covenant with God. As a boy, Isaac was to be sacrificed by his father as a burnt offering (**1**); however, God intervened and saved his life.

Isaac married Rebekah, with whom he had two sons, Esau and Jacob. God reconfirmed the promises he had made to Isaac's father. He died at an old age, after he had unwittingly blessed his son Jacob.

Jewish holiday plate from the 19th century with a depiction of the binding of Isaac by Abraham

» **Matriarchs and Patriarchs:** p. 69

Isaac's Blessing When Isaac felt that death was near, he wanted to bless his favorite son Esau. Jacob, however, approached him disguised as his brother (p. 83). The blessing of his father promised Jacob success and dominion over his brother (**2**). Isaac did not know he was deceived until Esau brought him his meal. By this time, it was too late to take back the blessing. The one he later gave to Esau was worth less than Jacob's.

Blessing

According to the Bible, blessings are healing powers from God. One example is the priest's blessing of Aaron (Numbers 6:24–26), which is used in Judaism and Christianity:
"The Lord bless you and keep you; the Lord make his face to shine upon you, and be gracious to you; the Lord lift up his countenance to you, and give you peace."

Figures and Stories Relevant to Isaac

God, see pp. 28–33

Angels, see pp. 42–43

Abraham, Isaac's Father, see pp. 60–63

The Tomb at Machpelah, see Abraham, p. 63

The Sacrifice / Binding of Isaac, see pp. 64–65

Sarah, Isaac's Mother, see pp. 68–69

Rebekah, Isaac's Wife, see pp. 82–83

Esau, Firstborn Son of Isaac, see pp. 84–85

Jacob, Second Son of Isaac, see pp. 88–91

God's Covenant With Israel, see pp. 142–143

Isaac Is Deceived

Genesis 27:6, 9–23

⁶ Rebekah said to her son Jacob, "I heard your father say to your brother Esau, … ⁹ Go to the flock, and get me two choice kids, so that I may prepare from them savory food for your father, such as he likes; ¹⁰ and you shall take it to your father to eat, so that he may bless you before he dies." ¹¹ But Jacob said to his mother Rebekah, "Look, my brother Esau is a hairy man, and I am a man of smooth skin. ¹² Perhaps my father will feel me, and I shall seem to be mocking him, and bring a curse on myself and not a blessing." ¹³ His mother said to him, "Let your curse be on me, my son; only obey my word, and go, get them for me." ¹⁴ So he went and got them and brought them to his mother; and his mother prepared savory food, such as his father loved. ¹⁵ Then Rebekah took the best garments of her elder son Esau, which were with her in the house, and put them on her younger son Jacob; ¹⁶ and she put the skins of the kids on his hands and on the smooth part of his neck. ¹⁷ Then she handed the savory food, and the bread that she had prepared, to her son Jacob. ¹⁸ So he went in to his father, and said, "My father"; and he said, "Here I am; who are you, my son?" ¹⁹ Jacob said to his father, "I am Esau your firstborn. I have done as you told me; now sit up and eat of my game, so that you may bless me."

²⁰ But Isaac said to his son, "How is it that you have found it so quickly, my son?" He answered, "Because the Lord your God granted me success." ²¹ Then Isaac said to Jacob, "Come

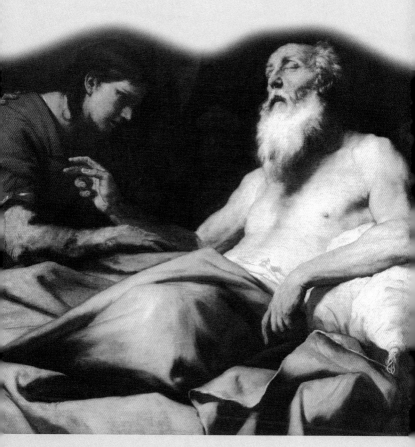

near, that I may feel you, my son, to know whether you are really my son Esau or not."

22 So Jacob went up to his father Isaac, who felt him and said, "The voice is Jacob's voice, but the hands are the hands of Esau."

23 He did not recognize him, because his hands were hairy like his brother Esau's hands; so he blessed him.

■ Rebekah was one of the matriarchs of the tribes of Israel

■ Rebekah was intelligent and determined

Genesis 24:1–28 Abraham's servant meets Rebekah

Genesis 27:1–40 Rebekah helps her favorite son Jacob to get the firstborn's blessing

"Drink, my lord," she said … "I will draw for your camels also, until they have finished drinking." Genesis 24:18–19

Rebekah

Along with Sarah, Leah, and Rachel, Rebekah is one of the four matriarchs of Israel. As Abraham did not want his son Isaac to marry a Canaanite, he sent his servant Eliezer back to his old homeland of Mesopotamia. A sign was supposed to help Eliezer choose a bride; the woman who was willing to wash his camels was to be brought back as a wife for Isaac. And indeed, as Eliezer was standing by a spring, a young and beautiful woman came along, who washed his camels: Rebekah (**1**). On the authority of Rebekah and her family, Eliezer took her to Canaan.

Fetching water is a traditional task for women

①

▶▶ **Matriarchs and Patriarchs:** p. 69

Rebekah Deceives Isaac

Rebekah appears to have been clever and confident. It was her decision to go with Eliezer and become Isaac's wife. Later, she intervened in the succession of her husband to ensure that her favorite son Jacob would become his heir. When Isaac was old and blind, he wanted to bless his firstborn Esau. He asked him to go out hunting and to prepare him a meal, as he liked it. Rebekah heard this and, in all haste, set a plan in

motion that would delude her husband and guarantee the firstborn's blessing for Jacob. She prepared a meal from the meat of two rams, dressed Jacob in Esau's attire, and covered his arms in pelts, as Esau was hairy and Jacob was not.

This ruse was successful and the blessing intended for Esau was given to Jacob (**2**). In order to protect Jacob from Esau's wrath, Rebekah sent him to her brother in Mesopotamia. Here she hoped that Jacob would marry one of his cousins.

Meetings by Water

For nomads, who traverse deserts with their herds, springs are vital. Much like today, water was the cause of many conflicts, such as when Abraham's and Lot's shepherds fought over access to a spring. However, wells were also a

place for men meeting women: Abraham's servant Eliezer found Isaac's wife Rebekah by a spring and Moses met his wife Zipporah by a fountain. In the New Testament, the Gospel of John depicts Jesus meeting a Samaritan woman by a spring.

» **Blessing:** p. 79

■ Esau was the progenitor of the Edomites

■ Esau was red-haired and hairy; he acted passionately and without consideration

Genesis 25:22 Esau and Jacob are already fighting in the womb

Genesis 25:29–34 Esau renounces his rights as the first-born over to his brother Jacob

Genesis 26:34–35 Esau marries Canaanite women

Genesis 27:41–45 Esau plans to kill Jacob

Genesis 33:1–16 After many years, Esau and Jacob finally reconcile

"Two nations are in your womb ... one shall be stronger than the other, the elder shall serve the younger." Genesis 25:23

Esau

Esau (**1**) was the firstborn of the twin boys of Isaac and Rebekah. He was a passionate hunter and the favorite of his father, but was tricked out of the blessing that Isaac wanted to bestow upon him before his death by his brother Jacob. Esau planned to kill him, but later managed to be reconciled with Jacob. He married Canaanite women, which caused his parents "great heartbreak."

In the Bible, Esau's descendants are identified as the Edomites, who were from the territory of Edom in southern Israel (**2**). They were in constant military conflict with the Israelites. In the later Jewish tradition, the brotherhood between Esau and Jacob became a model for the relationship between Jews and Christians, whereby Esau stood for the Christians and Jacob for the Jews.

⟩⟩ **The Descendants of Adam and Eve to David:** pp. 24–25

*Figures and Stories
Relevant to Esau*

Isaac, see pp. 78–79

Rebekah, Esau's Mother,
see pp. 82–83

Jacob, Esau's Younger Brother,
see pp. 88–91

The Edomites, see the
Neighboring Peoples of Israel
pp. 166–167

The Caananites, see
pp. 160–161

Esau Sells His Firstborn Right
Returning home one day, the exhausted Esau caught the scent of a lentil dish (**4**) that his brother Jacob had prepared. Esau asked Jacob to give him some of this "red stuff." But

Jacob said he would do so only if Esau relinquished his birthright (**3**) to him. Without much consideration, he gave up these rights, which did not seem to be very crucial to him. Aside from this, Esau caused his

parents much grief by cavorting with foreign women. Esau's sobriquet "the red" ("Edom" in Hebrew) was transferred to his descendants, who became known as the Edomites.

Esau and Jacob Reconcile
Enraged over the stolen birthright, Esau planned to kill his brother. However, Jacob fled to relatives of his mother's. When Jacob returned many years later, he feared that his brother was still plotting to take his life. Therefore, he sent Esau a gift of a large number of sheep, goats, cows, asses, and camels. When the two of them came face to face again, Esau fell around Jacob's neck and kissed his brother (**5**). Their issue was resolved, but the conflicts between their offspring, the Israelites and the Edomites, resurfaced time and time again.

■ Laban was Jacob's uncle and Rebekah's brother

Figures and Stories Relevant to Laban

"Come now, let us make a covenant, you and I; and let it be a witness between you and me." Genesis 31:44

Laban

Laban was Rebekah's brother, and thus Jacob's uncle. Jacob fled to him after duping his brother Esau out of the blessing of their father. Laban took Jacob in and gave him work as a shepherd (**1**). As a wage for seven years of work, he promised his daughter Rachel in marriage. On the wedding night, he brought his eldest daughter Leah to Jacob instead of Rachel. This went against their agreement, but Laban justified his actions by explaining that it was not customary for the younger daughters to be married before the eldest. After another seven years of service, Laban finally allowed Jacob to marry Rachel.

A sculpture from Mesopotamia from ca 1900 B.C.E.

Laban Searches for His Lost Idol When Jacob became rich while working in the service of Laban, the relationship between the two men cooled immensely. Therefore, Jacob furtively left one day with his wives to return to his family in Canaan. Laban followed Jacob because his family's idol, an image of God, was missing. Jacob, who did not know that Rachel had taken the idol with her and had hidden it under her saddle, told Laban to search through the camp. Whoever was found with the idol was to be killed. Laban searched through everything (**2**), but did not find anything as Rachel led him astray with a skillful pretext. As the idol was not found,

a dispute broke out between Laban and Jacob. However, one night Laban dreamed that God told him to make peace with Jacob. Hence the two men managed a reconciliation (**3**)

and made a contract: Jacob had to treat both Leah and Rachel well and take no further wives, and neither one of them was to cross each other's boundaries with hostile intentions.

■ Jacob was the third patriarch after Abraham and Isaac

■ Jacob received the name
Israel from God, meaning
"God's fighter"

Genesis 25:29–34 Jacob buys
his brother Esau's birthright

Genesis 27:1–40 Jacob de-
ceives his father and is blessed

Genesis 28:10–22 Jacob
dreams of a ladder to heaven
and constructs an altar

Genesis 29:1–14 Jacob flees
from his brother Esau to his
uncle Laban

Genesis 29:15–30 Jacob works
as a shepherd for Laban in order
to marry his daughters Rachel
and Leah

Genesis 32:23–33 Jacob wrestles with an angel and receives
the new name Israel from God

Genesis 37:12–36 Jacob's sons
assert that their youngest
brother Joseph is dead

Genesis 46:1–34 Jacob moves
in with Joseph in Egypt

Genesis 50:1–14 Jacob is
entombed in Hebron at Machpelah, the tomb of the patriarchs

But Jacob said, "I will not let you go, unless you bless me."
Genesis 32:26

Jacob

Jacob was the third biblical patriarch. He was
the younger of twin boys born to Isaac and
Rebekah. He bought his brother Esau's firstborn
rights for a plate of lentils and with his mother's
help he obtained, through deception, the blessing
that his father had wanted to give to Esau. Afterward, he fled to his uncle Laban, married Laban's
daughters, and became rich. Jacob was the actual
progenitor of the people of Israel, as the 12 Tribes
originated from his 12 sons. Impressive encounters
with God mark Jacob's story. He later settled in
Egypt, but was buried in Hebron like his forefathers.

Stories of the Patriarchs

In chapters 12–36 of Genesis,
the stories of the fathers and
mothers of Israel are told:
Abraham, Isaac, and Jacob,
as well as their wives Sarah,
Rebekah, Leah, and Rachel.
The patriarchs had sons who
were often quarreling. The
line of descendants was constantly endangered by

infertility, but was secured
through divine intervention.
According to the Bible, other
nations aside from the
Israelites emerged from
the patriarchs.

⨳ **Matriarchs and Patriarchs:** p. 69

Blessing From Isaac With his mother's help, Jacob managed to be blessed by his father Isaac (**1**) in place of his elder brother Esau. The blessing promised him prosperity and well-being, as well as dominion over his brother. Whoever Jacob blessed, should be blessed, and whoever he cursed, should be cursed.

Jacob's Dream of a Ladder to Heaven During his flight from Esau, Jacob dreamed of a ladder that reached from the ground toward heaven (**2**), with angels climbing up and down. God appeared to him and confirmed the promise he had made to Abraham that this land would be in his possession and that of his descendants. Jacob erected a stone at this site (**3**), which he called Bethel ("House of God"), and then later an altar.

Jacob Meets Rachel When Jacob arrived in Haran, he met Rachel (**4**), the daughter of his uncle Laban. She was watering her father's sheep (**5**) by a fountain. He introduced himself as her cousin and kissed her. In exchange for entering into Laban's service, Jacob asked to marry Rachel, who was the younger and more attractive of Laban's two daughters (pp. 94–95).

Jacob's Fight at Zarqa Jacob became a rich herd owner while in Laban's service. Laban's sons were jealous of him and Jacob decided to return to Canaan with his family and possessions. One night along the way, shortly before his renewed encounter with Esau (pp. 84–85), he met a stranger on the banks of the Zarqa River, who provoked him to a fight (**6**). The stranger struck a blow on Jacob's hips but could not defeat him. When morning came, he asked Jacob to let him go. Jacob responded: "I will not let you go, unless you bless me." Thus the stranger gave Jacob a new name, "Israel" ("God's fighter"), as he had fought with God and men, and won. The stranger would not, however, say his own name. In the end Jacob left the fight wounded but blessed. He called the site of the struggle Peniel ("God's face"), as he had seen God face to face there.

Jacob's Sons Bring Him a Bloody Cloak Jacob had 12 sons, but his first child with Rachel, Joseph, was his favorite. The preferential treatment Jacob gave him incurred the envy of his brothers. One day while they were with their herds, Jacob sent Joseph to them. They sold him to a caravan en route to Egypt and showed his cloak to Jacob, which they had smeared in goat's blood (**7**). Jacob believed that an animal had killed Joseph and was inconsolable.

Jacob Travels to Egypt When Jacob was told by his sons that Joseph, believed to be dead, was still alive, he became ecstatic and wanted to see him one last time before he died. He took his entire family to Egypt (**8**). Joseph approached his father, and as they met, Jacob fell around Joseph's neck, crying with joy. Joseph introduced his family to the pharaoh, who allowed them to live in Egypt.

Jacob's Death Before Jacob died at the age of 147 in Egypt, he blessed all of his sons. Jacob's last wish was to be entombed in the land of his forefathers rather than in Egypt. His sons brought his embalmed body back to Canaan and entombed him in a cave at Machpelah (**9**), which his grandfather Abraham had bought for the burial of Sarah. Jacob's parents Isaac and Rebekah, as well as his wife Leah, were all entombed there.

▶▶ **Blessing:** p. 79

Jacob's Dream—The Ladder to Heaven

Genesis 28:12–16

12 And he dreamed that there was a ladder set up on the earth, the top of it reaching to heaven; and the angels of God were ascending and descending on it. 13 And the Lord stood beside him and said, "I am the Lord, the God of Abraham your father and the God of Isaac; the land on which you lie I will give to you and to your offspring; 14 and your offspring shall be like the dust of the earth, and you shall spread abroad to the west and to the east and to the north and to the south; and all the families of the earth shall be blessed in you and in your off-spring. 15 Know that I am with you and will keep you wherever you go, and will bring you back to this land; for I will not leave you until I have done what I have promised you." 16 Then Jacob woke from his sleep and said, "Surely the Lord is in this place—and I did not know it!"

 **Dreams and Their Meanings:** p. 101

■ Leah and Rachel were Jacob's wives

■ Leah and Rachel were matriarchs of Israel

Genesis 29:1–19 Jacob meets his cousins Leah and Rachel, Laban's daughters

Genesis 31:17–21 Rachel hides Laban's household deities

Genesis 35:16–20 Rachel dies after the birth of Benjamin

Genesis 35:23–26 List of the 12 sons of Jacob with Leah and Rachel, as well as their handmaids Bilhah and Zilpah

Leah's eyes were lovely, and Rachel was graceful and beautiful.

Genesis 29:17

Leah and Rachel

When Jacob arrived at the house of his uncle Laban, he met his cousins Leah and Rachel (**1**). Leah was the elder, while Rachel was the younger and more beautiful of the two sisters. Jacob worked for his uncle for seven years in order to win Rachel's hand in marriage. On his wedding night, however, Jacob was given Leah, not Rachel, as his wife. Laban offered him Rachel's hand in marriage in exchange for another seven years of labor. Leah, the unloved wife, was the first to become pregnant, eventually having seven children. Because she was initially childless, Jacob had two sons with her handmaid Zilpah. Rachel also had trouble getting pregnant, so she told her husband to have children with her handmaid Bilhah. Finally, Rachel became pregnant with Joseph. She later died after the birth of her second son Benjamin. Rachel and Leah were two of the matriarchs of Israel.

Matriarchs and Patriarchs: p. 69

Rachel's Cunning When Jacob left Laban's household without saying a farewell, Rachel took the statue of the household deity with her (p. 87). Laban hurried after them and fought with Jacob over the missing idol. Jacob said that the person who had taken the statue would be punished with death. When Laban searched through the camp, Rachel hid the statue beneath her saddle and said that "the way of women" was upon her so she had to remain seated on the camel (**2**). Thus, she managed to keep Laban from discovering her theft.

Rachel's Death Rachel, unlike Leah, waited a long time before finally becoming pregnant. Her first son was Joseph. After the birth of her second son, she realized that she was going to die (**4**). She called the child Ben Oni ("son of my misfortune"), but Jacob renamed him Benjamin ("son of my right hand"). Jacob erected a stone memorial near present-day Bethlehem in remembrance of Rachel. Her grave (**3**) is visited to this day by infertile women, who pray to become pregnant.

Figures and Stories Relevant to Leah and Rachel

Laban, Father of Leah and Rachel, see pp. 86–87

Jacob, Cousin and Husband of Leah and Rachel, see pp. 88–91

Leah's and Rachel's Sons, see the Sons of Jacob, pp. 96–97

Joseph, the Elder of Rachel's Two Sons, see pp. 98–103

Leah's and Rachel's Offspring, Patriarchs of the Israelites, see the 12 Tribes of Israel, pp. 162–165

■ The 12 sons of Jacob were considered to be the forefathers of the 12 Tribes of Israel

Then Jacob called his sons, and said: "Gather around, that I may tell you what will happen to you in days to come." Genesis 49:1

The Sons of Jacob

Jacob conceived 12 sons between his wives Leah and Rachel and their handmaids Bilhah and Zilpah. A daughter from Leah is also mentioned, named Dinah.

Leah's sons were Reuben, Simeon, Levi, Judah, Issachar, and Zebulon. The sons of her handmaid Zilpah were Gad and Asher. Rachel was the mother of two sons: Joseph and Benjamin. Her handmaid Bilhah had Dan and Naphtali. According to the Bible, the 12 Tribes of Israel originated from Jacob's 12 sons. Joseph was Jacob's favorite son (p. 99), and for this he was hated by his brothers. They wanted to kill him; however, Reuben convinced them to simply throw Joseph into a pit (**1**). Later, they sold him to Egyptians (**2**). Here, Joseph became highly influential.

The Brothers Recognize Joseph

As a famine was raging in Canaan, Joseph's brothers went to Egypt to sell grain. They met Joseph, who had managed to gain great notoriety, but he did not identify himself. Only when they came to Egypt a second time—this time with their youngest brother Benjamin, who Jacob treasured—did Joseph reveal himself to his brothers (**3**). He did not blame them for selling him to the Egyptians because it put him in the position to help his family, thus they acted out God's will.

The Brothers Avenge Dinah

Shechem, who was a member of the Canaanite nation of the Hivites, raped Dinah, the daughter of Jacob and Leah. He wanted to marry her, so his father Hamor, who was the ruler over the land, implored Jacob to authorize the marriage on behalf of his son and was prepared to pay a dowry. Dinah's brothers demanded that Shechem, Hamor, and all the men of their nation be circumcised. Afterward, Dinah's brothers assailed the Hivites (**4**), who were defenseless due to their wounds, killed all the men and took all their women, children, and possessions. Jacob was ashamed of his sons, but they defended themselves by saying that they had to protect their family's honor.

■ Joseph was Jacob's favorite son

■ Joseph was a successful interpreter of dreams

■ Through Joseph's influence, the Israelites manage to get to Egypt

Genesis 37:1–11 Joseph tells his brothers of his dreams

Genesis 37:23–28 Joseph is sold by his brothers to Egyptians

Genesis 39:1–18 Potiphar's wife tries to seduce Joseph

Genesis 41:1–36 Joseph interprets the dreams of the pharaoh

Genesis 41:37–46 Joseph is appointed as the highest official in Egypt

Genesis 45:1–25 Joseph reveals his identity to his brothers

Genesis 48:1–22 Joseph's children Ephraim and Manasseh are blessed by their grandfather Jacob

Genesis 49:22–26 Joseph is blessed by his father Jacob

Genesis 50:15–26 Joseph forgives his brothers and dies in Egypt

Even though you intended to do harm to me, God intended it for good, in order to preserve a numerous people, as he is doing today.

Genesis 50:20

Joseph

Joseph is no longer considered to be one of the patriarchs of Israel, but is still one of the central figures of the last part of Genesis. His story forms the transition from the time of the patriarchs to the residence of the Israelites in Egypt. Joseph was the favorite

Joseph dreamt that his brothers would bow to him like ears of corn

son of Jacob and the firstborn of Rachel. As his father clearly favored him, he incurred the envy of his brothers. Their hatred was so fierce that they wanted to kill him. Instead, they sold him to a caravan headed to Egypt (**1**). Joseph was made a servant in the house of the Egyptian high official Potiphar. Potiphar soon made him the custodian of his entire estate because of Joseph's ability. ⏵⏵

⏵⏵ **Matriarchs and Patriarchs:** p. 69

Joseph's Dreams Joseph told his family about two of his dreams (**2**). In one, he was binding sheaves with his brothers. His sheaf stood upright, and those of his brothers bent over toward his. In a second dream, he saw the sun, the moon, and 11 stars—all of which bowed to him. Rebuking him, his father asked Joseph whether his parents and his brothers should likewise bow before him. His brothers were also annoyed that Joseph was promoting himself in this way.

Joseph in Islam

The Qur'an mentions Joseph (Yusuf in Arabic) in Surah 12. His story in the Qur'an is similar to that of the Bible, except with some additional material. For example, one day Potiphar's wife was entertaining female guests. When Joseph walked into the room, they were so taken with him that they did not notice the knives in their hands and accidentally cut themselves. The Qur'an also reports on the failed attempt of Potiphar's wife to seduce Joseph and her false accusations. She later appeared before the pharaoh and informed him that her allegations against Joseph were false.

Potiphar's wife tried to seduce Joseph, but failed and so took revenge on him with a false allegation. Joseph was consequently thrown in jail, where he interpreted the dreams of his fellow convicts. When the pharaoh needed a dream interpreter one day, someone remembered Joseph. He interpreted the pharaoh's dreams in a convincing way and also set out a plan of action, which meant that the pharaoh made him his highest official (**3**). Joseph married an Egyptian woman, Asenath, the daughter of a priest. ⏩

4

Potiphar's Wife In Egypt, Joseph was sold to the household of Potiphar, a high official to the pharaoh. Joseph was highly capable, and so Potiphar entrusted him with the upkeep of his household.

As Joseph was handsome, Potiphar's wife desired him and tried to seduce him, but he remained steadfast. One day, they were both alone in the house and Potiphar's wife tried again. Joseph fled (**4**), but

Potiphar's wife ripped off a part of his robe. When her husband returned, she claimed that Joseph had tried to seduce her, using the cloth as proof. Believing her, Potiphar had Joseph jailed.

⏩ **Sexuality in the Bible:** p. 107

5

6

Joseph Interprets the Dreams of the Pharaoh

While Joseph was in prison, the pharaoh had a dream (**5**,**6**) that no one could explain. First, he saw seven fat cows grazing on a pasture. Then, he saw seven emaciated cows, which came and ate the seven fat ones. In another dream, he saw seven luscious ears of corn. Then, he saw seven meager ears of corn that were scorched by the wind from the east. One of the pharaoh's officials remembered that Joseph had interpreted his dreams while he was in prison, and all that Joseph had predicted to him had come true. Hearing this, the pharaoh summoned Joseph from prison and he interpreted his dreams: the fat cows and the thick ears of corn were symbols for seven years of prosperity to come. The gaunt cows and paltry corn signified the seven bad years of famine that would come thereafter. Joseph advised the pharaoh to store provisions during the seven good years in anticipation of the famine. The interpretation made sense to the pharaoh and he made Joseph the administrator over all of Egypt.

Dreams and Their Meanings

Dreams in the Bible present the possibility of direct contact with God, such as Jacob's dream of a ladder to heaven (pp. 92–93), or Laban's dream, in which God ordered him to be friendly to Jacob. Dreams can show future events, such as the pharaoh's dream of the seven fat and seven thin cows. The language of dreams is symbolic, thus an interpretation is needed. However, not every interpretation is correct and dreams, like prophecies, can be wrong.

The Seven Good and the Seven Bad Years Joseph's politics in Egypt were very successful. During the years of plenty, he made provision for the coming years of hardship by having a portion of the harvest (**7**) stored away (**8**). When the famine began, Joseph sold the provisions to the Egyptians. The Egyptian people had to give all their money, then their livestock, and finally their fields for food. Finally, all of Egypt was the property of the pharaoh.

When the years of strife that Joseph had predicted began, the famine also struck Canaan. Joseph's brothers traveled to Egypt to buy grain. They encountered Joseph (**9**), but did not recognize him. After testing the honesty of his brothers, Joseph finally revealed his identity. In the end, he saw to it that his family could come to Egypt. After Jacob's death, Joseph's brothers were afraid that he might take his revenge on them, but Joseph had forgiven them. He reminded them of God's promise that He would one day lead them back into the land that was promised to their forefathers (p. 62).

Jacob Blesses Ephraim and Manasseh Joseph had two sons with his Egyptian wife, Manasseh and Ephraim. Their names were a play on Joseph's life and fate: Manasseh means "God let me forget my trou- bles," and Ephraim means "God let me grow in the land of my suffering." Hearing that his fa- ther was ill, Joseph brought both of his sons to Jacob to be blessed (**10**). Jacob blessed the second-born Ephraim with his right hand, and the first-born Manasseh with his left, so that he would obtain the lesser blessing. Joseph was upset, but Jacob insisted that a greater people would stem from the young Ephraim.

(10)

Figures and Stories Relevant to Joseph

Jacob, Joseph's Father, see pp. 88–91

Rachel, Joseph's Mother, see pp. 94–95

Joseph's Brothers, see the Sons of Jacob, pp. 96–97

The Egyptian Pharaoh, see the Egyptians, pp. 104–105

God's Covenant With Israel, see pp. 142–143

Manasseh and Ephraim, Joseph's Sons and Patriarchs, see the 12 Tribes of Israel, pp. 162–165

Mixed Marriages, see the Neighboring Peoples of Israel, pp. 166–167

⏩ **Blessing:** p. 79

■ Egypt was one of the great powers, which held the Israelites under its influence

■ The liberation from Egyptian bondage is a central theme in Jewish history and religion

Genesis 12:10–20 Abraham and Sarah move to Egypt because of a drought

Genesis 39–50 Joseph in Egypt

Genesis 42–43 Jacob's family goes to Egypt during a famine

Exodus 1 The Israelites are oppressed and Pharaoh demands that their newborn boys be drowned

Exodus 12:31–50 Moses leads the Israelites out of Egypt

I Kings 3:1 Solomon marries the Egyptian pharaoh's daughter

I Kings 14:25–26; II Chronicles 12:2–9 Pharaoh Shishak's military campaign against Judah

II Kings 23:29; II Chronicles 35:22–24 Pharaoh Nechoh kills King Josiah of Judah

I Maccabees 1:16–19 The Ptolemies lose control over Palestine to the Seleucids

By strength of hand the Lord brought us out of Egypt, from the house of slavery. Exodus 13:14

The Egyptians

Egypt was among the great powers of the ancient Middle East. Through various dynasties, the country experienced several golden ages after 3000 B.C.E. The last great dynasty was that of the Ptolemaic rulers, who again succeeded in establishing Egypt's domi-

Israelites carrying out forced labor in Egypt (illustration from a Jewish manuscript)

nance over the region (pp. 288–289). The country's great prosperity derived from its highly productive agriculture along the Nile River (**1**). Foreign peoples were also continuously drawn to the fruitful oasis of the Nile.

In addition to its politics, Egypt exercised significant cultural influence over the entire Middle East. Traces of this can be found in the Bible—for instance, the story of Joseph (pp. 98–103)—or in wisdom literature, such as the Psalms (pp. 222–223). Thus, the idea that the king is a son of God, as expressed in Psalm 2 and Psalm 110, builds on Egyptian traditions: pharaohs were seen as gods.

Israelites in Egypt Nomads came to Egypt in times of drought, from Canaan as well as from other lands (**2**). Ancient Egyptian historian Manetho describes a people called the Hyksos, who settled east of the eastern Nile Delta. Modern archaeologists confirm that the Hyksos were a Semitic people, originally from Canaan. Many biblical scholars have concluded that the Hyksos were the Israelites of the Bible, though not all. Clear archaeological evidence for the Israelites' bondage in Egypt and their escape from the country has not been found. Nevertheless, the Israelites' flight from slavery in Egypt forms the central theme of the Book of Exodus. God rescues his people from the pharaoh (**3**), leading them back to the Promised Land.

Figures and Stories Relevant to the Egyptians

Joseph, the Egyptian Pharaoh's Highest Official, see pp. 98–103

Moses, see pp. 110–115 and pp. 120–125

God's Covenant With Israel, see pp. 142–143

Neighboring Peoples of Israel, see pp. 166–167

Solomon, Son-in-Law of the Egyptian Pharaoh, see pp. 238–241

The Ptolemaic Kings of Egypt, see the Ptolemies and Seleucids, pp. 288–289

The Merneptah Stele

The oldest known reference to Israel can be found in an Egyptian inscription on the Merneptah Stele, which describes Pharaoh Merneptah's military campaign in Canaan in the late 13th century B.C.E. The pharaoh's victory over the Israelites is mentioned: "Israel is laid waste, its seed is no more." Although this statement would prove false, the reference remains the earliest archaeological evidence for Israel's existence in Canaan.

▶▶ **The Mesha Stele:** p. 167

■ Tamar has her father-in-law Judah's children

Genesis 38:6–11 When Tamar's husband dies, she is expected to bear children to his brothers

Genesis 38:14–23 Judah meets Tamar, who is disguised as a prostitute, and sleeps with her

Genesis 38:24–26 Judah wants to punish the pregnant Tamar, but he sees that he was unjust

Then Judah said to Onan, "Go in to your brother's wife and perform the duty of a brother-in-law to her; raise up offspring for your brother." Genesis 38:8

Tamar and Onan

Judah's eldest son Er was married to Tamar. Because Er was "wicked in the sight of the Lord," God killed him. As Er died childless, Judah asked his second son to marry Tamar and have children with her, who would be considered Er's descendants. Onan

Judah presented his signet ring as a pledge to the disguised Tamar

married Tamar and slept with her, but he "spillt his seed on the ground" because he did not want to give offspring to his dead brother in this way. God was displeased with this action and killed Onan as well for his disobedience. Judah's third son, Shelah, was next in line to marry Tamar, but Judah was afraid that Shelah may also be killed by God for disobedience. He put Tamar off, never offering Shelah to her in marriage. In response, Tamar devised a plan to become pregnant and thus secure her position within the family.

Sexuality in the Bible

According to biblical understanding, sexuality is a gift from God and an integral part of the human experience. As with other human interactions, there are specific rules for sexual intercourse, which are found with the guidelines for cleanliness in the Book of Leviticus and effect both men and women. For example, it mandates that there should be a period of sexual abstinence immediately after a woman menetretes or has a child. In addition, the emission of semen makes a man unclean until the following day, and so he must wait to make a sacrifice in the Temple. There are many other specific commandments against incest and adultery.

» **Polygamy in the Ancient Middle East:** p. 229

Tamar's Deception Disguised, Tamar waited by the road for her father-in-law, Judah. When Judah saw the veiled woman (**1**), he took her for a prostitute and promised her a goat if she slept with him. Since he did not have a goat with him, he gave her his ring as a pledge. When he tried to fulfill his pledge, he could not find the "harlot." Tamar's plan worked; she became pregnant. When Judah heard this, he believed Tamar had dishonored his family and wanted to burn her to death (**2**). But when she showed him the ring, Judah realized that he had been unjust to her. Tamar bore twin sons; one of them, Perez, is an ancestor of King David.

Figures and Stories Relevant to Tamar and Onan

Judah, Tamar's Father-in-Law and Son of Jacob and Leah; see Jacob's Sons, pp. 95–96

David, Descendant of Tamar, see pp. 216–221

▶▶ **The Descendants of Adam and Eve to David:** pp. 24–25

Moses in the Basket of Rushes

Exodus 1:22, 2:1–10

22 Then Pharaoh commanded all his people, "Every boy that is born to the Hebrews you shall throw into the Nile, but you shall let every girl live."
1 Now a man from the house of Levi went and married a Levite woman.
2 The woman conceived and bore a son; and when she saw that he was a fine baby, she hid him for three months.
3 When she could hide him no longer she got a papyrus basket for him, and plastered it with bitumen and pitch; she put the child in it and placed it among the reeds on the bank of the river.
4 His sister stood at a distance, to see what would happen to him. 5 The daughter of Pharaoh came down to bathe at the river, while her attendants walked beside the river. She saw the basket among the reeds and sent her maid to bring it. 6 When she opened it, she saw the child. He was crying, and she took pity on him. "This must be one of the Hebrews' children," she said.
7 Then his sister said to Pharaoh's daughter, "Shall I go and get you a nurse from the Hebrew women to nurse the child for you?"
8 Pharaoh's daughter said to her, "Yes." So the girl went and called the child's mother.
9 Pharaoh's daughter said to her, "Take this child and nurse it for me, and I will give you your wages." So the woman took the child and nursed it.
10 When the child grew up, she brought him to Pharaoh's daughter, and she took him as her son. She named him Moses, "because," she said, "I drew him out of the water."

■ Moses led the Israelites out of Egypt to the land of Canaan

■ Moses was the first and most important prophet of the people of Israel

Exodus 2:1–10 The infant Moses is found in the rushes by the pharaoh's daughter and she takes him in

Exodus 2:15 Moses flees from the angry pharaoh to Midian

Exodus 2:16–22 Moses marries Zipporah, a Midianite

Exodus 3:1–22 God appears to Moses in a burning thorn bush

Exodus 4:10–17 Moses is afraid to speak to the pharaoh

Exodus 7–12 Because the pharaoh refuses to listen to Moses, God punishes the Egyptians with ten plagues

Exodus 13:17–22 God leads the Israelites, taking the form of a pillar of clouds and fire

Exodus 14:5–9 When Moses and the Israelites leave Egypt, they are pursued by the pharaoh's army

Exodus 14:26–31 The Israelites cross the Red Sea with God's help

Exodus 16:1–36 In the desert, God feeds the people with manna and quail *p.120 »*

By a prophet the Lord brought Israel up from Egypt,
and by a prophet he was guarded.

Hosea 12:13

Moses

Moses' Childhood, Exile, and Calling

Moses is one of the main figures of the Bible. God appeared to him within a burning thorn bush. Under Moses, the people of Israel left Egypt and formed a covenant with God at Mount Sinai.

The story of Moses begins with his rescue as an infant. The Egyptian pharaoh at the time of Moses' birth no longer remembered Joseph and his services to the kingdom (pp. 98–101). He made the Israelites perform forced labor and was also disturbed by their growing population. He commanded the Egyptians to drown the Israelites' male children in the Nile. Aware of the danger to her newborn son, Moses' mother placed him in a woven basket, and cast it out into the water. The pharaoh's daughter came across the crying child (**1**) and took pity on it, later giving it the name Moses. Through a ruse, his mother was able to act as his nursemaid.

①

Moses Flees One day, Moses, who had grown up at the royal court, observed the Israelites performing forced labor for the

pharaoh. Witnessing an Israelite being beaten by an Egyptian (**2**), he killed the Egyptian in anger. Word of it reached the pharaoh, and Moses, fearing for his life, fled to Midian.

Moses and Zipporah In Midian, Moses was sitting by a well (**3**), when the daughters of the priest Jethro arrived to water their sheep. Other shepherds attempted to drive the young women away from the well, but Moses helped them give water to their animals. Impressed by the young man's helpfulness, Jethro offered Moses his daughter Zipporah in marriage. They wed and bore a son. Moses called him Gershom, a name that evokes exile in a foreign land.

The Burning Bush While herding his sheep one day in the desert, Moses reached Horeb, the "mountain of God." There he saw a thorn bush that was on fire, but not consumed by the flames. Then he heard a voice calling his name, commanding him to remove his shoes, as he was standing on holy ground. Moses saw that it was the God of Abraham (**4**). God recognized the Israelites' plight and wanted to free them. When Moses asked his name, he answered, "I am that I am." Thus, God did not reveal his identity, but promised to help his people.

St. Catherine's Monastery

In the Bible, the "mountain of God" is interchangeably called Horeb and Sinai, which may point to the influence of different traditions. Today, a Greek Orthodox monastery stands at the foot of Mount Sinai, founded in the sixth century and named after St. Catherine. Its grounds contain a thorn bush said to be the one in which God appeared to Moses.

⏩ **Meetings by Water:** p. 83   **Manifestations of God:** p. 317

Moses and Aaron Moses returned to Egypt with his wife Zipporah and his son (**1**). When Moses learned that God expected him to speak to the pharaoh, he was afraid: he had no talent for speaking. Yet God did not accept this, and insisted on teaching Moses what to say. Still, Moses remained reluctant: "My Lord, send who you will send." Upon hearing this, God became angry and sharply rebuked Moses. Nevertheless, he allowed Moses' more eloquent brother Aaron to accompany him. Together, they went to the pharaoh to demand that he let the Israelites go (**3**).

"Let My People Go"

Returning to Egypt, Moses told the Israelites about God's plan to free them from bondage. He went to the pharaoh (**2**) and demanded that he interrupt the work so that the Israelites could celebrate a festival in the desert and make sacrifices to their God. However, the pharaoh refused: his heart was "hardened" and he was not open to God's will. Instead, he made the Israelites' work even more grueling: the straw they needed to produce bricks (**4**) was no longer delivered to them; they had to gather it themselves. Thus, the Israelites' suffering was even greater under their harsh working conditions. Moses protested to God: rather than improving, the situation had become worse. Yet God affirmed his promise to free the Israelites from bondage in Egypt and lead them to the land promised to their ancestors. By liberating them, God would demonstrate his power and glory.

▶▶ **The Promised Land:** p. 122

A Miracle Before the Pharaoh Together, Moses and his brother Aaron presented their demand to the pharaoh, insisting that he let the Israelites go. They attempted to emphasize their request with a miracle: when Aaron threw his staff to the ground, it turned into a live serpent (**5**). Then, the pharaoh called for his magicians, who threw down their staffs, which also transformed into snakes. Aaron's serpent swallowed those of the magicians, but the pharaoh still refused to free the Israelites—just as God predicted since he had "hardened the pharaoh's heart."

First Plagues After this, God afflicted Egypt with a series of plagues. First, the water in the rivers turned to blood. The fish died, and the water became undrinkable. Next, large numbers of frogs and insects tormented the people (**6,7**). These were followed by diseases: livestock plagues and painful boils. Then, hail and locusts lay waste to the land, followed by three days of total darkness, which brought life to a halt.

The Tenth Plague The pharaoh still did not change his mind; he even refused to meet with Moses. God announced another, even more dreadful plague: the death of the firstborn. Every firstborn son from an Egyptian family died. The pharaoh himself lost his eldest son (**8,9**). The grief and despair were enormous: every household was mourning a dead child.

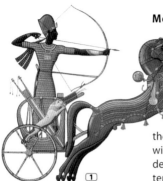

Moses Leads the Israelites Out of Egypt

Only after the death of every firstborn Egyptian son were the Israelites finally permitted by the pharaoh to set out for the desert. However, he soon realized that they were escaping, and he sent his army after them. By the time the Israelites reached the Red Sea, the Egyptians' battle chariots (**1**) had caught up with them. The people were frightened and near despair. On God's direction, however, Moses extended his arm, raising his staff, and the sea divided. A strip of dry land appeared, allowing the Israelites to walk safely across to the other side. When the Egyptians followed, the masses of water rushed back together, and the soldiers were drowned.

In remembrance of this night, the Israelites were commanded to celebrate the Passover (pp. 118–119) every year. The head of each household was to slaughter a lamb and roast it over a fire.

Drowning of the Egyptians
According to a Jewish tale, the angels wanted to break into a joyful song when the Israelites reached the shore and their Egyptian pursuers drowned (**2**). But God rebuked them: "The work of my hands drowns in the sea, and you want to sing?"

Figures and Stories Relevant to Moses

God, see pp. 28–33

Angels, see pp. 42–43

Joseph, an Israelite and High Council to the Pharaoh, see pp. 98–103

The Pharaoh, King of Egypt, see the Egyptians, pp. 104–105

Miriam, Moses' Sister, see pp. 134–135

Aaron, Moses' Brother, see pp. 136–137

God's Convenant With Israel, see pp. 142–143

Zipporah, Moses' Wife, a Midianite, see the Neighboring Tribes of the Peoples of Israel, pp. 166–167

p.125 ››

The Israelites' Victory Song After God saved them from the pursuing Egyptians, Moses and the Israelites lifted their voices in a hymn of praise (**3**), recorded in Exodus 15. The prophets Miriam—Moses' sister—and Aaron joined the women of Israel in their song: "This is my God, and I will praise him ... The Lord is a warrior; the Lord is his name. Pharaoh's chariots and his army he cast into the sea; his picked officers were sunk in the Red Sea."

Manna and Quail As they wandered through the desert, the Israelites became increasingly dissatisfied. Longing for the rich meat stews of Egypt, they complained to Moses and Aaron. God heard the people's protests and provided them with food: in the evening, it rained quail from heaven (**4**), and in the morning the Israelites found piles of small, round kernels covering their camp. "Man hu?" they asked: "What is this?" "Manna, bread to eat," Moses replied. The Israelites were only supposed to take as much manna as they needed for each day. To satisfy their thirst, Moses made water flow from a stone (**5**).

The Parting of the Red Sea

Exodus 14:26–31

26 Then the Lord said to Moses, "Stretch out your hand over the sea, so that the water may come back upon the Egyptians, upon their chariots and chariot drivers." ²⁷ So Moses stretched out his hand over the sea, and at dawn the sea returned to its normal depth. As the Egyptians fled before it, the Lord tossed the Egyptians into the sea. ²⁸ The waters returned and covered the chariots and the chariot drivers, the entire army of Pharaoh that had followed them into the sea; not one of them remained.

²⁹ But the Israelites walked on dry ground through the sea, the waters forming a wall for them on their right and on their left. ³⁰ Thus the Lord saved Israel that day from the Egyptians; and Israel saw the Egyptians dead on the seashore. ³¹ Israel saw the great work that the Lord did against the Egyptians. So the people feared the Lord and believed in the Lord and in his servant Moses.

Passover

The Jewish holiday of Passover is celebrated in remembrance of the Israelites' liberation from Egypt. The festival, which begins in springtime on the 14th day of the month Nisan, lasts seven days—or eight days in the diaspora. Until the destruction of the Temple (pp. 368–369), Passover was a time of pilgrimage. Believers traveled to Jerusalem, and a lamb was slaughtered and eaten.

On the evening of the Seder, the Haggadah, or "story," is read. It contains texts, prayers, and songs, as well as explanations of the holiday's emblematic rituals and foods. The central event of Passover is a meal (**4,5**), which includes wine (**1**) and symbolic foods. Rituals are performed in remembrance of the experiences of slavery and liberation. The Haggadah states: "This is the bread of poverty, which our ancestors ate in the land of Egypt."

The Seder Plate All of the foods on the Seder plate (**2**) are symbolic. The charosset, a paste made from apples and nuts, represents the mortar of the bricks the Israelites were forced to produce. Bitter herbs symbolize life in bondage. A bone is reminiscent of the lamb's blood used to mark the houses. An egg symbolizes sacrifices made at the temple. A sprig symbolizes the fruits of the new land, while saltwater represents the Israelites' tears. The matzo (**3**) stands for the unleavened bread baked by the Israelites, in their haste to leave Egypt.

▶▶ The Temple in Jerusalem: pp. 368–369

« p.110

■ Moses received the Ten Commandments from God

Exodus 19:3–20:21 On Mount Sinai, God gives Moses the Ten Commandments

Exodus 24:1–8 God forms a covenant with the Israelites

Exodus 32:1–6 The Israelites pray to a golden calf

Exodus 35:4–40:33 The construction of the Tabernacle

Numbers 27:12–23 Joshua becomes Moses' successor

Deuteronomy 4–30 Moses recites God's Ten Commandments

Deuteronomy 34 Moses names Joshua successor and dies

Wanderings in the Desert

After their escape at the Red Sea, the Israelites traveled through the desert under Moses' leadership. However, their wanderings did not lead them directly to the Promised Land; their first destination was the Sinai Peninsula (**2**). Along the way, the Israelites lost confidence in Moses, complaining to him about their fears of dying of hunger or thirst in the desert. God came to their aid, providing food and water (p. 115). Here, the biblical text conveys the people's complaints not merely as resistance against Moses, but mistrust in God himself.

The Israelites finally arrived at the "mountain of God," Mount Sinai or Horeb, as it is also called in the Bible. In this place, God offered to form a covenant with the people of Israel. After liberating them from slavery (**1**), he wanted to set them apart from other nations by making them his chosen people (pp. 132–133). The laws of the Torah, which were revealed by God on Mount Sinai (pp. 130–131) formed part of this covenant.

⟫ **God's Chosen People:** pp. 132–133   **God's Covenant With Israel:** pp. 142–143

The Israelites at Mount Sinai When the Israelites arrived at Mount Sinai (**3**), God made his offer: if the Israelites agreed to a covenant and promised to uphold his Commandments, they would become his chosen people. Moses conveyed this to the people, who unanimously agreed: "All that the Lord has said we will do." After three days, Moses led the people to the mountain, where God revealed himself. The earth shook, a cloud of smoke rose, and a trumpet blast was heard. They were forbidden to step on the foot of the mountain.

The Covenant With God
Moses climbed the mountain, where God spoke to him and gave him the Ten Commandments (**4**). The first of the Commandments (pp. 126–127) was tied to the Israelites' liberation from Egypt, forming the foundation of the covenant between God and the people of Israel. In addition, God gave Moses instructions regarding religious services and worship, holidays, and civil and criminal law, especially the protection of the poor and the weak. Afterward, the people promised to follow the rules, and the covenant was sealed with a sacrificial ritual and feast.

The Golden Calf When Moses was on the mountain, the people became restless. Aaron, Moses' brother, created an idol of a golden calf (**5**), and the Israelites gave sacrifices to it (**6**). God was enraged and wanted to destroy them, but Moses reminded him of his promise to Abraham, and they were spared.

▷▷ **Sacrifices:** p. 45   **Manifestations of God:** p. 317

The Laws of God

In Judaism, God did not just reveal the written Torah, the five books of Moses, to him on Mount Sinai, but also their interpretation, the oral Torah. According to the oral traditional conception, these were passed verbally from generation to generation until they were written in the Talmud (p. 503). The Ten Commandments (**2**) are only a small part of the 613 laws and prohibitions. They regulate the relationship between God and humankind, as well as between humans with one another.

Behavior has a particular value in Judaism. It is dependent upon the practice of the will of God, who has expressed himself in his laws. Therefore, holiness is not derived from one's forefathers. Holy people become so by giving themselves to God, loving him, and acting according to his will, as was said by the religious philosopher Abraham Joseph Heschel.

The Ark of the Covenant On Mount Sinai, Moses received exact instructions for the construction of the Tabernacle (**3**), a type of sanctified tent that would act as a sanctum for the Ark of the Covenant (**1**) containing the tablets of the law. Moreover, there was an altar, golden candlesticks, a table for the showbread, and a copper basin for sacrifices. Sacrifices were made by the priests, who were sanctified and wore special garments.

The Promised Land

Along with his promise of a great lineage and rich blessings (p. 62) to the patriarchs—and later to the whole populace of Israel—God gave the land of Canaan to the Israelites. They did not obtain this land out of merit, but rather because God, out of free love, had bound himself to them. However, the ownership of the Promised Land was entwined with obedience to the laws. If the Israelites were to contravene these laws then the land of milk and honey would not bear any fruit. The severest punishment for disobedience would be banishment from the land.

▶▶ **Matriarchs and Patriarchs:** p. 69   **The Tabernacle:** p. 162

The Land of Milk and Honey

Moses sent scouts to the Promised Land to investigate its fertility and its inhabitants. The men returned after 40 days, bringing with them a grape that was so large that it had to be carried by two men on a pole (**4**), as well as figs and pomegranates. The land was fertile (**5**), flowing with milk and honey. Many powerful tribes, however, already lived there. Out of fear, the Israelites wanted to return to Egypt. This incited God's wrath, as they did not trust in his promise. Thus, he decreed that they would spend 40 years in the desert. Only their descendants would be allowed to enter the Promised Land.

Moses Speaks With God

The relationship between Moses and God was unique. Moses was one of the few people to see God face to face (**6**). In the Tabernacle, God spoke with Moses "as one speaks to a friend" (Exodus 33:11). The Bible reports that when Moses asked to see God in his full glory, God placed him on a rock so that he would only see him from behind, as a human would die if they were to view God in the true fullness of his glory.

Rebellion of Korah's Mob

Korah, Dathan, Abiram, and their followers rose against Moses' and Aaron's claims to power. They insisted that the people, and not just the priests, should be able to present offerings to God. They prepared their own sacrifices; however, the Earth opened and engulfed the leaders of the rebellion, while the others were consumed by flames (**7**).

End of the Journey

Along their journey through the desert, the people complained continuously about the lack of water and nourishment. As punishment, God sent snakes (**1**) to bite the Israelites, who realized their sins and promised to change. Moses erected an iron snake: whoever was bitten and saw the snake would survive (**2**).

After 40 years of migration, the Israelites finally reached the Promised Land. However, God did not let Moses accompany them because he had misused his power in the past. Before his death, Moses gave a long speech, which encompasses the fifth book of the Torah. He reminded the people to follow the laws of God. Thus, this book was called Deuteronomy, "Repetition of the Laws." His words were recorded and housed within the Ark.

A memorial on Mount Nebo in present-day Jordan depicts the iron snake, which Moses is supposed to have built for the Israelites during their migration

Moses Passes Leadership to Joshua As Moses knew that he was not allowed to enter the Promised Land, he appointed his trusted servant (**3**) Joshua as his successor. Under his leadership, the Israelites went on to conquer the Promised Land. Moses encouraged and strengthened Joshua, so that he would not have any fear. He assured Joshua that God was going to be with him and the Israelites; God would deliver the land to the Israelites that he had promised to their ancestors.

Death of Moses Moses blessed the Tribes of Israel before his death, each tribe receiving its own blessing. Then, as ordered by God, he ascended Mount Nebo and saw the Promised Land (**5**) from its summit. He died at the age of 120 (**4**) and his gravesite remains unknown. The Israelites mourned him for 30 days. The Bible says of him: "Never since has there arisen a prophet like Moses, whom the Lord knew face to face. He was unequalled for all the signs and wonders that the Lord sent him to perform in the land of Egypt."

The Ten Commandments

Bar Mitzvah At age 13, Jewish boys have reached religious maturity. During their Bar Mitzvah (Hebrew: "son of the law"), the boys read from the Torah for the first time (**1**) in the synagogue.

Israel received the Torah on Mount Sinai (pp. 130–131) through an intense appearance by God, in which the mountain smoked and shook, and thunder and lightning raged (p. 121). God announced the Ten Commandments (**3**) to the Israelites, and their fear was so great that they asked Moses to speak with him alone. The Decalogue ("ten words") begins with God's introduction of himself and his works: "I am the Lord your God, who brought you out of the land of Egypt, out of the house of slavery." The relationship between God and Israel is based on this liberation, and it forms their covenant. The Ten Commandments are: do not worship other gods; do not create a carved image; do not abuse the name of God; keep the Sabbath holy; honor your parents; do not murder; do not commit adultery; do not steal; do not bear false witness against your neighbor; do not covet what belongs to your neighbor (**2**) (Exodus 20).

⏩ **God's Covenant With Israel:** pp. 142–143

Sukkoth—The Feast of Tabernacles

Sukkoth, the Feast of Tabernacles, is celebrated in remembrance of the huts in which the Israelites lived in during their migration through the desert (**1**). The festival is celebrated in the autumn; it begins five days after Yom Kippur (pp. 138–139) and lasts a week. Simchat Torah, the day of rejoicing the Torah, is celebrated on the eighth or ninth day. God is thanked for his gift and people dance with the Torah in the synagogue or the street.

Meals are eaten in leaft huts (**2**). Those inside should be able to see the stars through the roof. Characteristic for Sukkoth is the lulav, a bouquet made of a palm and a willow branch, myrtle and an etrog (**3**), which is a type of citrus fruit.

>> Moses Leads the Israelites Through the Wilderness: p. 120

The Torah

The word Torah (Hebrew: "teachings," "law") has several meanings. It not only identifies individual instructions from God, but also the five books of Moses in their entirety (Greek: Pentateuch), and moreover, the combined laws of God and the teachings for the people of Israel.

The Torah was given to the Israelites on Mount Sinai (p. 121), a place that is far removed from everyday life both in terms of time and space. According to Jewish understanding, God presented both a written and an oral Torah on Sinai. The former was condensed into the Pentateuch, and the latter into the later Jewish lore of the Talmud (p. 503) and the Midrash. The laws of the Torah encompass the whole spectrum of life: the relationship between God and humanity, as well as the various relationships within humankind.

The Torah formed the central point of life for the people of Israel. It was the link between God and the Israelites. By obeying the Torah, they strengthened the covenant they had made on Sinai day by day.

Learning in the Jewish Tradition The Torah makes a two demand: it must be obeyed and it must be studied (**1**). There is a debate in the Jewish tradition over which one is more important. One possible answer sounds like a paradox: Studying is more important because it leads to the practice.

Shrine of the Torah In the synagogues (**2**), the Torah—divided into 52 weekly portions—is read through once over the year (**4**). The Torah used in services is handwritten on parchment. The scribes need about a year to transcribe one copy of the Torah. If it is damaged, the copy is buried or kept secure in a genizah. The Torah is encased in the synagogue, draped in a mantle (or cabinet) made of velvet, the apexes are topped by crowns, and a plate adorns the front (**3**).

⏩ **God's Covenant With Israel:** pp. 142–143 **Synagogues:** p. 368

▶▶ **God's Covenant With Israel:** pp. 142–143

God's Chosen People

Exodus 19:3–8

3 Then Moses went up to God; the Lord called to him from the mountain, saying, "Thus you shall say to the house of Jacob, and tell the Israelites: 4 You have seen what I did to the Egyptians, and how I bore you on eagles' wings and brought you to myself. 5 Now therefore, if you obey my voice and keep my covenant, you shall be my treasured possession out of all the peoples. Indeed, the whole earth is mine, 6 but you shall be for me a priestly kingdom and a holy nation. These are the words that you shall speak to the Israelites." 7 So Moses came, summoned the elders of the people, and set before them all these words that the Lord had commanded him. 8 The people all answered as one: "Everything that the Lord has spoken we will do." Moses reported the words of the people to the Lord.

■ Miriam was Moses' sister
■ In Exodus, Miriam is identified as a prophetess

Exodus 2:1–10 Miriam observes Moses being saved by the daughter of the pharaoh

Exodus 15:20–21 Miriam sings a song of thanks for the rescue by the Red Sea

Numbers 12:1–15 When Miriam criticizes Moses, she contracts leprosy

Numbers 12:13 Moses prays for Miriam to become healthy

Micah 6:4 Miriam leads the Israelites with Moses and Aaron

Numbers 20:1 Miriam is buried in Kadesh

"Has the Lord spoken only through Moses? Has he not spoken through us also?" Numbers 12:2

Miriam

Miriam is mentioned not only in the five books of Moses, but also by the prophet Micah, who identifies her as the person who, together with Moses and Aaron, led the people of Israel out of Egypt (Micah 6:4). Miriam is the most important female figure in Exodus. She was the elder sister of Moses and Aaron. Even as a girl, she made sure that her brothers were safe. After leaving Egypt, she led the Israelite women in a dance and sang a song of praise to God. The Bible calls her, like her brother Moses, a prophetess. She later rebelled with her brother Aaron against Moses' authority. They questioned why God spoke only through Moses. God invited the three of them into the meeting tent and then harshly censured Miriam and Aaron. Thereafter Miriam became "white as snow" and was struck down with leprosy. Abiding by the rules set out for lepers, she had to spend seven nights removed from the camp, during which time the people stayed in the same spot. She then returned to the camp and the Israelites continued their journey. Miriam died in Kadesh and was buried there.

Liberal Judaism and Female Rabbis

There are numerous positions of leadership open to women in Judaism. In outside of Orthodox Judaism, they can be ordained as rabbis and cantors. The first female rabbi was Regina Jonas, who was ordained in Berlin in 1935. She was murdered by the National Socialists in Auschwitz in 1944.

Women have been ordained as rabbis in the U.S. by Reform Judaism since 1974 and also by Conservative Judaism since 1984. There have been discussions about the ordination of women in Orthodox Judaism; some women have even received a private orthodox semicha (ordination).

Figures and Stories Relevant to Miriam

God, see pp. 28–33

The Egyptians, see pp. 104–105

Moses, Miriam's Brother, see pp. 110–115 and 120–125

The Parting of the Red Sea, see pp. 116–117

Aaron, Miriam's Brother, see pp. 136–137

The Song of Victory by the Red Sea as a Psalm, see the Psalms, pp. 222–223

Micah, see the Minor Prophets, pp. 330–333

Miriam and the Daughter of the Pharaoh

After Moses was put into the Nile River in a basket by his mother (p. 110), his elder sister observed the progress of her newborn brother from the riverbank. The daughter of the pharaoh found the boy and felt sympathy for him. Miriam used this opportunity and asked the princess if they were looking for a wet nurse for the child (**1**). The princess agreed and thus Miriam fetched her mother so that she could breast-feed her son. She even received a reward from the pharaoh for her services. Thus, through Miriam's actions it was possible for Moses to be brought up in his own family until he was old enough to move in with the princess in the court of the pharaoh.

Miriam's Song of Victory

After the flight from Egypt, the crossing of the Red Sea, and the liberation of the Israelites, Moses and Miriam praised God (p. 115). She took a drum, gathered the women of Israel, and sang a song of thanks (**2**). "Sing to the Lord, for he has triumphed gloriously; horse and rider he has thrown into the sea." (Exodus 15:21).

■ Aaron was Moses' brother

■ Aaron made a golden calf to be worshiped by the Israelites

■ Aaron was Moses' delegate to the Israelites

Exodus 4:27 Aaron meets Moses, who is returning to Egypt

Exodus 4:28–31 Aaron shares Moses' words with the Israelites

Exodus 7:1–13 Aaron throws a staff onto the ground, which transforms into a snake

Exodus 12:31–42 Aaron and Moses lead the Israelites out of Egypt together

Exodus 16:2 During the Exodus, Aaron and Moses are constantly interrupted by the grievances of the people

Exodus 29:1–44 Aaron and his line of descendants are ordained as priests

Exodus 32:1–6 Aaron is asked by the Israelites to make gods for them and makes a golden calf for them to pray to

Numbers 12:1 Aaron and his sister Miriam criticize Moses' marriage with a Kushite woman

Deuteronomy 10:6 Aaron dies in Moserah and is buried; his son succeeds him

Then bring near to you your brother Aaron, and his sons with him, from among the Israelites, to serve me as priests. Exodus 28:1

Aaron

The Bible refers to Moses' brother Aaron (**1**) as a prophet. This eloquent man accompanied Moses in his negotiations with the pharaoh (pp. 112–113). When challenged, he threw his staff to the ground and it turned into a snake. His snake swallowed those of the Egyptian magicians, who performed the same trick. While Moses was away for an extended period on Mount Sinai, Aaron collected gold from the Israelites and created a golden idol of a calf (**2**). He presented it to the people with these words: "These are your gods, Israel, who led you out of Egypt!" (Exodus 32:4). God was irate and wanted to kill the Israelites, but Moses convinced him otherwise.

Aaron and Moses When Moses was told by God to lead the people of Israel out of Egypt, God placed his articulate brother by his side (**3**). Together, they persuaded the Israelites to leave. Later, Aaron and his sister Miriam criticized Moses many times (p. 134) and even challenged his claim to power. In spite of this, he was elected to the office of high priest.

Figures and Stories Relevant to Aaron

God, see pp. 28–33

Pharaoh, see the Egyptians, see pp. 104–105

Moses, Aaron's Brother, see pp. 110–115 and 120–125

Miriam, Aaron's Sister, see pp. 134–135

The Levites, see the 12 Tribes of Israel, pp.162–165

Aaron the Priest God appointed Aaron from the tribe of Levi and his offspring as priests. It was their duty to present the offerings of the people on the altar, at first in the Tabernacle (p. 162) and later in the Temple. They were also responsible for holy objects (**4**, **5**) such as the Ark of the Covenant, the golden candlesticks, a transportable altar, a table for ceremonial bread, and a copper basin for sacrifices. The priests wore special garments consisting of over and under robes, a breastpiece, a tunic, a headband, and a belt. The finest materials and cloth were used for them: reds, blues, and purples, linen, gold, scarlets. On the breast piece could be found 12 jewels inscribed with the names of the 12 Tribes.

High Priests: p. 234　**The Temple in Jerusalem:** pp. 368–369

Yom Kippur— The Day of Atonement

Yom Kippur is a major holiday on the Jewish calendar (**1**). According to biblical understanding, the day brings purification. To this end, goats were symbolically laden with the sins of the people and sacrificed. It was only on Yom Kippur that the high priests could enter the inner sanctum of the Temple. Since the destruction of the Temple, the holiday has been celebrated through fasting and prayer (**2**). Making peace with others is a prerequisite for reconciliation with God. The ten days that precede Yom Kippur are known as the "days of repentance" and their goal is reflection and renunciation from wrongdoing.

Blowing of the Shofar
On Yom Kippur and Rosh Hashanah (the New Year's festival), a shofar (**3**)—a ram's horn—is blown. The sound of the shofar has several meanings: it reminds Jews that God is the Lord of the world and calls them to repent. It also reminds them of the sacrifice of Abraham, as well as a reminder of the coming of the Messiah.

>> The Temple in Jerusalem: pp. 368–369

Kapparah A small minority of Jews still practice the striking of the "kapparah," in which sins are transferred to a chicken by waving it over someone's head (**4**). The chicken is finally presented as a sacrifice (Hebrew: "kapparah"). This ceremony is a reminder of the transfer of sins to the scapegoat, as described in Leviticus 16.

4

■ Balaam was a seer, who defended Israel

■ Balaam and his donkey were a favorite motif for medieval art

■ The story of the clever donkey is a plea against cruelty to animals

Numbers 22:1–6 King Balak tells Balaam to curse the Israelites

Numbers 22:9–20 God tells Balaam not to curse the Israelites but to bless them

Numbers 22:21–30 When Balaam's donkey sees an angel, it halts and does not want to continue

Numbers 22:31–35 God also lets Balaam see the angel

Numbers 24:1–25 Balaam blesses the Israelites rather than cursing them

Joshua 13:22 Balaam is slain by the Israelites

But the donkey said to Balaam, "Am I not your donkey, which you have ridden all your life to this day? Have I been in the habit of treating you in this way?" Numbers 22:30

Balaam and His Donkey

En route to Canaan, the Israelites arrived in the land of the Moabites. Balak, the king of the Moabites, sent emissaries to Balaam, a seer, to demand that he curse the Israelites. Balak hoped to defeat the Israelites in battle. During the night, God spoke to Balaam and warned him against cursing the Israelites. The Moabites, however, coerced him until he gave in. Traveling with his donkey (**1**) to Balak, Balaam encountered an angel, who instructed him to do only what God had told him. When he arrived, Balaam presented God with a sacrifice. To Balak's outrage, however, he did not curse the Israelites. Balaam replied that he could not act against the word of the God of Israel. He prophesied that a "star from Jacob" and a "scepter from Israel" would emerge and that the Israelites would conquer the land.

Figures and Stories Relevant to Balaam

God, see pp. 28–33

Angels, see pp. 42–43

The Israelites, see the 12 Tribes of Israel, pp. 162–165

The Moabites, see the Neighboring Peoples of Israel, pp. 166–167

Jesus of Nazareth, see pp. 402–409 and 414–419

Animals in the Bible

Humanity should simultaneously use and respect the world as God's creation, which is reflected in the law against having animals work on the Sabbath. Animals have served as sacrifices, as when lambs' blood on doorposts saved the Israelites' firstborns in Egypt. On the Day of Atonement, a scapegoat symbolically took on the sins of the people. This is also the role of Jesus in the New Testament, who is called the Lamb of God.

>> **Curses:** p. 55   **Blessing:** p. 79   **Dreams:** p. 101

An Angel Encounters Balaam's Donkey

Balaam accompanied the emissaries of King Balak on his donkey. Along the way, an angel with a sword, who was invisible to humans, stepped in front of his donkey (**2**), which deviated from the path. Balaam whipped it to try to bring it back on course to no avail. God let the donkey speak, and it asked Balaam why he had beat it three times. Then God opened Balaam's eyes so that he could also see the angel. He told him to continue on his path, but to do only what God had ordered.

God's Covenant With Israel

God's devotion to humankind is described in the Bible as a "covenant." It was God (p. 48) who made a covenant with Noah as a promise that he would never again wipe out the human race. The sign of this covenant, which includes all of humankind, is the rainbow (**2**). Then God made a covenant with Abraham (p. 62) in which God promised Abraham numerous progeny and possession of the land of Canaan. This covenant applied to Abraham and his offspring and its sign is circumcision. This covenant was renewed for the entire people of Israel on Mount Sinai after their Exodus from Egypt (**1**), God promised: "I will be your God, and you will be my people." Israel was bound to obey God's laws (pp. 121–122).

The prophet Jeremiah spoke of how the people of Israel would form a "new covenant" with God at the end of days. The novelty of such a covenant was that it would be written onto the hearts of the Israelites, so that they would fulfill it of their own accord. In the Christian tradition, this promise is attributed to Jesus Christ, through whom God made a covenant with the world.

As they crossed the River Jordan and entered the Promised Land, the Israelites carried the Ark of the Covenant, which held God's commandments.

» **God's Chosen People:** pp. 132–133

Hear, O Israel!

Deuteronomy 6:4–9

⁴ Hear, O Israel: The Lord is our
God, the Lord alone.
⁵ You shall love the Lord your God
with all your heart, and with all your
soul, and with all your might.
⁶ Keep these words that I am commanding you today in your heart.
⁷ Recite them to your children and talk
about them when you are at home and
when you are away, when you lie down
and when you rise.
⁸ Bind them as a sign on your hand, fix
them as an emblem on your forehead,
⁹ and write them on the doorposts of
your house and on your gates.

*During specific prayers, some Jews wear
boxes on their forehead and arms, in
which special biblical texts such as the
Hear, O Israel! (Hebrew: Shema Yisrael)
are kept. The boxes, known
as tefillin, are
secured
with
prayer
straps.*

From the Conquest of Canaan to the Time of the Judges

Delilah betrayed the secret source of Samson's enormous strength to his enemy, the Philistines

From the Conquest o

p. 154

p. 183

* The dating of events before the later kingdoms of Israel and Judah is highly debated and is viewed by many scholars as largely unhistorical.

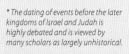

p. 171

Canaan to the Judges

p. 161

p. 168

p. 188

1100   1050   1000

p. 195

p. 197

From the Conquest of Canaan to the Time of the Judges

While the five books of Moses detail biblical history from the creation of the world to Moses' death, the acquisition and division of the Promised Land lies at the center of the Book of Joshua. The Book of Judges details the Israelites' experiences from the moment they enter Canaan, throughout the time of the judges. This period ends with the era of the kings. In the Book of Joshua (**1**), the conquest of Canaan by the Israelites is described as a successful military campaign that was made possible purely because God stood by them and intervened for their benefit. In return for this divine intervention, God required that the Israelites follow the laws of the covenant made on Mount Sinai, which are gathered in the Torah. At first, the Book of Joshua describes the celebration of Passover, which commemorates the liberation of the Israelites from Egyptian slavery by God. The circumcision of males—an act symbolic of the covenant between God and the people of Israel—is also central to this holiday.

After Joshua, his name meaning "Yahweh is salvation," had conquered the land of Canaan, it was split up between the 12 Tribes of Israel. The tribes of Reuben, Gad, and a portion of Manasseh settled the land east of the Jordan, and the remaining tribes settled in the west. As they inherited the high priesthood, the tribe of Levi—also known as the Levites—were not allotted a particular region but rather established an array of cities throughout the Promised Land. At the end of the Book of Joshua, Joshua called a meeting of the tribes. Here, he called upon the Israelites to make a decision: they had to choose between the various gods of the local populace or God. The people unanimously chose God, who had led them out of Egypt. Afterward, Joshua renewed the covenant between God and Israel, and the Israelites agreed to follow the Ten Commandments.

The story of the Israelite military conquest of the Promised Land in the Book of Joshua is not consistent with archaeological research. For example, although the cities Tel Hazor, Aphek, Lachish, and ② Megiddo were destroyed, it was through a long process lasting one hundred years, not through an Israelite military campaign. Thus, the causes of these cities' falls were likely due to a breakdown in the social order. The cities of Ai and Jericho have similar stories, in that it is still unclear whether outside enemies or internal unrest were responsible for their disintegration. In the Book of Joshua, the conquest of Jericho is described as a miraculous event in which the Israelites' trumpets were used to bring down the city's walls.

There are many different hypotheses regarding the Israelite settlement in Canaan. Some researchers believe that it was a peaceful migration of nomads (**2**); others see the Israelites as a part of the local Canaanite population, from whom they gradually seceded. Most historians agree that the Book of Joshua was not a contemporary construction, but rather was written hundreds of years after the settlement. In its current form, it most likely originates from the time during or just after the exile—after 586 B.C.E. The violent nature of the military conquest of the Promised Land often shocks today's readers. However, the Book of Joshua can also be understood within the context of Israel and Judah's desire for sovereignty.

Among other things, the Book of Judges describes Israel just after the conquest and before the establishment of the kingship. A recurring theme found

throughout the narrative of Judges was the disobedience of the Israelites—often by falling into idolatry—and God's punishment by letting them be besieged by their enemies. Weary of the subjugation, the Israelites always turn back to God. Hearing their cries, God allows a judge to emerge, who can lead the people to win back their freedom. The term "judge" used here is certainly misleading: They were prophets and priests, as well as political and military leaders. Their duty was to redeem Israel—with God's help—and that is why they were referred to as "saviors" (Hebrew: "moshia"). The judges of Israel included Othniel, Ehud, Shagmar, Deborah and Barak, Gideon, Jephtha, and Samson.

Like Joshua, the Book of Judges is not a description of historical facts, but rather a theological interpretation. Despite reservations about a kingship, which consistently arise within the text, the conclusive statement during the time of the judges was: "At that time there was no king in Israel; each person did what he found to be right." Left to their own devices, the Israelites periodically rejected God and turned to idolatry. This disregard of the Torah led to chaos, immorality, and corruption. Yet God pitied his people and allowed judges to appear during times of crisis. The time of the Judges is the background for the story of the Moabite Ruth (**4**), who remained faithful to her Israelite mother-in-law Naomi and God. Like most books of the Bible, the authoring of Judges occurred over time. Most historians believe that the texts date back to the time of exile, thus after 586 B.C.E. The office of the judge ended when the prophet and priest Samuel (**3**) anointed the first king of Israel, Saul.

The Taking of Jericho

Joshua 6:13, 16, 20–21

13 *The seven priests carrying the seven trumpets of rams' horns before the ark of the Lord passed on, blowing the trumpets continually. The armed men went before them, and the rearguard came after the ark of the Lord, while the trumpets blew continually.*
16 *And at the seventh time, when the priests had blown the trumpets, Joshua said to the people, "Shout! For the Lord has given you the city."*
20 *So the people shouted, and the trumpets were blown. As soon as the people heard the sound of the trumpets, they raised a great shout, and the wall fell down flat; so the people charged straight ahead into the city and captured it.*
21 *Then they devoted to destruction by the edge of the sword all in the city, both men and women, young and old, oxen, sheep, and donkeys.*

A horn from Megiddo in Israel from the time of the settlement of the 12 Tribes in Canaan (second–first century B.C.E.). With God's help the Israelites made the walls of Jericho cave in with noise and shrieking.

■ Joshua was Moses' successor

■ Joshua led the Israelites during the acquisition of the lands of Canaan

Deuteronomy 31:1–8 Moses names Joshua his successor

Joshua 2:1–24 Joshua sends emissaries to Jericho

Joshua 3:1–17 The Israelites cross the Jordan

Joshua 4:1–24 Joshua and the Israelites erect 12 stones

Joshua 6:1–27 Joshua and the Israelites conquer Jericho

Joshua 10:12–15 Joshua makes the sun stand still

Joshua 13–21 Joshua divides the lands among the 12 Tribes

Joshua 24:29–33 Joshua dies and is buried in Timnath-serah

Be strong and courageous; for you shall put this people in possession of the land that I swore to their ancestors to give them.

Joshua 1:6

Joshua

Shortly before his death, Moses appointed Joshua as his successor. The name Joshua (Hebrew: Je-hoshuah) means "God will help" or "God will save." This corresponds to the central message of the Book of Joshua. Joshua's task was to lead the Israelites, who had been migrating through the desert for 40 years, from the east over the River Jordan and into the Promised Land of Canaan. Then, he had to conquer it, and to divide it among the 12 Tribes of Israel. ⟫⟫

①

Jericho Jericho (**1**), which is described as being heavily fortified, was conquered by the Israelites. According to God's instructions, Joshua had the Israelite soldiers walk around the city walls once a day for six days. On the seventh day, the priests walked around the walls, carrying the Ark of the Covenant (**2**). Suddenly, trumpets sounded and the soldiers let out a battle cry, bursting the city walls open. The Israelites took over the city and killed all the in-**②** habitants, except Rahab.

Moses Anoints Joshua Upon his death, Moses named Joshua as his successor (p. 125). Joshua and Caleb were the only people to have survived both the Exodus from Egypt and the settlement in the Promised Land. Moses, who was not allowed to enter the Promised Land, blessed Joshua by laying his hand upon him (**3**). God promised Joshua that he would act with him as he had done with Moses: "Do not be frightened or dismayed, for the Lord your God is with you wherever you go." The people promised to follow Joshua as they had followed Moses.

Passage Over the Jordan
The first time the Israelites set foot in the Promised Land was after crossing the River Jordan. The Ark of the Covenant, which held the tablets of the law, was carried by priests at the head of the procession (**4**). When they walked into the river with the Ark, the waters receded and the Israelites were able to walk across it with dry feet, just as when Moses had parted the Red Sea (pp. 116–117). Joshua told the people that this miracle was a sign from God: just as the waters had given way to them, all the peoples of the land of Canaan would also retreat. A memorial was constructed from 12 stones in remembrance of this event, as every tribe had taken a stone from the riverbed of the Jordan.

> **Figures and Stories Relevant to Joshua**
>
> **God**, see pp. 28–33
>
> **Moses**, Prophet and Leader of the Israelites During the Exodus From Egypt, see pp. 110–115 and 120–125
>
> **God's Covenant With Israel**, see pp. 142–143
>
> **The Canaanites**, Inhabitants of the Land of Canaan, see pp. 160–161
>
> **The 12 Tribes of Israel**, see pp. 162–165
>
> **Inhabitants of the Land of Canaan**, see the Neighboring Peoples of Israel, pp. 166–167

⟫ **The Promised Land:** p. 122   **Jericho:** p. 160

The Bible narrates how the Israelites conquered one city after another during their acquisition of the land (**6**). This was not due to their military superiority, but rather because God was on their side. Judging by archaeological finds (**7**), the Israelites—contrary to the biblical account—was not accomplished by force, but rather through peace.

Rahab acknowledged the greatness of the God of Israel. She helped the Israelites conquer her home city.

Joshua Spares Rahab Before the conquest of Jericho, Joshua sent emissaries to the city, who were taken in by the prostitute Rahab. When men of the king hunted for the "spies," they hid on Rahab's roof and fled. She acknowledged the greatness of the God of Israel, "for the Lord your God is the God in the heavens above and the earth below." When the Israelites conquered Jericho, they killed all of its inhabitants, except for Rahab and her family (**5**).

Joshua Commands the Sun After Joshua had conquered the cities of Jericho and Ai, the king of Jerusalem became afraid of the advancing Israelite troops and sought local allies to help him. Five kings and their armies pledged their support, but God sent large stones from heaven, which killed many of the enemy soldiers. In order to defeat his enemies, Joshua ordered the sun not to move (**8**). Thus, it did not set until the Israelites had wiped out every last one of their opponents (p. 167).

Joshua's Death Reaching old age, Joshua summoned the Tribes together in Shechem (**9**) and asked them whether they wanted to serve the God of their forefathers or the gods of the Canaanites. They unanimously opted for God and renewed the covenant. Joshua died at age 110 and was buried in Timnath-serah.

⟫ **God's Covenant With Israel:** pp. 142–143

■ God led the Israelites into the land of Canaan

Joshua 3:10 The military success of the Israelites is based on God's support

Joshua 6 The Israelites conquer the Canaanite city of Jericho

Judges 1:1–7 The Israelites defeat Adonibezek

Judges 2:6–23 The Israelites pray to Canaanite gods

Judges 4:1–24 Yael kills the Canaanite captain Sisera

II Samuel 5:6–10 David conquers the Jebusite city of Jerusalem

I Kings 9:20–21 Solomon makes the Canaanites his slaves

You shall make no covenant with them and their gods.

Exodus 23:32

The Canaanites

Canaan is the biblical name for the land promised to the Israelites by God, and Canaanites the name for the inhabitants. The name also serves as an umbrella term for the other peoples of this land. The Bible also mentions, among others, the Hivites, Jebusites, Amorites, and Perizzites. They were all politically autonomous, living in individual city-states under city-sovereigns and kings. The land ① was taken from them by the Israelites.

God repeatedly warned the Israelites not to form any alliances with the people of Canaan, as they prayed to false gods (**1**), whereas the Israelites could only serve God. As is described in the Book of Judges, the Israelites continuously turned from the correct path of worshiping God and following his Commandments. They engaged in aspects of the Canaanite lifestyle, such as the worshiping of idols. As punishment, God delivered them into the hands of the Canaanites, until he saw the suffering of his people and sent a savior to liberate them.

Jericho

According to the Bible, Jericho was overtaken and destroyed by the Israelites with the help of God (p. 156). Archaeological finds suggest that the city, one of the oldest of the world, had very few inhabitants—if any—at the time of the Israelite settlement. Also, the walls of the city had already been destroyed. Many scholars propose that the military invasion narrated in the Bible is not historically accurate.

>> The Promised Land: p. 122

The Battle Against Adonibezek After Joshua's death, the Israelites took up the war against the Canaanites and God stood by their side once again. After they had beaten the enemy armies, Adonibezek, one of the enemy commanders, fled, but the Israelites chased him down and attacked him. They hacked off his thumbs and big toes (**2**), as he had done to others before. He recognized the justice of God: "As I have done, so has God repaid me."

David Conquers Jerusalem
Joshua 15:63 reports that the Israelites initially could not conquer the Jebusite city of Jerusalem, and so for a long time the city remained an enclave in the territories of the tribes of Judah and Benjamin. It was not until the reign of King David that the fortified city fell to the Israelites (**4**). His commander Joab penetrated the city through a water shaft, thus making the conquest possible. David made Jerusalem his capital and enlarged it with the help of Phoenician craftsmen. The rest of the Canaanites were later made to do forced labor by David's son Solomon.

▶ Jerusalem: pp. 226–227

Figures and Stories Relevant to the Canaanites

Yael Kills Sisera Deborah and Barak's campaign against the Canaanite king Jabin and his captain Sisera is reported in the Book of Judges (pp. 170–171). Defeated by the Israelite forces, Sisera was on the run. Yael invited him into her home, gave him something to drink, and prepared him a bed. Once he had fallen asleep, she took one of the tent pegs and plunged it through his temple (**3**).

■ The 12 Tribes of Israel were the offspring of Jacob's 12 sons

■ According to the biblical depiction, God was involved in the history of the Tribes from the outset

Exodus 40:34–38 The Tabernacle as a meeting place between humankind and God

Joshua 13–21 Joshua divides the land among the Tribes

Joshua 21:43–45 Fulfillment of God's promise to Abraham: the land of Canaan for the Israelites and safety from their enemies

Judges 1:1–7 The Israelites defeat the Canaanite commander Adonibezek

Judges 19:1–30 The concubine of a Levite is raped by Benjamites in Gibeah

Judges 20:1–48 The tribe of Benjamin is punished for the rape

Judges 21:1–25 The Israelites restore women to the tribe of Benjamin

II Kings 17:1–6 The northern kingdom of Israel is conquered by the Assyrians, ten of the 12 Tribes completely disappear from biblical lore

All these are the 12 Tribes of Israel, and this is what their father said to them when he blessed them, blessing each one of them with a suitable blessing. Genesis 49:28

The 12 Tribes of Israel

The Bible begins with the creation, and then turns to specific people after the Flood, namely the matriarchs and patriarchs of Israel. The history of Israel is narrated as a family affair: from Abraham through Isaac to Jacob and his 12 sons. Jacob's sons with his wife Leah were Reuben, Simeon, Levi, Judah, Issachar, and Zebulun. Leah also had Jacob's only mentioned daughter, Dinah. Jacob had Gad and Asher with Leah's handmaid Zilpah. His favorite wife Rachel gave birth to Joseph and Benjamin. Joseph was the father of Manasseh and Ephraim. Rachel's handmaid Bihah gave birth to Dan and Naphtali. ⟫

The Tabernacle was the most important sanctum for all the Israelites, where they could communicate with God.

The Tabernacle

The construction of the "meeting tent," also known as the Tabernacle, is described in Exodus. It was a living space for God and a place where God and humankind could interact. At its center was the inner sanctum with the Ark of the Covenant, which could only be entered once a year. It is a point of contention among scholars whether the tent really existed or whether it was a retrospective construction.

⟫ **Patriarchs and Matriarchs:** p. 69

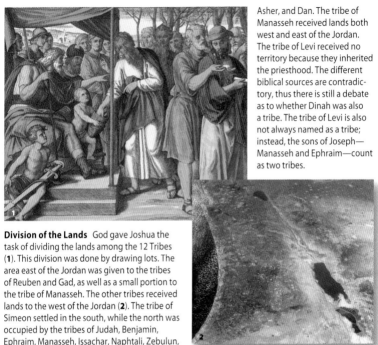

Asher, and Dan. The tribe of Manasseh received lands both west and east of the Jordan. The tribe of Levi received no territory because they inherited the priesthood. The different biblical sources are contradictory, thus there is still a debate as to whether Dinah was also a tribe. The tribe of Levi is also not always named as a tribe; instead, the sons of Joseph—Manasseh and Ephraim—count as two tribes.

Division of the Lands God gave Joshua the task of dividing the lands among the 12 Tribes (**1**). This division was done by drawing lots. The area east of the Jordan was given to the tribes of Reuben and Gad, as well as a small portion to the tribe of Manasseh. The other tribes received lands to the west of the Jordan (**2**). The tribe of Simeon settled in the south, while the north was occupied by the tribes of Judah, Benjamin, Ephraim, Manasseh, Issachar, Naphtali, Zebulun,

Battling the Canaanites
After Joshua's death, the Israelites fought a renewed war against the Canaanites over land. The Canaanites did not present a united front as they were led by individual sovereigns and kings. They were inferior to the Israelites, who fought together, and so one city after another fell to the Israelites. Adonibezek, a Canaanite king, tried to flee from the triumphant Israelites. When he was caught, his thumbs and big toes were cut off (p. 161).

The descendants of Jacob's 12 sons and grandsons formed the 12 Tribes of Israel. When they had moved into the Promised Land, Joshua (**4**) assigned each of the Tribes their territory according to lots. God's promise, which he had first made to Abraham (p. 62) and then confirmed with Israel on Mount Sinai (pp. 121–122), had been fulfilled. The Israelites inhabited the land and God "gave them peace" from their enemies. Some biblical scholars consider the lore of the 12 Tribes to be without historic merit.

Rape at Gibeah The legal relationship between the Tribes is demonstrated in Judges 19 with the story of the rape at Gibeah: En route to their home, a Levite and his concubine entered Benjamite territory. After searching a long time for shelter, they were taken in by an old man in the city of Gibeah. Then, some local men demanded that the old man hand over his guest to them so that they could rape him. Refusing, the old man offered them his own daughter and the guest's concubine instead. However, the men remained persistent. Finally, the guest threw his concubine out of the house and she was repeatedly raped by the locals. At dawn, the woman crawled to the door and died on the threshold. The man loaded the corpse onto his donkey and, when he arrived at home, he divided it into 12 pieces (**5**), sending one to each of the Tribes as a sign to avenge this disgrace.

Figures and Stories Relevant to the 12 Tribes of Israel

God, see pp. 28–33

Abraham, see pp. 60–63

Isaac, see pp. 78–79

Jacob, see pp. 88–91

Leah and Rachel, see pp. 94–95

God's Covenant With Israel, see pp. 142–143

Joshua, see pp. 156–159

The Canaanites, see pp. 160–161

Punishment of the Tribe of Benjamin The Israelites wanted to avenge the rape at Gibeah, thus they demanded that the tribe of Benjamin deliver the men of Gibeah so that they could be put to death. The Benjamites refused and started a campaign against the other tribes. The Benjamites were eventually defeated (**6**), and the Israelites made a pact to never give them their daughters.

However, they later regretted this decision, as it meant that the tribe might die out, thus leaving their lands exposed to the Canaanites. They did not want to break their vow, so they permitted the Benjamites to kidnap women during a celebration in Shiloh (**7**). The Bible comments: "In those days there was no king in Israel; all the people did what was right in their own eyes."

The Lost Tribes

With the conquest of the northern kingdom of Israel by the Assyrians in 722 B.C.E., a large proportion of the population resettled and all traces of ten of the 12 Tribes were lost. There have been many attempts in history to identify the descendants of the lost tribes, such as the Bnei Menashe (Hebrew: "sons of Manasseh") in India or the Falasha in Ethiopia. Both are recognized as Jews by the state of Israel. Even the Samaritans (p. 409) trace their lineage back to the 12 Tribes.

- The Amalekites were an enemy of Israel

- The Ammonites, the Amorites, the Edomites, the Midianites, the Moabites, and the Amalekites are sometimes referred to as the Canaanites

- God always gave Israel's neighbors the upper hand to punish their unfaithfulness

- According to the Bible, all peoples were related to Israel

Genesis 19:36–38 Lot is the patriarch of the Moabites and the Ammonites

Genesis 36 Esau, Isaac's son, is the patriarch of the Edomites and the Amalekites

Exodus 2:20–22 Moses marries the Midianite Zipporah

Numbers 13:29 Moses' scouts investigate the Canaanites

Joshua 10 Joshua conquers the south of Canaan

Judges 6:1 Because the Israelites are unfaithful to God, he lets the Midianites conquer them

Judges 7 Gideon conquers the Midianites

Ruth 4:13–17 Boaz marries Ruth the Moabite

I Kings 16:31 King Ahab marries Jezebel from Phoenicia

Remember what Amalek did to you on your journey out of Egypt, … you shall blot out the remembrance of Amalek from under heaven; do not forget. Deuteronomy 25:17, 19

The Neighboring Peoples of Israel

Alongside Egypt, Assyria, and Babylon—the great powers that had a great influence in the region for better or for worse—the Bible mentions an array of smaller populations and nations. At the time of the Israelite settlement, the Ammonites, Amorites, Edomites, Midianites, Moabites, and Amalekites all appear in the Bible, sometimes under the general term of "Canaanites." The Amalekites were considered Israel's main nemesis, as they attacked and killed many of the Israelites during their migration to Canaan. God ordered the Israelites to remember this incident, and to annihilate the Amalekites. Torah scribes follow this order up to today, as they initially record the word "Amalekite" during their transcriptions, but afterward scratch it out.

Hebrew uses an Aramaic alphabet, which is a testament to the close cultural contact between ancient Israel and its neighbors

Women From Different Cultures In spite of the biblical ban against the Israelites marrying people from different cultures, there are many examples of mixed marriages in the Bible. Moses, for example, married Zipporah (**1**), the daughter of a Midianite priest (p. 111), while Boaz married the Moabite Ruth, who was King David's matriarch (p. 191).

⏩ **From the Descendants of Adam and Eve to David:** pp. 24–25

Joshua Kills the Amorite Kings Terrified of the approaching Israelites (p. 159), the kings of Jerusalem, Hebron, Lachish, Jarmut, and Eglon made an alliance in hopes of creating an impenetrable defense. However, God was with the Israelites and the armies of the Amorite kings were struck down (**2**). The five kings fled into a cave where they were found by Joshua's men and taken into custody. Joshua executed them and hung each of their bodies from a tree (**3**).

Gideon's Victory Over the Midianites Because of their misconduct, God let the Midianites take over the Israelites. After seven years of foreign rule, Gideon, a judge, was commanded by God to liberate Israel and regain their national sovereignty (p. 174). To ensure that the Israelites did not see their victory as their own, God ordered Gideon to fight against the Midianites with an army of only 300 men. With God's help, Gideon confused the enemy so that they fought among each other, then fled (**4**).

The Mesha Stele

The Mesha Stele was discovered in eastern Jordan during excavations in the 19th century. The tablet records the Moabite king Mesha's defeat of the Israelite king Omri in the ninth century B.C.E. (p. 249): "I am Mesha, son of Kamoshiat the Moabite king ... Omri was a king of Israel and oppressed Moab ... thus spoke Kamosh [Moabite god]: 'Go conquer Nebo against Israel!'" Sources outside of the Bible and archaeological evidence often conflict with biblical texts. The Old Testament interprets history theologically, thus it is not a history book. Instead, it is a collection of stories about the experiences Israelites had with their God.

▶ The Merneptah Stele: p. 105

The Cult of Baal

The Bible describes Baal as the main god of the Canaanites. He was often represented and worshiped in the form of a mountain, weather, or fertility god (**1**). At times, he appeared alongside a female goddess named Ashera. The word "Baal" can be translated as "lord," "master," "owner," "king," or "god."

Each Canaanite city had its own Baal god. According to the Bible, serving Baal meant idol worship, something the Israelites were forbidden by God after the creation of the covenant on Mount Sinai. Judges 2:11 states that the Israelites displeased God by praying to the "Baals," which is used in plural here to encompass all the neighboring societies' gods. Constant campaigns against Baal suggest that the Israelites were worshiping both Baal and the God of Abraham, and that they gradually turned to monotheism.

One vicious attack against the Baal cult in the Bible occurred when King Ahab invited the prophet Elijah and the Baal priests to meet on Mount Carmel for a competition to show the people who was the living God (p. 308) (**2**). When Baal did not answer the call of his priests to show his power and Elijah's God did, the people recognized the God of Israel (I Kings 18:39). Afterward, Elijah slaughtered Baal's priests.

①

In Roman times, Baal was often identified with Jupiter (Greek: Zeus), or with the sun god Helios (Greek: Apollo). One of the largest standing Roman temples today is located in the ancient Baal cult city of Baalbek in Lebanon.

⏩ **God:** pp. 28–33   **God's Judgment on Mount Carmel:** pp. 310–311

■ Deborah was a judge

■ Deborah was one of the few female prophets

■ Yael helped Deborah and her commander Barak to victory over Sisera

Judges 4:1–3 During Deborah's term of office, the Israelites become unfaithful to God and are ruled by their enemies as punishment

Judges 4:6–16 Deborah calls on Barak to go into battle against the Canaanite captain Sisera

Judges 4:17–24 Yael kills Sisera

Judges 5:1–31 After their victory over Sisera, Deborah sings a victory song

The peasantry prospered in Israel, they grew fat on plunder, because you arose, Deborah, arose as a mother in Israel. Judges 5:7

Deborah

Deborah and Barak are two judges in the Bible. One thing that all judges have in common is that they rescued the Israelites. This can be understood in two ways: in a military capacity, as the judges were successful commanders, and in the sense that they led

the Israelites back on the correct path to God. It was unusual that Deborah, a woman, took up a position of leadership. She was also described as a prophet.

During Deborah's term as a judge, the Israelites once again displeased God, and so he delivered them into the hands of their enemies. They were ruled by the Canaanite king Jabin for 20 years. The Israelites turned to God and he heard their pleas. Deborah told Barak to wage a battle against Jabin. She prophesied his victory, but told him that the fame would go to a woman. The Israelites faced their enemies' chariots (**1**) on Mount Tabor (**2**).

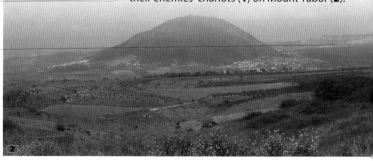

Yael Deborah and Barak began a campaign against the Canaanite king Jabin. When the Canaanite captain Sisera advanced with 900 chariots, God frightened the Canaanites. Sisera fled, leaving his army behind, which was utterly destroyed by the Israelites.

During his flight, Sisera came to the tent of Heber, a Kenite who lived in peace with King Jabin. Yael, Heber's wife, invited him in and gave him something to drink and a blanket so that he could sleep. When he had fallen asleep, she took a peg and bashed it through his temple (**3**). When Barak searched for Sisera, Yael showed him his dead body.

Deborah's Victory Song

Deborah's victory song was aimed at warning away the foreign kings and princes, who had threatened the Israelites and would threaten them again. The central point of the song is God's rescue of the Israelites from Egypt. As in the Psalms, God is addressed directly and praised.

Figures and Stories Relevant to Deborah

God, see pp. 28–33

The Canaanites, see pp. 160–161

The 12 Tribes of Israel, see pp. 162–165

▷▷ **The Psalms:** pp. 222–225

The Victory Song of Deborah

Judges 5:6–7, 12, 24–27

6 In the days of Shamgar son of Anath, in the days of Jael, caravans ceased and travelers kept to the byways. **7** The peasantry prospered in Israel, they grew fat on plunder, because you arose, Deborah, arose as a mother in Israel. **12** Awake, awake, Deborah! Awake, awake, utter a song! Arise, Barak, lead away your captives, O son of Abinoam. **24** Most blessed of women be Jael, the wife of Heber the Kenite, of tent-dwelling women most blessed. **25** He asked water and she gave him milk, she brought him curds in a lordly bowl.

26 She put her hand to the tent-peg and her right hand to the workmen's mallet; she struck Sisera a blow, she crushed his head, she shattered and pierced his temple. 27 He sank, he fell, he lay still at her feet; at her feet he sank, he fell; where he sank, there he fell dead.

■ Gideon was a judge of Israel

■ Gideon freed the Israelites from Midianite domination

Judges 6:11–24 Gideon demands a sign from God during his vocation

Judges 6:25–32 Gideon destroys an altar to Baal

Judges 7:1–25 Gideon is victorious over the Midianites

Judges 8:22–23 The Israelites want to make Gideon king, but he declines

Judges 8:24–27 Gideon lapses into worshiping false idols

Judges 8:32 Gideon dies

Gideon said to them, "I will not rule over you, and my son will not rule over you; the Lord will rule over you." Judges 8:23

Gideon

Gideon was one of the judges of the Old Testament. During his time in office, the Israelites had once again left the right path and God had delivered them into the hands of the Midianites. When God called upon Gideon, the judge demanded a sign. An angel told him to present a sacrifice, which Gideon fastened to a rock (**3**). Suddenly, a fire erupted from the rock and consumed the offering. Gideon was then certain and he went about fulfilling his task.

Gideon gathered the men of Israel for the military campaign. God told him to reduce the army so that the victory would be his and not the Israelites'; thus, whoever was fearful and half-hearted could return home. However, the army was still too large in God's eyes. Gideon then brought the army to a spring, and whoever drank without using their hands would go into battle (**1**). Thus, only 300 men were left to fight against the Midianites and Amalekites. Gideon and his army surrounded the enemy camp and, in the night, blew trumpets. The enemy was so confused that they fought against one another and then fled. Gideon scored a great victory for the Israelites.

Gideon Fights Against Baal God ordered Gideon to tear down an altar sanctified to Baal. Together with ten other men, he tore the altar down and erected a new one to God in its place (**2**). The next day, Baal's supporters ordered Gideon's father Joash to deliver his son to them to be stoned. He refused and said that whoever fought for Baal would die. Gideon received a new name: Jerubbaal ("he who fights Baal").

Gideon Collects the Rings of the Midianites
The Israelites offered Gideon the title of king, but he refused on the basis that only God could be the true lord of the Israelites. Instead, he asked for a portion of the spoils of war and so the Israelites gave him the Midianite rings (**4**). Gideon made an ephod from the gold, which he placed in his hometown. Praying to it, he slipped into idol worship. However, the Midianites were still unable to inflict damage on Israel as long as he lived.

■ Abimelech was the king of Shechem in Israel

"Which is better for you, that all seventy of the sons of Jerubbaal rule over you, or that one rule over you?" Judges 9:2

Abimelech

Abimelech was the son of Gideon the judge and his concubine. He had 70 half-brothers—all of whom counted as Gideon's heirs. He suggested to the inhabitants of Shechem that they make him their king, instead of having 70 rulers. They agreed and gave him silver. With this silver he recruited mercenaries, whom he used to kill almost all of his half-brothers. Only Jotham was able to escape, and he cursed Abimelech and the Shechemites. Abimelech was not able to hold his leadership for long and died a violent death. His story reflects Israel's volatility before a central kingship.

Judges 9:1–6 Abimelech becomes the king of Shechem

Judges 9:5 Abimelech kills 69 of his half-brothers

Judges 9:7–20 Jotham curses Shechem and Abimelech

Judges 9:22–25 An evil spirit causes a rift between Abimelech and the Shechemites

Judges 9:34–49 Abimelech destroys Shechem and all of its inhabitants

Judges 9:50 Abimelech besieges and conquers Thebez

Judges 9:51–54 Abimelech is fatally wounded by a woman and has his armsbearer kill him

Figures and Stories Relevant to Abimelech

God, see pp. 28–33

Curses, see p. 55

The Mark of Cain, see p. 45

Gideon, Abimelech's Father, see pp. 174–175

King of Shechem Abimelech was made king by the inhabitants of Shechem (**2**). However God punished both Abimelech for the murder of his brothers and the Shechemites for their lack of loyalty to the house of Gideon. An evil spirit caused a rift between Abimelech and the Shechemites. When the Shechemites turned away from him, he conquered the city and killed its populace. Thus, the curse against them was fulfilled.

Abimelech's Death in Thebez
Abimelech tried to enforce his leadership with all his might. After the destruction of Shechem, he continued on to the city of Thebez, which he besieged and conquered. Most of the population had taken shelter within a castle. When Abimelech neared the fortress with his men, a woman threw a stone at him, which hit him on the head and injured him badly. He called over his armsbearer and ordered that he kill him with a sword (**3**), so that no one could say that he had died at the hands of a woman. The curse made by Jotham on his half-brother Abimelech was thus satisfied by God, who avenged the brutal murder of Gideon's sons.

■ Jephtha was a judge and successful military commander for the Israelites

■ Jephtha killed his daughter to fulfill his vow

Judges 11:4–11 Jephtha becomes Israel's commander

Judges 11:30–31 Jephtha makes a vow before battle, to sacrifice the first thing that he encounters after returning home from a victory

Judges 11:32–33 Jephtha defeats the Ammonites

Judges 11:34–39 Jephtha encounters his daughter when he returns home and remains true to his vow by sacrificing her

Judges 12:1–6 Jephtha fights against the Ephraimites

Judges 12:7 Jephtha dies

If you will give the Ammonites into my hand, then whoever comes out of the doors of my house to meet me, when I return victorious from the Ammonites, shall be the Lord's. Judges 11:30–31

Jephtha and His Daughter

Jephtha, the son of Gilead and a prostitute, was another judge from the Old Testament. His half-brothers did not want him to have a part of their father's legacy, so they drove him away.

When the Israelites were being threatened by the Ammonites, they asked Jephtha, who was a good soldier, to be

Head of an Ammonite king from ca 700 B.C.E.

their military commander. He agreed, but only under the condition that he would become their political leader as well. Before the campaign, he vowed that he would sacrifice whatever approached him first upon his return home, if he were victorious. He was successful against the Ammonites, but this triumph was overshadowed by a personal tragedy.

Shibboleth

The Israelite tribe of the Ephraimites had a peculiar accent. They would, for instance, pronounce the word "shibboleth" (Hebrew: ear of corn) as "sibboleth." During a war with the Ephraimites, Jephtha placed his men on the fords of the Jordan. Whenever a man came along, they forced him to say "shibboleth." If he said "sibboleth," he would be killed. The word has since come to mean a password in some languages.

Jephtha' Daughter Receives Her Father

When Jephtha returned from his victory over the Ammonites, his sole child came out to greet him (**1**). She was leading a group of women in a dance, as it was an Israelite tradition to welcome the homecoming soldiers from a military campaign with dancing, singing, and drumming (**2**). When Jephtha set his eyes upon his daughter, he tore his clothes in anguish, as he felt duty-bound to the vow that he had made to God before his campaign.

Death of Jephtha's Daughter

Jephtha's daughter told her father to keep his vow; however, she asked for two months to prepare herself to die. Together with her female friends, she went into the mountains and bemoaned her fate (**3**). After the allotted time, she returned and Jephtha killed his daughter (**4**) and presented her as a burnt offering to God. The Bible reports that it became customary among Israelite women to mourn four days out of the year in remembrance of the sacrifice of Jephtha's daughter. However, the story is a violation of the Torah, which forbids the use of humans in sacrificial offerings. Jephtha remained a judge after his daughter's death. He led a second successful campaign against the tribe of Ephraim, which had not supported him against the Ammonites.

Figures and Stories Relevant to Jephtha and His Daughter

The Tribe of Ephraim, see the 12 Tribes of Israel, pp. 162–165

The Ammonites, see the Neighboring Peoples of Israel, pp. 166–167

⏩ **Mourning Rituals:** p. 346

Samson's Secret—Delilah Leads to Samson's Downfall

Judges 16:4–5, 17–19

4 *After this he fell in love with a woman in the valley of Sorek, whose name was Delilah.* **5** *The lords of the Philistines came to her and said to her, "Coax him, and find out what makes his strength so great, and how we may overpower him, so that we may bind him in order to subdue him; and we will each give you eleven hundred pieces of silver." ...* **17** *So he told her his whole secret, and said to her, "A razor has never come upon my head; for I have been a Nazirite to God from my mother's womb. If my head were shaved, then my strength would leave me; I would become weak, and be like anyone else."*

A comb with a depiction of Samson

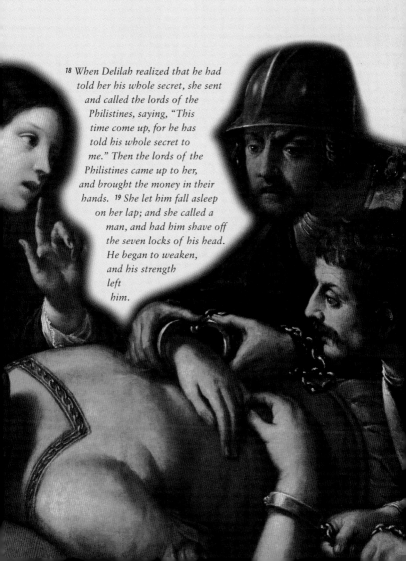

18 When Delilah realized that he had told her his whole secret, she sent and called the lords of the Philistines, saying, "This time come up, for he has told his whole secret to me." Then the lords of the Philistines came up to her, and brought the money in their hands. 19 She let him fall asleep on her lap; and she called a man, and had him shave off the seven locks of his head. He began to weaken, and his strength left him.

■ Samson was a judge

■ Samson became a symbol of superhuman strength

Judges 13:2–5 An angel announces Samson's birth

Judges 14:1–20 Samson marries a Philistine

Judges 15:1–5 Samson catches 300 foxes and sends them with torches in their tails through the fields of the Philistines

Judges 15:9–16 Samson kills 1,000 men with the jawbone of a donkey

Judges 16:1–3 Samson carries the city gates of Gaza

Judges 16:4–19 Delilah learns the secret of Samson's strength

It is he who shall begin to deliver Israel from the hand of the Philistines. Judges 13:5

Samson

Samson was also one of the judges of Israel. His story carries many fantastical traits. Even his birth has been linked to a miracle, as his father Manoah and his wife initially could not have any children. Nevertheless, an angel appeared to Manoah's wife and announced that she would bear a son, who would be a man for God and would save the Israelites from the Philistines. He also said that her son should never cut his hair.

As promised, a boy was born and he was named Samson. As he grew, the spirit of God began to stir him (Judges 13:25). ▶▶

(1)

Samson's Change of Heart
Samson disowned his wife after marrying her, but later on he changed his mind. When he wanted to visit her, his father-in-law informed him that she had a new husband and offered him her younger sister as a replacement. Samson was angry and captured 300 foxes (**1**), which he tied together by the tail in pairs, and fastened torches to their tails and had them run through the Philistines' cornfields (**2**). The Philistines took their revenge out on Samson's wife by setting her on fire.

(2)

Samson Defeats a Lion One day, Samson encountered a lion and ripped it apart with his bare hands, "as one might tear apart a kid" (**3**). After a few days, he returned to the spot where he had killed the lion and saw that a swarm of bees had settled in its cadaver and were producing honey. Samson took the honey and ate it. This unusually acquired honey later was the answer to a riddle that Samson posed to his wedding guests.

Figures and Stories Relevant to Samson

God, see pp. 28–33

Angels, see pp. 42–43

Samson's Secret, see pp. 180–181

Samson's Revenge, see pp. 186–187

The Philistines, Enemy of Samson and the Israelites, see pp. 188–189

Samson's Wedding During Samson's wedding (**4**) to a Philistine woman, he presented his guests with a riddle: "Out of the eater came something to eat / Out of the strong came something sweet." If they were able to solve it, he would reward them with expensive robes. Unable to solve it, they turned to Samson's wife, who got the answer from him after she had wept for seven days. She passed it on and the guests exclaimed to Samson: "What is sweeter than honey? What is stronger than a lion?" Angered, he went to the city of Ashkelon and he killed 30 men. He took their clothes and gave them to the guests who had solved his riddle. He let his wife to return to her family. She was later married to one of his companions.

Samson was a passionate, vengeful, and rash man, and immense power grew from his rage. He once killed 1,000 men with the jawbone of a donkey (**5**); another time he ripped the gates of the Philistine city of Gaza from their hinges (**6**). Samson had a weakness for women, which constantly landed him in trouble and eventually led to him falling into the hands of his enemies.

Samson and Delilah After Samson had fallen in love with Delilah, she was visited by some Philistines, who wanted to learn the secret of his strength. They promised her 1,000 pieces of silver for this information. Delilah tried to worm the secret out of Samson. He misinformed her three times, but then she accused him of not loving her and his resistance melted (**7**).

Samson Is Taken Prisoner and Blinded

Samson finally let himself be swayed by Delilah's prodding and divulged to her that his hair could never be cut. Consequently, she revealed this secret to the Philistines. When Samson was sleeping with Delilah, a Philistine cut off his hair, which was the source of Samson's superhuman strength. Samson lost his power, and the Philistines were able to take him prisoner as a defenseless man. They cut out his eyes (**8**), locked him in chains, and threw him into a jail, where he had to turn a millstone (**9**). The Philistines were overjoyed that they had finally beaten him and threw a great celebration. They praised their god Dagon for delivering Samson into their hands and presented him with a sacrifice.

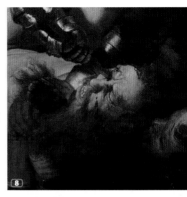

Samson Destroys the Temple of the Philistines

Samson's hair grew again while he was in prison. When the Philistines held a celebration for their god Dagon, they brought him out so as to humiliate him and amuse themselves. Samson pleaded to God to give him back his strength so that he could take his revenge on the Philistines. The blind Samson grappled the two middle columns holding up the temple of Dagon, threw his weight against them, and collapsed the entire temple (**10,11**). Samson died but took down thousands of Philistines with him. His brothers later buried him in the grave of their father.

Samson's Revenge—Samson Destroys the Temple of Dagon and Numerous Philistines

Judges 16:23–25, 28–30

23 The Philistines gathered to offer a great sacrifice to their god Dagon, and to rejoice; for they said, "Our god has given Samson our enemy into our hand." **24** When the people saw him, they praised their god; for they said, "Our god has given our enemy into our hand, the ravager of our country, who has killed many of us." **25** And when their hearts were merry, they said, "Call Samson, and let him entertain us." So they called Samson out of the prison, and he performed for them. They made him stand between the pillars. **28** Samson called to the Lord and said, "Lord God, remember me and strengthen me only this once, O God, so that with this one act of revenge I may pay back the Philistines for my two eyes." **29** And Samson grasped the two middle pillars on which the house rested, and he leaned his weight against them, his right hand on the one and his left hand on the other. **30** Samson said, "Let me die with the Philistines." He strained with all his might; and the house fell on the lords and all the people who were in it. So those he killed at his death were more than those he had killed during his life.

■ Due to their military strength, the Philistines were a large threat for the Israelites

Judges 16:4–22 The Philistine Delilah draws out the secret of Samson's strength and the Philistines overpower him

I Samuel 5:1–2 The Philistines make an offering to their god Dagon

Judges 16:26–30 Samson destroys the Philistines' temple

I Samuel 17 The young David defeats the giant Philistine Goliath

I Samuel 27:1–4 David flees from King Saul to the Philistines

Did I not bring Israel up from the land of Egypt, and the Philistines from Caphtor and the Arameans from Kir? Amos 9:7

The Philistines

In 1200 B.C.E., the Philistines settled on the coastal plains in the southern part of Canaan. Their technical knowledge and military strength—exemplified by their chariots—enabled them to take command over the area. The Old Testament often refers to hostilities between the Israelites and the Philistines during the time of the judges, as well as the reigns of King Saul and King David. However, there were occasionally periods of peace and friendship, which explains Samson's marriage to a Philistine and David finding asylum from Saul in the Philistine city of Gath. The name of the region—Palestine—originated with the Philistines. In 135 C.E., after the suppression of the second Jewish revolt, the Romans renamed the Judea province Palestine.

The fertility goddess, Astarte; sculpture from the Philistine city of Gaza

The Sea Peoples

The Philistines may have stemmed from the "sea peoples." Some scholars believe they originated from the Aegean; however, others contest that they were not an ethnic group at all, but rather an alliance of sailors. Regardless, their attacks spread fear, as an Egyptian inscription from 12 B.C.E. states: "The foreign nations are conspiring on their islands … no nation could withstand their weaponry."

David and Goliath The Philistine soldier Goliath was not only protected due to his sheer size: He also wore a helmet, scaled armor, and greaves (leg armor). While the men of Israel were afraid of him, David, a young shepherd, asked: "Who is this uncircumcised Philistine, who scorns the armies of the living God?" He went up against Goliath and defeated him with the shepherd's weapon of a slingshot (**1**) (p. 214).

Philistine Cities The Philistines lived on the southern coastal plains of Canaan. Their five cities—Ashdod (**2**), Ashkelon, Ekron, Gath, and Gaza—reached their pinnacle during the 10th and 11th centuries B.C.E. This was due to their military, and a monopoly on iron production, as well as their comparatively weak neighbors. The Philistine army of career soldiers was equipped with chariots. The Philistines' hegemony ended with their fall to the Assyrians in 723 B.C.E.

Samson Samson had killed many Philistines through various confrontations (**3**). They were finally able to capture him by the betrayal of him by a woman. Although defeated, he destroyed their temple and killed hundreds of Philistines.

■ The Moabite woman Ruth was King David's matriarch

■ Ruth went back to Bethlehem together with her mother-in-law

Ruth 1:1–22 After the death of her husband, Ruth moves to Bethlehem with her mother-in-law Naomi

Ruth 2 During fieldwork, Ruth meets Boaz

Ruth 3 Ruth takes Naomi's advice to stay with Boaz and start a relationship with him

Ruth 4:13–22 Ruth and Boaz are married and have a son, Obed, the grandfather of King David

---

Figures and Stories Relevant to Ruth and Naomi

The Moabites, see the Neighboring Peoples of Israel, pp. 166–167

David, Ruth's Grandson With Boaz and King of Israel, see pp. 216–221

Jesus of Nazareth, a Descendant of Ruth, see pp. 402–409 and 414–419

Where you go, I will go; where you lodge, I will lodge; your people shall be my people, and your God my God. Ruth 1:16

Ruth and Naomi

The Book of Ruth is one of the few biblical books that bears the name of a woman. The novella of Ruth and Naomi is set during the time of the judges and begins with a raging famine in Israel. Facing these conditions, Elimelech, his wife Naomi, and their sons left their hometown of Bethlehem and moved to Moab. While Elimelech died abroad, his sons Machlon and Chilion took Moabite wives, which was then forbidden. After Machlon and Chilion both died, Naomi decided to return to Israel. Her two daughters-in-law Ruth and Orpa wanted to accompany her; however, Orpa allowed Naomi to convince her that it would be better for her to stay in Moab. But, Ruth's attachment to Naomi proved to be stronger than any argument. She spoke the very words that are often used as marriage vows in Christian services: "Where you go, I will go."

Ruth's solidarity is not just referring to Naomi, but also to her God. Her story has a close relationship to the harvest (**1**), and is thus read in synagogues during the celebration of Shabuoth (p. 192).

 **The Family Tree of David:** pp. 208–209

Ruth Meets Boaz Life in Bethlehem was very difficult for Naomi and her Moabite daughter-in-law Ruth. As neither of them had any close male relations, they could not claim their deceased husbands' inheritances. However, Ruth did not give up. She made use of the right of the poor and gleaned in the fields of Boaz, a relative of Naomi's husband Elimelech, in order to support her and her mother-in-law. One day, Boaz met Ruth and took her in his care (2) so that she would not be harassed by the men, and invited her to eat with him. When Ruth told Naomi that she had met Boaz, Naomi told her to go to him in the evening, and then to "uncover his feet" and to lie next to him. When Ruth followed Naomi's advice, Boaz asked her to stay with him. Together they were able to retrieve the inheritance of Ruth's deceased husband. Ruth and Boaz married and had a son named Obed (3). Naomi continued to live with Ruth and Boaz, and took care of Obed. Their neighbors praised Ruth; she was worth more to Naomi than seven sons. Obed later had a son named Jesse, who was the father of King David. Thus, Ruth was David's grandmother, and is listed as one of Jesus' matriarchs in the Gospels of Matthew and Luke in the New Testament.

Shabuoth—
The Feast of Weeks

The Feast of Weeks, also called Shabuoth (Hebrew: "weeks"), begins 50 days after Passover. Shabuoth was one of the three festivals during which the Israelites would go to the Temple in Jerusalem. As an offering, pilgrims brought God the first yield of the new harvest. Since the Temple's destruction, the theological basis of the festival has been changed to celebrate God's gift of the Torah on Mount Sinai (**1**). Today, the Ten Commandments and the Book of Ruth are read during Shabuoth services; the latter is meant to show believers that their loyalty to the Torah should be as strong as Ruth's was to Naomi.

Religious Festivals	
Eid Ul-Adha	pp. 72–73
Passover	pp. 118–119
Sukkoth	pp. 128–129
Yom Kippur	pp. 138–139
Shabuoth	**pp. 192–193**
Purim	pp. 284–285
Hanukkah	pp. 294–295
Christmas	pp. 400–401
Easter	pp. 426–427
Pentecost	pp. 470–471

Harvest Festival In the Bible, Shabuoth is also known as Yom Ha-Bikkurim, or "celebration of the first fruit" (**4**). On this day, the synagogues are decorated with plants. There are processions (**3**), and at night the faithful study the Torah. Sweet milk-based food is eaten as, according to the Song of Solomon, the Torah is milk and honey (**2**) under the tongue.

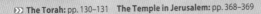

>> The Torah: pp. 130–131   The Temple in Jerusalem: pp. 368–369

■ Samuel was the last judge of Israel

■ When the people wanted to make him king, he refused

Then Samuel said to all the house of Israel, "If you are returning to the Lord with all your heart, then put away the foreign gods ... and he will deliver you out of the hand of the Philistines." I Samuel 7:3

Samuel

The story of Samuel, who acts as a prophet, a priest, and a judge, occurred during a time when there was still no kingship in Israel. Samuel's birth was a miracle, as his mother Hannah was "heartsick" that she could not have children. She cried and prayed to God in the Temple (**1**), until the priest Eli promised that she would give birth to a child. Hannah called her son Samuel, meaning "heard by God," because God heard her prayer and gave her a gift. Deciding that she should serve God in some way, Samuel later became Eli's apprentice and his successor.

Due to external pressures, especially from the Philistines, times were hard for Israel. During one battle, the Israelites took the Ark of the Covenant into battle with them against the Philistines. The Israelite army was defeated and many men died. ▷

Hannah Brings Samuel to Eli

Hannah believed her son Samuel was a gift from God; thus, she wanted to thank him by having her son dedicate his life to the Temple. After her son was weaned, Hannah and her husband Elkanah visited the Temple. They brought God a rich offering and gave their son to the priest Eli (**2**). Hannah was happy that God had fulfilled her wish and praised and glorified him with a song in I Samuel 2:1. This hymn contains many elements from the *Magnificat* that Mary sang when she was pregnant with Jesus (pp. 384–385).

God Appears to Samuel One night, Samuel heard someone calling his name and, assuming it was Eli, went to the priest (**3**), who insisted it was not him. Yet, even as Samuel lay down, he still heard his name. By the third time, he realized that God was calling him. God told him that he was going to judge Eli and his sons, because his sons were "worthless men" and Eli let them get away with it. Eli later died when he heard that his sons were killed in a battle against the Philistines.

》 **The Psalms:** pp. 222–223

Among the dead were Eli's sons Hofni and Pinhas. The Ark of the Covenant fell into the Philistines' hands (**4**); however, God plagued them with disease until they sent it back to the Israelites with rich peace offerings. Samuel, who succeeded Eli as priest and judge, promised the Israelites that God would save them from their enemies if they refrained from idolatry. The people gave their word and the promise was fulfilled. Later, he anointed Saul as the first king of Israel. He abdicated the office of judge, but continued to enforce the will of God.

Samuel Anoints Saul

Samuel's sons, Joel and Abijah, were his successors; however, they were selfish men. Thus, the Israelites demanded that a king be appointed, like the neighboring societies. Samuel was displeased because he believed that only God should rule Israel; however, God told him to listen to the people. Under God's command, Samuel anointed Saul as king (**5**) (p. 211).

Anointment

The ritual of anointing priests, prophets, and kings with special anointing oil as a part of an initiation into their office is found throughout the Old Testament. It was also possible to anoint objects, such as the Tabernacle and the Ark of the Covenant. An anointed person was referred to as a Messiah (Hebrew: "Mashiach") and was often given a specific role to fulfill, whether it be as a priest, prophet, or king. Expectations were also linked to them, such as the Persian king Cyrus II, who was designated as God's anointed. He allowed the Jews to return to Israel from the Babylonian captivity (pp. 280–281). The sobriquet "the anointed one" was also given to Jesus (p. 404).

⏩ **The Tabernacle:** p. 162

Samuel Condemns Saul God ordered King Saul to strike down the Amalekites, the arch-enemy of Israel, and to kill the entire populace along with their livestock. The military campaign against the Amalekites was successful, but Saul ignored God's orders, sparing their king Agag and keeping the good animals for himself. Samuel confronted him and said that his disobedience was as much a sin as idolatry. Repentant, Saul asked for forgiveness, which Samuel refused to grant (p. 211). As he turned to go, Saul grabbed his cloak, tearing off a piece. To Samuel, this meant that God had likewise wrenched the kingdom away from Saul. In the end Samuel killed the Amalekite king Agag himself (**6**).

6

7

> ### *Figures and Stories Relevant to Samuel*
>
> God, see pp. 28–33
>
> The Amalekites, see the Neighboring Peoples of Israel, pp. 166–167
>
> The Philistines, see pp. 188–189
>
> Saul, see pp. 210–213
>
> David, see pp. 216–221
>
> The Kings of Israel, see pp. 248–251

Samuel Anoints David
Samuel pitied Saul's fate; however, God told him to anoint another king. He ordered him to fill his horn with oil and set out. Eventually, Samuel came across Jesse from the city of Bethlehem. Samuel met Jesse's eldest of eight sons, but he was not who God had chosen. Instead, the new king of Israel was David, Jesse's youngest son, who was herding sheep. He was summoned and then anointed by Samuel (**7**) (p. 216).

Samuel Kills King Agag

I Samuel 15:27–33

²⁷ As Samuel turned to go away, Saul caught hold of the hem of his robe, and it tore. ²⁸ And Samuel said to him, "The Lord has torn the kingdom of Israel from you this very day, and has given it to a neigh-bor of yours, who is better than you. ²⁹ Moreover, the Glory of Israel will not recant or change his mind; for he is not a mortal, that he should change his mind."

³⁰ Then Saul said, "I have sinned; yet honour me now before the elders of my people and before Israel, and return with me, so that I may worship the Lord your God." ³¹ So Samuel turned back after Saul; and Saul worshiped the Lord. ³² Then Samuel said, "Bring Agag king of the Amalekites here to

me." And Agag came to him haltingly. Agag said, "Surely this is the bitterness of death." **33** But Samuel said, "As your sword has made women childless, so your mother shall be childless among women." And Samuel hewed Agag in pieces before the Lord in Gilgal.

The Era of the Kings of Israel and Judah

Gallery of Old Testament kings on the façade of the Notre Dame Cathedral in Paris

The Era of the Kings

Kings of the Kingdom of Israel and Their Surroundings

p. 216

1050*   1000   950   900   850

p. 228

p. 230

* Starting from the time of the later kingdoms, some biblical stories are supported by other evidence, such as archaeological finds, non-biblical primary sources, and other results of research.

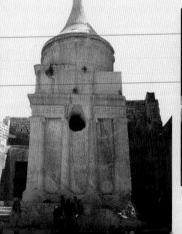

# of Israel and Judah

p. 252

The Kings of Israel

p. 248

p. 209

800   750   700   650   600   550

The Kings of Judah

p. 254

p. 256

The Era of the Kings of Israel and Judah

The most complete description of the era of the kings is found in the two books of Samuel and both books of Kings. Like the books of Joshua and Judges, these writings evidently arose over an extended period of time. They likely took on their current form, for the most part, during the time of Babylonian exile. A shorter view of the same time period is provided by the two books of Chronicles, which were probably written after the Jews' return from exile. During the era of the judges, the Israelites were little more than a loose confederation of tribes. Only in times of external threat did the 12 Tribes come together under charismatic leaders: the judges. For a long time, the introduction of a monarchy was viewed as a challenge to God's authority. No supposedly divine king—as in Egypt, for example—should rule over Israel, but God alone.

Nevertheless, the need for unified leadership became increasingly pressing, especially near the end of the judges epoch, when the Israelites faced a dangerous enemy in the form of the Philistines. When the people of Israel demanded a king in light of the continuing threat from the Philistines, the prophet Samuel, who also served as a judge, at first refused. He pointed out the ① problems posed by a monarchy, but the Israelites did not change their minds. Finally, with help from God, Samuel anointed the Benjaminite Saul as the first king of Israel. After Saul's first military success, the Tribes confirmed his legitimacy as king: thus, the acclamation of the people was added to Saul's divine calling. The individual tribes—which had previously been politically independent, only forming temporary military alliances—now placed themselves under a common ruler. The temporary office of judge was replaced by the institution of the monarchy.

2

Saul's reign was still strongly reminiscent of that of the judges, since he was first and foremost a military ruler, a leader in the fight against external enemies. When he was later defeated by the Philistines, he also forfeited his life (**2**). His successor David (**1**), from the tribe of Judah, was finally able to eliminate the threat posed by the Philistines. The transfer of power from Saul to David was not free of conflict, however. Only after several years of civil war was David able take his place as king over all the tribes of Israel. Then he began a campaign to conquer Israel's neighboring peoples and built up an empire.

Many researchers doubt that all of the events described in the Bible reflect historical facts. In particular, the stories of the first kings, Saul, David, and Solomon—who are not mentioned by any source outside the Bible—are viewed as descriptions of idealized rulers from the perspective of later times. David can be seen as the model of a king chosen by God. For centuries, hopes for a savior sent by God, the Messiah, were linked to his reign. The New Testament also builds upon references to David, since from a Christian perspective, Jesus of Nazareth was the new David, the long-awaited savior.

After David's death, his son Solomon (**4**) succeeded him. Solomon's numerous public building projects reached unprecedented heights of splendor. Among them was the new Temple in Jerusalem (**3**), which was especially significant because it centralized the worship of Yaweh (God) along with political power in the kingdom. Solomon, renowned for his wisdom, appears in the Bible as a cosmopolitan and educated king with international connections.

Soon after Solomon's death, the differences among the Tribes once again arose: the ten northern tribes revolted against the tyrannical leadership of Solomon's son Rehoboam, choosing their own king, Jeroboam. The division into a northern kingdom (Israel) and a southern kingdom (Judah) continued through the following centuries. In the northern kingdom, several dynasties succeeded each other in bloody struggles for succession. The southern kingdom included little more than the settlement area of the tribes of Benjamin and Judah. In their ancestral lands, the descendants of David maintained their hold on power. In addition to political struggles and threats from great powers such as the Egyptians, Assyrians, and Babylonians, numerous internal religious conflicts arose among the Israelites. The prophets of Yaweh exercised great

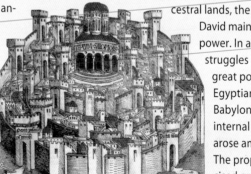

influence in the political sphere. They served as royal advisers, but they could also become dangerous enemies for the rulers. Prophets were often involved in overthrowing disliked rulers who did not serve their interests. Even the most powerful kings faced equally influential prophets who warned and criticized them, such as Samuel under King Saul, Nathan under King David, and Elijah under Ahab. The prophets' condemnation of the rulers, as described in the Bible, is unparalleled in the Middle East for its severity: the kings of ancient Israel, with their human weaknesses, are very different from rulers of other lands who stood far above their subjects and were worshiped as divine.

Again and again, the kings of Israel acted in ways that are "displeasing to the Lord," as the Bible reports, and in return, they and their people were punished by God. In retribution for the Israelites' actions, God allowed them to be defeated by their enemies.

As with the idealized early kings, it is clear here as well that the Bible is less interested in the precise narration of historical events than in a theological interpretation of history. In the end, the Israelites lost their independence as a further punishment from God: the northern kingdom of Israel was conquered by the Assyrians in 722 B.C.E., while the southern kingdom of Judah was taken over by the Babylonians in 587 B.C.E. A significant proportion of the population was sent into exile in Babylon. ④

The Family Tree

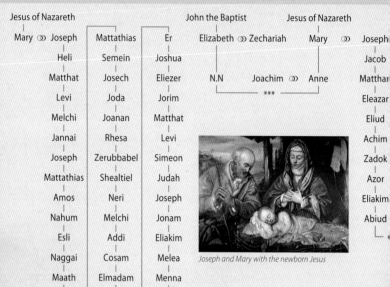

Jesus of Nazareth
|
Mary ⚭ Joseph
|
Heli
|
Matthat
|
Levi
|
Melchi
|
Jannai
|
Joseph
|
Mattathias
|
Amos
|
Nahum
|
Esli
|
Naggai
|
Maath

Mattathias
|
Semein
|
Josech
|
Joda
|
Joanan
|
Rhesa
|
Zerubbabel
|
Shealtiel
|
Neri
|
Melchi
|
Addi
|
Cosam
|
Elmadam

Er
|
Joshua
|
Eliezer
|
Jorim
|
Matthat
|
Levi
|
Simeon
|
Judah
|
Joseph
|
Jonam
|
Eliakim
|
Melea
|
Menna

John the Baptist
|
Elizabeth ⚭ Zechariah
|
N.N   Joachim ⚭ Anne
    |_____***_____|

Jesus of Nazareth
|
Mary ⚭ Joseph
|
Jacob
|
Matthar
|
Eleazar
|
Eliud
|
Achim
|
Zadok
|
Azor
|
Eliakim
|
Abiud

Joseph and Mary with the newborn Jesus

Mattath

Amnon   Chileab   Absalom   Tamar   Adonijah   Nathan
              Abigail,
Joab   Ahinoam   Widow of Nabal   Maacah   Haggith
                ⚭   ⚭   ⚭

Zeruiah   Eliab   Abinadab   Shimea   Nethanael   Radda

Joab and Absalom

* Jesus' genealogy
according to Luke 3:23–31

** Genealogy of Jesus according to Matthew
1:13–16

*** Family of Elizabeth and Mary according
to the Christian tradition

Ruth a
Naom

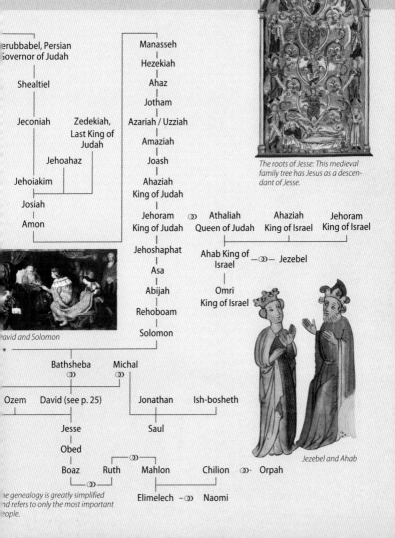

# of David

Zerubbabel, Persian
Governor of Judah

Shealtiel

Jeconiah

Jehoiakim

Josiah

Amon

Zedekiah,
Last King of
Judah

Jehoahaz

Manasseh

Hezekiah

Ahaz

Jotham

Azariah / Uzziah

Amaziah

Joash

Ahaziah
King of Judah

Jehoram
King of Judah

Jehoshaphat

Asa

Abijah

Rehoboam

Solomon

Athaliah
Queen of Judah

Ahaziah
King of Israel

Jehoram
King of Israel

Ahab King of
Israel — ⚭ — Jezebel

Omri
King of Israel

The roots of Jesse: This medieval
family tree has Jesus as a descendant of Jesse.

David and Solomon

Bathsheba   Michal
⚭   ⚭

Ozem   David (see p. 25)

Jesse

Obed

Boaz   Ruth   Mahlon   Chilion ⚭· Orpah
└─⚭─┘   └──⚭──┘

Elimelech – ⚭ – Naomi

Jonathan   Ish-bosheth

Saul

Jezebel and Ahab

David (see p. 25)

The genealogy is greatly simplified
and refers to only the most important
people.

■ Saul was the first king of the Israelites

And the spirit of God came upon Saul in power when he heard these words, and his anger was greatly kindled. I Samuel 11:6

Saul

Belonging to the tribe of Benjamin, Saul ("prayed for") was the first Israelite king. The Bible describes him as having a stately appearance and being a successful military commander. He led the Israelites in ongoing wars against their neighboring enemies, such as the Philistines. It was primarily through these conflicts that the 12 Tribes gradually became a unified state. However, after Saul had achieved victory over the Amalekites, God repudiated him for failing to wipe them out entirely.

Later, the biblical reports of Saul lay heavy emphasis on his state of mind. He was described as being melancholic, depressive, and psychologically unstable—suffering caused by God's punishment. Some scholars attest that Saul's rapturous states and influences of the "evil spirit" suggest epilepsy. Saul's melancholy reached its climax with his suicide after a failed battle against the Philistines in the Gilboa Mountains of northern Israel (**1**). **»**

Saul Is Anointed King As the reigning judge, Samuel, grew older, the people of Israel asked him to instate a new king due to the warmongering of the neighboring enemy states. Displeased that the people would rather have a king than a religious leader (p. 196), Samuel prayed to God. Samuel pronounced Saul, a simple young man, as the first king of the Israelites and anointed him with oil (**2**). After Saul's victory against the Ammonites, he was accepted by the people and elected the king of Gigal. Next, he had to lead the people of Israel into battle against the Philistines, who held Israelite lands in their possession.

Saul Is Condemned Samuel gave Saul the task of destroying the Amalekites, who were enemies of the Israelites, and killing every last one of them. Although Saul went into battle and annihilated the Amalekites, he spared their king, Agag, as well as taking the best animals as spoils. This disobedience angered God. Samuel accused the king of stealing from the battle spoils (**3**). As Saul had disregarded the word of God, he was now to be repudiated by God and could no longer be the king of Israel. Seeing his error, Saul repented and Samuel executed the Amalekite king.

Anointment: p. 196

During his illness, Saul attempted to soothe his mood swings with music. It was because of this that David, a talented lyre player, entered the king's court. However, with David's growing popularity, Saul began to view him as a rival. His feelings toward David constantly fluctuated. At times he would love and respect him; other times he would hate and seek to kill him (**4**). In the end, David was selected as Saul's successor.

David and Jonathan Upon David's arrival at the king's court, Jonathan, the eldest son of King Saul, befriended the young musician. As a sign of their friendship he gave David his clothes, armor, sword, bow, and belt. Jonathan's father, however, became jealous of David's popularity and military success. Eventually Saul's jealousy grew to such an extent that he decided to murder David. Jonathan warned his friend of his father's murderous plot and helped David to escape (**5**). Appealing to Saul's conscience, Jonathan sought to prevent the murder attempt by reminding his father of David's good works and pointing out the complete irrationality of his hatred. Through these efforts Jonathan pacified his father and David was able to remain at the royal court.

David Spares Saul Fearing for his life, David fled into the mountains under the pursuit of Saul. Resting in a cave, Saul failed to notice that David and his companions were hiding at the back. David quietly cut off a corner from Saul's cloak. Regretting this immediately, he ordered his men not to attack. As Saul exited the cave, David showed him the piece of material he had cut from his cloak (**6**) and used it to demonstrate that he had the chance to kill Saul but his intentions were good.

Saul and the Witch of En-Dor

Fearful of the approaching threat of the Philistines, Saul prayed to God for advice but received no reply. Seeking answers, he disguised himself one night and visited a necromancer in En-Dor (**7**). When he requested that she summon the ghost of the dead judge Samuel, the witch saw that she was in the presence of King Saul in disguise. Upon this realization, she fears for her life because Saul had previously exiled all the necromancers of the land. After calming her down and promising not to do her any harm, Saul saw a man in priestly robes appear—the ghost of Samuel. Saul complained to him about his distress: the growing threat of the Philistines, God turning his back on him, and his own lack of counsel or a plan of action.

Samuel's reply reminded Saul that God had reproached him and given his kingship to his successor, David. Saul later suffered defeat by the Philistines in the Gilboa Mountains and was badly wounded. To avoid being ignobly ridiculed by the Philistines before being killed, Saul demanded that his arms bearer stab him with his sword, but he was refused. Thus Saul fell upon his own sword and died (**8**). His sons also lost their lives in the battle. David later had the bodies of Saul and Jonathan, his beloved friend,

entombed. He sang a song of mourning, which bore witness to his deep pain.

David and Goliath—David Defeats the Giant Philistine With One Stone

I Samuel 17:23–24, 49–51

23 As he talked with them, the champion, the Philistine of Gath, Goliath by name, came up out of the ranks of the Philistines, and spoke the same words as before. And David heard him.
24 All the Israelites, when they saw the man, fled from him and were very much afraid.
49 David put his hand in his bag, took out a stone, slung it, and struck the Philistine on his forehead; the stone sank into his forehead, and he fell face down on the ground.
50 So David prevailed over the Philistine with a sling and a stone, striking down the Philistine and killing him; there was no sword in David's hand.
51 Then David ran and stood over the Philistine; he grasped his sword, drew it out of its sheath, and killed him; then he cut off his head with it. When the Philistines saw that their champion was dead, they fled.

⏩ The Philistines: pp. 188–189

■ David was founder of a dynasty of kings who reigned until the capture of Jerusalem in 587 B.C.E.

■ He was a victorious military commander

■ He is described in the Bible as passionate and musically gifted

"The Lord, who saved me from the paw of the lion and from the paw of the bear, will save me from the hand of this Philistine."

I Samuel 17:37

David

The Bible describes David ("beloved") as being exceptionally handsome with blond hair, blue eyes, and a stately figure. At the court of King Saul, the talented musician soon earned friends and admirers. David also made a name for himself as a military commander. His popularity was based on his kindly appearance and impassioned character. He was largely led by his emotions rather than strategic deliberations. ⏵⏵

The lyre is associated with David

I Samuel 16:21–23 David arrives as a musician at King Saul's court

I Samuel 17:48–49 David battles against the Philistine Goliath

I Samuel 18:1–4 David's friendship with Jonathan

I Samuel 18:5–9 Saul's jealousy

I Samuel 18:10; 19:1 Saul attempts to murder David

I Samuel 24:5–8; 26:9–11 David spares Saul's life

I Samuel 27 David escapes to the Philistines

II Samuel 5 David becomes king after Saul's suicide

II Samuel 6 David takes the Ark of the Covenant to Jerusalem

II Samuel 11:4–5 David commits adultery with Bathsheba

II Samuel 12:1–14 Penitent David is forgiven

I Kings 1:28–53 David names Solomon as his successor

①

David Is Anointed After God had condemned King Saul, Samuel sought a new king (p. 197) for his people. God sent Samuel to search among the sons of Jesse from the tribe of Judah in Bethlehem. He was first introduced to Jesse's eldest sons, but it was not until he met David, the youngest son, that God gave him a sign that he had found the new king. Samuel immediately anointed David with consecrated oil (1).

⏵⏵ **Anointment:** p. 196

The Triumph of David

Courageous and confident in the support of God, David went into battle for King Saul against the Philistines. Right at the beginning, David conquered the giant Goliath (pp. 214–215). Soon David was so successful that he rose from being a lowly arms bearer to the army commander. As he returned from yet another victory over the Philistines, the people received him jubilantly. Women from all over Israel adorned themselves in jewelry and thronged round the victorious commander (**2**).

David and His Music

As mentioned in the Bible, David had great musical abilities that brought him into Saul's court. David composed a stirring song of mourning for the dead Saul and his fallen friend Jonathan. He also authored many of the psalms, which brought David fame as an accomplished musician, a notion that is reaffirmed and referenced in music history.

2

They even sang a victory song in honor of David: "Saul slew a thousand, but David tens of thousands." Hearing this, Saul was enraged with jealousy. He also feared that David would bring his leadership into dispute and would seize his crown. In spite of this, the king tried to align himself with David and gave him the hand of his daughter Michal in marriage. Saul's son Jonathan also had a close relationship with David and protected him against King Saul's outbreaks of rage.

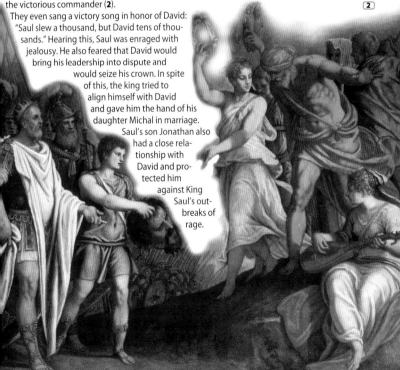

However, the latest historical research casts doubt on this idealized David (**3**). In the Bible, he built a great empire as Saul's successor. His reign might have taken place in the early tenth century B.C.E. Some allege that his greatest feat was trimming the autonomy of the Israelite tribes. Others doubt that his power was this great; for them David is the ideal model of a king (**4**).

David and Abigail David sent his servants to Nabal to ask him to supply his men as reciprocation for the aid he had previously given to Nabal's people. Nabal showed his avarice by claiming not to know David and sending his servants away. Hearing this, David was irate and armed himself for battle. However, one of Nabal's men had reported these events to Abigail, the beautiful and wise wife of Nabal. Riding to David with bread, wine, and cake, she apologized for the foolishness of her husband and was blessed by David (**5**). After Nabal's death, David took Abigail as his wife.

6

David Spares Saul's Life

Hearing reports by the people of Sif that David was staying in a nearby desert, the raging king followed him without delay. Discovering that Saul was after him, David found his camp and came across him sleeping. David's warrior Abishai was pleased that God had delivered Saul into his hands and wanted to impale the king with his spear (**6**). David told him that Saul was anointed by God and God would smite him in his own time. David did not want to lay a hand on the anointed king and thus he spared Saul's life yet again (p. 212).

Michal Saves David

Influenced by the evil spirit, Saul once more wanted to kill David. He tried twice to impale David against a wall; however, David was able to save himself. Saul consequently had David's house watched in order to kill him the next morning. David's wife Michal, the daughter of the king, saved her husband by helping him escape from a window (**7**). As David fled, she took an idol, covered it with goat hair, goat pelt, and clothing, and laid it next to her in bed as a decoy. With the arrival of Saul's men, Michal claimed that David was lying ill.

7

The elaborate examples that illustrate David's emotions, his penitence for his mistakes (**9**), and the motivations behind his actions are unparalleled in the Old Testament. In spite of—or possibly directly because of—his passionate nature and his human weaknesses, David has become the archetype of the ordained kings. The Christian tradition draws a parallel to David in Jesus Christ. Apart from being his descendant, Jesus is also viewed as a regal figure—a Messiah. In the New Testament, David is presented as a prototype of Jesus who is also given kingly titles.

David in Battle With the ascension of Hanun as the Ammonite king, David wanted to continue the relationship that he had had with Hanun's deceased father. To express his sympathy, David sent envoys to Hanun. However, the Ammonites were distrustful and took the envoys for spies. Hanun mistreated them by shaving half of their beards and cutting away their clothes. After this provocation, David went to war with the Ammonites (**8**). They asked the neighboring Aramaeans for help, but they too had already been defeated by David. The Israelites conquered the Ammonite capital of Rabba and completely subjugated their domains. Through this and other campaigns David stretched his power to the northeast and the Euphrates.

The Star of David

The hexagram (six-cornered shape) was used in the Middle Ages by Jews, Christians, and Muslims. As a talisman, it served to ward off demons, spirits, and fire. From the start of the modern era, the hexagram, known as the "Star of David," became an increasingly Jewish symbol. The First Zionist Congress in Basel in 1897 declared the Star of David a national emblem, and in 1948 it became a part of the flag of Israel. With the Nazis, a yellow Star of David was used to demarcate the Jewish population. The Star of David is full of symbolism: the six triangles represent the six days of creation, while the large hexagon in the middle represents the seventh, the day of rest.

David Brings the Ark of the Covenant to Jerusalem After Saul's death, it was several years until all the tribes recognized David as their king. Under his leadership, the Israelites built the stronghold of Zion, present-day Jerusalem. Here David erected his capital city, which he expanded into the "City of David." In an awesome procession (**10**) led by the king, the holy Ark of the Covenant—a sign of the bond between God and the Israelites—was brought to Jerusalem. David's wife Michal observed the festivities and became angry at the frivolity of her husband. Seeing his behavior as unbecoming, she reproached him for it. Because of this lack of understanding, God punished Michal by making her barren.

David Anoints Solomon David had decided that his son Solomon would be his successor, but Solomon's stepbrother Adonijah claimed the throne. Bathsheba, Solomon's mother, informed David and he had Solomon anointed (**11**).

The Psalms

The book of Psalms (**2**) is a collection of 150 sacred poems. Many have been traditionally accredited to King David (**1**). Psalms are found at different points in the Bible, ascribed to historically significant events. For example, there is the song of victory sung after crossing the Red Sea in Exodus 15, as well as David's song of thanksgiving in I Chronicles 16, and Hannah's song of praise in I Samuel 2. The Psalms are a feature of ancient Israelite literature, as God appears in them as a partner in a dialogue with man, sharing a bond.

The Psalms could have acted as the incitement, the foundation, or even the expression of personal prayer. Their themes have universal value as they address existential questions of misery, lamentation, desires, praise, and thanks. The Psalms are still part of the prayer books of the Chrisstian churches today. Texts such as Psalm 23, "The Lord is my Shepherd," are some of the most well-known and well-loved passages of the Bible. Many people continue to use them as a means of support in difficult situations.

Intoning the Psalms

In ancient Israel, music was a vital part of social life and was present during victory celebrations and general festivities. Psalm 150, "The Great Hallelujah," calls upon all musical instruments and beings—everything that has the "breath of God"—to praise the Lord. In Judaism and in Catholic Mass (**3**), the Psalms are a part of the liturgy. In Protestantism, many Psalms have been set to music as hymns (**4**).

▷▷ **David and His Music:** p. 217

gnā misericordiam   misericordia

misericordiam   tuam

The Good Shepherd—Trusting in God's Leadership and Protection

Psalm 23

"A Psalm of David"
1 The Lord is my shepherd, I shall not want.
2 He makes me lie down in green pastures; he leads me beside still waters;
3 he restores my soul. He leads me in right paths for his name's sake.
4 Even though I walk through the darkest valley, I fear no evil; for you are with me; your rod and your staff—they comfort me.
5 You prepare a table before me in the presence of my enemies; you anoint my head with oil; my cup overflows.
6 Surely goodness and mercy shall follow me all the days of my life, and I shall dwell in the house of the Lord my whole life long.

>> Jesus' Parable of the Lost Sheep: p. 408

Jerusalem—Zion

Jerusalem is accepted as one of the oldest cities in the world. As early as the 19th century B.C.E., Jerusalem is mentioned in Egyptian sources. Historians, archaeologists, and believers have a great interest in the origins of this city; however, excavations are difficult (**1**). New Testament Jerusalem lies about 13 to 15 feet (four to five meters) beneath today's city.

Another name for Jerusalem is "Zion." This was the name of the stronghold conquered by David, later called the City of David. It was here that he erected the capital of his kingdom. In the time of Solomon, the word "Zion" referred to the Temple Mount. This led to the location of Zion being equated with the location of God's presence. As a theological concept, Zion stood for an unassailable spot, the domicile of God. Thus Jerusalem quickly became far more than an average city: it became a symbol-laden, holy place, a religious middle ground for Jews, Christians, and Muslims. World maps from the Middle Ages (**3**) place Jerusalem in the middle, the boundary between heaven and earth.

The Temple Mount The Temple Mount (**2**) lies in the southeast of the Old City of Jerusalem. It was here that Solomon erected the first temple. Today, two of the most important Islamic sanctuaries are found on the mountain: the Dome of the Rock and the Al-Aqsa Mosque. For Jews, the site still has religious meaning and they assemble together there by the Wailing Wall. This forms the western boundary of the former temple district and is the only thing remaining from the Herodian temple of the Roman era.

▶ **Jerusalem Under Herod the Great:** p. 364   **Temple in Jerusalem:** pp. 368–369

■ Bathsheba was a beautiful and willful woman

■ She secured her son Solomon's succession to the kingship

David sent someone to inquire about the woman. It was reported, "This is Bathsheba ... the wife of Uriah the Hittite." II Samuel 11:3

Bathsheba

When David caught sight of Bathsheba bathing (**1**), he summoned her to him and the couple had an affair. As Bathsheba became pregnant, David tried to attribute the paternity to her husband, Uriah, a soldier. When this did not work, David sent Uriah into battle. With Uriah's death, David married Bathsheba. As punishment for their adulterous affair, their first child died. Afterward, David recognized his error and repented

A Hittite warrior— Bathsheba's first husband, Uriah, was a Hittite.

before God, who blessed him and Bathsheba with a second son: the future king Solomon. The story of Bathsheba exemplifies not only penitence, but also the mercy of God toward human weakness.

»» Sexuality in the Bible: p. 106

2

Bathsheba's Son Dies

David's adultery with Bathsheba counts as one of several dishonorable acts in his life. When she became pregnant, he even tried to pass the paternity on to her husband Uriah. He bade Uriah to take a furlough from the war and stay with Bathsheba, but Uriah declined. In order to legitimize the affair and the pregnancy, David then had Uriah sent back into the war against the Ammonites and charged his men with the task of positioning Uriah at the front line. The plan was successful and Uriah soon was killed in battle, leaving David free to marry Bathsheba. David was unaware of any wrongdoing on his part until a sermon held by Nathan the prophet confronted him with the unrighteousness of his behavior. David's life would be spared due to his penitent nature, but Nathan predicted an early death for his son. The first child of Bathsheba and David died soon after its birth (**2**). Deeply penitent, David prayed to God for forgiveness.

Polygamy in the Ancient Middle East

Polygamy ("many marriages") was a royal privilege in the ancient Middle East: Bathsheba was one of eight wives of King David. Marriages often served to solidify political unions between rulers, such as Solomon's marriage to an Egyptian princess. A special type of polygamy was the levirate marriage: Should a man die childless, it became the duty of his brother to sire an heir with his widowed sister-in-law. This responsibility was famously balked by Onan, who was ultimately punished by God. Whereas Christianity was oriented toward monogamy from the outset, polygamy was allowed by Jewish law well into the Middle Ages.

≫ **Tamar and Onan:** pp. 106–107

■ David had many children with different wives

■ David's sons strove after their father's crown

II Samuel 13 Amnon rapes his sister Tamar

II Samuel 15 Absalom's revolt

II Samuel 18:1–18 Absalom's death and memorial

But Absalom spoke to Amnon neither good nor bad; for Absalom hated Amnon, because he had raped his sister Tamar. II Samuel 13:22

David's Children

David had many children of which around 20 are mentioned in the Bible. Along with Adonijah, who prevailed against his half-brother Solomon in becoming David's successor, another son, Absalom, plays a significant role. He initially appears as his sister Tamar's avenger, who was raped by their half-brother Amnon. Later, Absalom revolts against his father and demands the throne for himself, forcing David to flee from Jerusalem. In the end, Absalom is killed against the will of the king. David appears to be a docile, perhaps even weak father. He is dependent on his sons, spoils them, and continuously forgives them for their shortcomings.

Absalom's Tomb

In II Samuel 18:18, it is reported that Absalom had a memorial ("a pillar") built for him because he was aware that his sons would not carry on his memory. For a long time, a stone monument in the Kidron Valley, east of the Old City of Jerusalem, was considered to be Absalom's memorial. However, the building is in the Hellenistic style from the first century B.C.E, which is not contemporaneous with King David. Nevertheless, for centuries the inhabitants of Jerusalem have carried on the custom of coming to this grave with their children and pelting it with rocks. It is their way of remembering the brutal death of Absalom, who was stabbed and stoned. The site and story both serve to show children what fate follows someone who rebels against their own father.

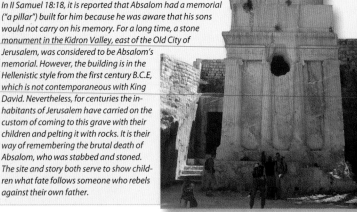

Amnon's Depravity With Tamar

Amnon, the half-brother of Tamar and Absalom, yearned so much after Tamar that he could not eat and feigned illness. As Amnon asked Tamar for help, she came to his bedside (**1**) and he forcibly violated her. Afterward, he became tired of her and sent her away, leaving Tamar to live a life of disgrace. David was furious, but he forgave his eldest son. Absalom, on the other hand, hated Amnon and waited to avenge his sister. Two years later at a party, he murdered the drunken Amnon.

Absalom's Death

After killing Amnon, it was years before Absalom could once again appear before his father; however, this peace did not last. Absalom used his popularity among the people to make himself king. David sent soldiers out against Absalom but ordered them to spare his son. As a fight ensued in the forest of Ephraim, Absalom rode under a tree and his long hair became entangled, leaving him hanging in the branches. David's general, Joab, ordered his men to kill the defenseless Absalom, but his soldiers refused as they recalled David's order. Joab stabbed Absalom (**2**) before attacking his body with stones.

■ Joab was the most important of David's military generals

■ He arbitrarily interfered with the rising disputes over David's crown

Joab sounded the trumpet and all the people stopped; they no longer pursued Israel or engaged in battle any further. II Samuel 2:28

Joab

The stories of Joab provide insight into King David's political situation. The people of Israel did not immediately accept David's rule, and there were many challengers to his crown, such as Saul's offspring, especially his son Ish-bosheth, who had powerful supporters. Additionally, many of the tribes refused to accept a king from another tribe. The tale of Abner and Joab shows the role of family ties—Joab was David's nephew—in politics of the time. Furthermore, an arbitrary act by Joab, the killing of Absalom (**1**) against the king's orders, proves that David's power was not absolute. When Joab sided with Adonijah after David's death, Solomon had him killed.

Joab Kills Abner In the disputes of succession after Saul's death, Abner supported Saul's son Ish-bosheth, but later helped David secure the crown. Joab wanted to avenge the murder of his brother Asahel by Abner. Therefore, he ambushed and stabbed him to death (**2**). Learning of this, David distanced himself from the murder, as he did not want to align his leadership with a cowardly, bloody deed. Despite this, Joab remained one of his most important soldiers (**3**).

The Downfall of Sheba

Sheba, of the tribe of Benjamin, refused to subjugate himself to the king from the tribe of Judah. David charged Joab with the task of ending this uprising.

When Joab heard that Sheba was hiding in Abel-Beth-Maachah, he wanted to storm and destroy the city. However, a local woman promised Joab that she would deliver him

Sheba's head if he would spare the city. After agreement, she conferred with her fellow inhabitants and they overpowered Sheba, throwing his head over the wall to Joab (**4**).

Figures and Stories Relevant to Joab

■ Zadok was the progenitor of a long line of high priests

■ The position of high priest stayed within his family until the era of the Maccabees

II Samuel 15:24–35 Zadok supports David against Absalom

I Kings 1:38–39 Zadok anoints Solomon as king

I Chronicles 15:11–28 Zadok helps bring the Ark of the Covenant to Jerusalem

So Zadok and Abiathar carried the Ark of God back to Jerusalem, and they remained there. II Samuel 15:29

Zadok

The meaning of Zadok's name in Hebrew, "God has proven himself righteous," was a leitmotif throughout his life. The priest was involved in multiple political affairs in order to defend the wishes of the rightful, God-elected ruler. He remained steadfast by David during the uprising of Absalom and he supported Solomon in his confrontations with Adonijah. For his loyalty, Zadok attained the position of high priest. By rewarding the virtuous, God made his works apparent here as well. The office of high priest remained a hereditary privilege passed through Zadok's offspring, the "Zadokites." The Zadokites acted as the religious leaders of Israel until the time of the Maccabees in the second century B.C.E.

An altar stone for offering from the ancient Israel era

High Priests

The high priest held the highest religious office in ancient Israel, the very first being Aaron. The high priest was in charge of the priesthood in the Temple of Jerusalem, observed holy services, and had sole access to the inner sanctum. His garments included a turban, a blue-purple robe, and a gold disk bedecked with jewels. Due to the prominent position of the high priest, who had vocation until his death, he also had vast political influence. This was especially true under the Maccabees, who were simultaneously high priests and political leaders. The office disappeared with the destruction of the Temple by the Romans in the first century B.C.E.

Figures and Stories Relevant to Zadok

Ark of the Covenant, see Moses, p. 122

David, King of Israel, see pp. 216–221

Solomon, see pp. 238–241

Nathan, a Prophet, see pp. 304–305

Adonijah and Absalom, see David's Children, pp. 230–231

Bathsheba, Compatriot in the Anointing of Her Son Solomon as David's Heir, see pp. 228–229

❯❯ **Aaron:** pp. 136–137   **The Maccabees:** pp. 290–293   **Caiaphas:** pp. 462–463

Zadok Anoints Solomon as King During the battles over succession, Zadok the priest sided with Solomon. In order to disinherit his son Adonijah, David gave Zadok, Nathan the prophet, and the military commander Benajah the task of publicly declaring Solomon king and David's successor in a splendid ceremony. Following David's orders, Zadok, Nathan, and Benajah placed Solomon on the king's mule and used a horn of oil to anoint the young man as the new king of Israel by the Gihon Spring (**1**). The ceremony made it perfectly clear that David had appointed Solomon as his successor. Later, Solomon had Adonijah and his supporters killed, whereas Zadok and Benajah were rewarded with eminent positions.

Solomon's Judgment— Two Women Fighting Over One Child

I Kings 3:16–28

¹⁶ *Later, two women who were prostitutes came to the king and stood before him.* ¹⁷ *One woman said, "Please, my lord, this woman and I live in the same house; and I gave birth while she was in the house.* ¹⁸ *Then on the third day after I gave birth, this woman also gave birth. We were together; there was no one else with us in the house, only the two of us were in the house.* ¹⁹ *Then this woman's son died in the night, because she lay on him.* ²⁰ *She got up in the middle of the night and took my son from beside me while your servant slept. She laid him at her breast, and laid her dead son at my breast.* ²¹ *When I rose in the morning to nurse my son, I saw that he was dead; but when I looked at him closely in the morning, clearly it was not the son I had borne."* ²² *But the other woman said, "No, the living son is mine, and the dead son is yours." The first said, "No, the dead son is yours, and the living son is mine." So they argued before the king.* ²³ *Then the king said, "One says, 'This is my son that is alive, and your son is dead'; while the other says, 'Not so! Your son is dead, and my son is the living one.'"* ²⁴ *So the king said, "Bring me a sword," and they brought a sword before the king.* ²⁵ *The king said, "Divide*

the living boy in two; then give half to one, and half to the other." ²⁶ *But the woman whose son was alive said to the king—because compassion for her son burned within her—"Please, my lord,*

ive her the living boy; certainly do not
ill him!" The other said, "It shall be
either mine nor yours; divide it."
⁷ Then the king responded: "Give the
rst woman the living boy; do not kill

him. She is his mother." **28** All Israel
heard of the judgment that the king had
rendered; and they stood in awe of the
king, because they perceived that the wisdom of God was in him, to execute justice.

■ Solomon was famous for his wisdom; under his rule, the kingdom of Israel experienced a golden age

■ Thanks to Solomon's Temple, Jerusalem became a religious and cultural center

Thus King Solomon excelled all the kings of the earth in riches and in wisdom. 1 Kings 10:23

Solomon

Solomon's name means "peace" or "prosperity"—a prophetic name, since his reign is marked by external peace and domestic prosperity. The Bible presents Solomon (**1**) as the model of a wise ruler. His "Solomonic judgment" (**2**) is especially famous: When two women argued before him over a child, Solomon used a ruse to uncover the rightful mother's identity. He announced that he would divide the child in half. Horrified, the true mother surrendered the baby rather than seeing it killed, which convinced Solomon that her claim was valid. »

Solomon's Request for Wisdom One night, God appeared to Solomon in a dream (**3**) and wanted to grant Solomon a wish. He confessed that, as a young, inexperienced ruler, he was filled with doubts and fears about the great responsibilities of his position. The attention and expectations of his people are focused on him. Thus, he asked God to grant him the wisdom to lead effectively and make prudent judgments. Pleased that Solomon asked for wisdom rather than riches and fame, God not only fulfilled Solomon's wish, but also gave him wealth and a long life.

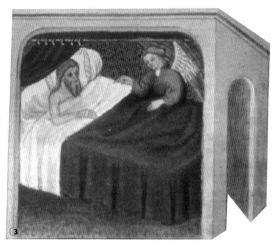

Megiddo and Armageddon

Megiddo, today in northern Israel, is one of the most significant archaeological sites from biblical times. Priceless ivory carvings have been discovered in excavations there. Thanks to Megiddo's strategically favorable location—on the fertile Jesreel Plain, at the convergence of several trade routes—Solomon ordered its strengthening into a fortress. Megiddo is the site of great battles in the Bible: In Judges 5:19, the kings of Canaan fought at the "waters of Megiddo." In II Kings 23:29, the Egyptians pursued Josiah to Megiddo, killing him there. Finally, in the Book of Revelation (16:16), Armageddon—the "Mountain of Megiddo" (Hebrew: "har megiddo")—is the setting of the final battle of good and evil.

Dreams: p. 101

Many scholars today think that Solomon was a historical person. In earlier accounts, his rule was dated to about 965 to 926 B.C.E. Solomon followed his father, David (p. 221); yet in contrast to his father, who conquered a substantial empire, Solomon was no warrior. He maintained close economic and diplomatic ties with his neighbors. Domestically, he strengthened his empire through wise leadership and the construction of fortified cities. Solomon's most famous project is the Temple in Jerusalem.

Yet maintaining the royal court and carrying out building projects placed an enormous burden on the people, who provided forced labor and paid high taxes. Solomon's tolerance of foreign cults was also criticized. The Tribes revolted after Solomon's death, turning from the house of David (p. 254).

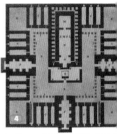

Solomon's Temple Solomon carried out his father David's plan to build a temple in Jerusalem. Within 11 years, an enormous and magnificent building arose, completely covered in gold (**4**). The Holy of Holies (**5**) lay within several courtyards, which were entered only by the high priest. The Temple was constructed next to the royal palace so as to centralize political power and religious life under the sole control of the king.

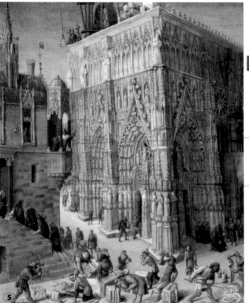

>> **The Temple in Jerusalem:** pp. 368–369

Solomon's Pagan Worship

Many of Solomon's wives were foreign, and he allowed them to retain their native religions. In the end, the women persuaded the aging king to pray to their gods as well as his own (**7**). As punishment, God denied Solomon's son and successor the leadership over Israel. Only one of the 12 Tribes remained faithful. Thus, God punished Solomon and still kept the promise he made to David that his family would rule forever.

Solomon's Marriages

Solomon's peaceful relations with his neighbors—such as the Phoenician king Hiram—were reinforced through strategic marriages. The daughter of the Egyptian pharaoh (**6**) received an entire city from her father as a dowry. Yet he also disobeyed God since many of his one thousand wives came from peoples with whom the Israelites were not supposed to ally themselves.

Solomon's Song of Love

King Solomon was long regarded as the author of the "Song of Songs," or "Song of Solomon." The tribute to sexuality in this erotic work proved too explicit for many Jewish and Christian theologians. They preferred to interpret the text as an allegory of God's love, with God or Christ in the role of the bridegroom, and the people of Israel, the Christian Church, or the individual believer as the bride. Consisting of only 117 verses, it is the shortest book of the Hebrew Bible.

» **Sexuality in the Bible:** p. 106

Wisdom Literature

Wisdom includes insight into the natural and divine order of the world. Knowledge arises from experience, through which people come to understand the relationship between actions and their consequences. This theme is addressed in many biblical stories: Good deeds lead to good results, while evil actions produce evil.

Among the Bible's teachings on wisdom are the Book of Job, the Book of Proverbs, the Wisdom of Solomon, Ecclesiastes, the Wisdom of Ben Sira, and some of the Psalms. King Solomon (**3**) was long believed to be the author of several of these writings on wisdom. Today, he is viewed as having compiled or commissioned at least some of them during his reign.

Job and Ecclesiastes The books of Job and Ecclesiastes focus on those who seek wisdom. In the Book of Job, a man's trust in God is put to an extreme test (**1**). This raises the question of God's justice and the connection between actions and consequences. The Book of Ecclesiastes is philosophical and addresses universal themes such as human happiness and the impermanence of life: "To everything there is a season…"

>> **Job:** pp. 346–349

Book of Proverbs The Bible's collection of proverbs includes sayings on everyday subjects such as trust, laziness, and dishonesty. Thus, lazy people are advised to follow the example of the industrious ant (**2**). At times, wisdom is personified by a woman. This has been interpreted, especially by many feminist theologians (p. 500), as signifying a feminine aspect of God's nature.

■ Numerous legends surround the magnificent Queen of Sheba; however, her true name and heritage remain unknown

I Kings 10:1–13; II Chronicles 9:1–12 The Queen of Sheba visits Solomon

I Kings 10:4–7; II Chronicles 9:5 The Queen is impressed by Solomon's wealth and wisdom

I Kings 10:10; II Chronicles 9:9 The Queen presents Solomon with precious gifts

II Chronicles 9:8 The Queen of Sheba praises the God of Israel

Matthew 12:42; Luke 11:31 The "Queen of the South" on Judgment Day

①

When the Queen of Sheba heard of the fame of Solomon, she came to test him with hard questions. I Kings 10:1

The Queen of Sheba

The Queen of Sheba has long been a subject of speculation, since the queen's true name and the location of her empire are still unclear. Many researchers point to modern-day Yemen as the queen's homeland. In biblical times, a state centered on the capital city of Marib (**1**) was located there. Another theory places the kingdom of Sheba in Ethiopia, which maintained close cultural and economic ties with southern Arabia for many years.

Although it is not clear that the Queen of Sheba was truly a historical person, from a theological point of view the description of her visit in the Bible underscores Solomon's fame, as even the most remote lands had heard of Israel's wise ruler. The story also illustrates Solomon's diplomatic relations with foreign leaders. In the New Testament, the Queen of Sheba appears as the "Queen of the South," who will assess people's worthiness on Judgment Day.

The Meeting of the Queen of Sheba and King Solomon

Having heard tales in her country about Solomon's wealth and wisdom, the Queen of Sheba did not believe them, so decided to visit the king of Israel and confirm the tales for herself. Accompanied by a great entourage, she traveled to Jerusalem, bringing precious gifts of gold and spices to Solomon. To test his knowledge, she posed him a series of riddles. Solomon was able to answer everything correctly (**2**), and expressed limitless knowledge of everything. Fascinated by the king and impressed by his wealth, the Queen of Sheba praised the God of Israel that had brought such a ruler as Solomon to the throne. After she delivered her generous gifts—and Solomon fulfilled her every wish in return—the Queen of Sheba traveled back to her homeland.

Ethiopian Traditions

According to Ethiopian tradition, Solomon and the Queen of Sheba had a son together: Menelik. The Solomonic dynasty, which ruled Ethiopia until 1974, traces its roots to him. The last Ethiopian emperor, Haile Selassie—known previously as Ras Tafari Makonnen—is still revered by Rastafarians today. For them, this presumed descendant of David and Solomon was the Messiah foretold in the Bible (p. 404), or the "Lion of Judah" mentioned in Revelation 5:5; "Conquering Lion of the Tribe of Judah" was among the emperor's official titles. The Rastafari movement arose in the 1930s among the black population of Jamaica.

■ The Phoenicians were known for their sailing skills, trade, and colonization

■ Each Phoenician city had its own Baal (god)

Joshua 13:6 Joshua wants to conquer the Phoenician lands

II Samuel 5:11 Hiram supports King David

I Kings 5:1–12 Hiram of Tyre and King Solomon make a contract regarding the construction of the Temple

I Kings 9:26–28; I Kings 10:22 Solomon and Hiram equip trade fleets

I Kings 11:5 Solomon prays to the Phoenician goddess Astarte

I Kings 16:31 King Ahab prays to the gods of his Phoenician wife Jezebel

I Kings 19:2 Jezebel and Elijah

King Hiram of Tyre having supplied Solomon with cedar and cypress timber and gold, as much as he desired. I Kings 9:6–16

The Phoenicians

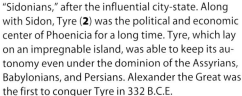

The Phoenicians lived in city-states on the coast of present-day Lebanon and Syria. Their name is derived from "phoinix," which is Greek for purple, the color of a costly dye made from the shells of the "banded dye-murex" snail. The Bible refers to them also as the "Sidonians," after the influential city-state. Along with Sidon, Tyre (**2**) was the political and economic center of Phoenicia for a long time. Tyre, which lay on an impregnable island, was able to keep its autonomy even under the dominion of the Assyrians, Babylonians, and Persians. Alexander the Great was the first to conquer Tyre in 332 B.C.E.

The Phoenician city-states were ruled by kings and patrician families. As excellent sailors, the Phoenicians managed to control the whole of the Mediterranean for a while—even advancing into the Atlantic. Their international contacts led to cultural diversity, which is reflected by the Egyptian influences in their art (**1**). The Phoenicians' own cultural acheivements include an alphabet.

The Cedar Forests of Lebanon Cedar wood, along with the production of purple dye, formed the basis of the Phoenicians' wealth. They used the wood in the construction of merchant and military fleets. The wood was also exported and sold at exorbitant prices to regions where there were few to no forested areas, such as Egypt, Mesopotamia, and Israel. The cedar forests in present-day Lebanon (**3**) are only a portion of the original. The overuse of natural resources was one of the reasons for the Phoenicians' downfall.

Hiram and Solomon In the first half of the tenth century B.C.E., Tyre experienced an enormous boom under the rule of King Hiram I. Hiram was a contemporary of King Solomon and the Bible states that the two rulers had a close relationship. Hiram supplied Solomon during the construction of the Temple (p. 240). He not only delivered cedar (**4**), but also put craftsmen and architects at Solomon's disposal. Researchers have noticed similarities between the Temple in Jerusalem and the temples that were built at the same time in Phoenicia. These comparisons substantiate biblical statements about the appearance of the Temple of Solomon. Hiram and Solomon also equipped one another for trade expeditions in the Red Sea and the Mediterranean.

Figures and Stories Relevant to the Phoenicians

The Cult of Baal, see pp. 168–169

Solomon's Temple, see Solomon, pp. 238–241

Ahab and Jezebel, see the Kings of Israel, pp 248–251

The Slaying of the Baal Priests by the Prophet Elijah, see Elijah, pp. 306–309

Jezebel and Ahab After Solomon's death, there was still political contact between the Phoenicians and the Israelites. King Ahab of Israel married the Phoenician princess Jezebel in order to strengthen the military alliance with her father (**5**). The Bible describes how Ahab worshiped Jezebel's Phoenician gods. This led to a negative portrayal of Jezebel. She was an opponent of the prophet Elijah, as he fought against the Baal cult that she supported.

■ Solomon's kingdom was split into the north and south after his death

■ In the northern kingdom of Israel, the dynasties changed in rapid succession

■ The kings supported increasingly more foreign cults

But Jehu was not careful to follow the law of the Lord the God of Israel with all his heart. II Kings 10:31

The Kings of Israel

Seal of King Jeroboam

After Solomon's death around 926 B.C.E., the kingdom founded by his father collapsed. Old rivalries broke out between the tribes and led to a split between the northern kingdom of Israel and the southern kingdom of Judah. Samaria became the northern capital in 876 B.C.E. (**1**).

The first king of the northern kingdom, Jeroboam I, had served as an official in Solomon's court until he was forced to flee to Egypt because he was involved in a conspiracy. When Solomon died, he fought against Solomon's son and successor Rehoboam for power. In the end, ten of the 12 Tribes of Israel aligned themselves with Jeroboam.

The political situation in the kingdom of Israel was highly unstable, as dynasties changed in rapid succession and usurpers continued to seek power. Altercations arose between the kings and the religious leaders—the prophets. They contributed to ⟫

①

Jeroboam's New Sanctums

After the division of the kingdom, the north lacked a religious center of worship, as the Yahweh cult was concentrated in Jerusalem. Fearing that his people would migrate to the south, Jeroboam had idols of bulls manufactured (**2**) and established sanctums in Dan (**3**) and Bethel with a new sacrificial cult.

The Death of Zimri Zimri became the king of Israel in 882 B.C.E.; however, he only ruled for seven days. When the people heard that he had murdered his predecessor Elah, they declared the military commander Omri (**5**) as their king. When Omri and his army overtook the capital of Tirzah, Zimri killed himself by starting a fire (**4**). During his rule, Omri later transferred the capital to Samaria. The Omride dynasty ruled over the northern kingdom of Israel until around 845 B.C.E. **5**

the downfall of many rulers with their public criticisms (**5**). These prophets included Elijah, Elisha, and Hosea.

In time, external pressures mounted against the kingdom of Israel, which had become dependent on the Assyrians. It fell with the conquest of Samaria by the Assyrians in 722 B.C.E. and the deportation of the upper class—a fate similar to that of the kingdom of Judah (p. 257).

Elijah With Ahab and Jezebel
Omri's son, King Ahab, was married to the Phoenician princess Jezebel (p. 247). She supported the Baal cult and convinced her husband to join. This provoked intense opposition from the prophet Elijah (p. 308), who judged the behavior of the king harshly. After the murder of Naboth, God appeared to Elijah and charged him with the task of cursing Ahab and Jezebel (**6**) so that they might die a similarly violent death. As Ahab later showed true remorse, God reconsidered his judgment on Ahab. His offspring would be murdered and wild animals would eat their corpses, like that of Jezebel.

Naboth's Vineyard King Ahab wanted to purchase Naboth's vineyard, as it was in the vicinity of his court, but Naboth refused to sell his father's inheritance. Ahab gave up, but Jezebel, convinced of the prerogatives of kings, persisted. She told two men to slur Naboth and claim that he had blasphemed against God and the king. The plan worked and Naboth was stoned to death (**7**). Ahab was then able to take the vineyard as his property.

Jehu and the End of the Omride Dynasty

With the help of the prophet Elisha, the military commander Jehu ended the reign of the Omride dynasty in 845 B.C.E. and, as Elijah had prophesied, Jezebel, Ahab's sons, and the supporters of Baal were killed. Jezebel was thrown out of a window (**8,9**) and dogs ate her body. As Ahab had managed considerable success in battle, Jehu was subjugated by the Assyrians and was forced to pay tributes to their king, Shalmaneser III (**10**). After an era of prosperity under Jehu's great-grandson Jeroboam II, decline began. Jehu's dynasty was toppled in 747 B.C.E.

■ The Assyrians were feared warriors

■ Assyria was the most important power, next to Babylon, at the time of the kingdoms of Israel and Judah

II Kings 17:1–6 The Assyrians conquer the kingdom of Israel

II Kings 18:13–19:37; II Chronicles 32:1–23 The Assyrians besiege Jerusalem and are pushed back by God

Isaiah 10:5–34; 14:24–27; 31:4–9; 31:27–33 Isaiah on the downfall of the Assyrians

Ezekiel 23 The kingdoms of Israel and Judah act like whores

Ah, Assyria, the rod of my anger—the club in their hands is my fury! Isaiah 10:5

The Assyrians

The central area occupied by the Assyrians with their capital of Assur lay to the north of present-day Iraq. Through brutal military campaigns, the Assyrians terrorized their neighbors. They were able to gain control over the Middle East and parts of Egypt.

In the eighth century B.C.E., the Neo-Assyrian Kingdom became an empire. In 722 B.C.E., the Assyrian king Shalmaneser V conquered the northern kingdom of Israel and deported a part of the population (p. 250). The southern kingdom of Judah fell under the Assyrian rule. It was not until 612 B.C.E. that the Assyrian Empire finally fell with the capture of Nineveh (**1**) by the Babylonians.

The Assyrians appear in the Bible as instruments of God used to punish the sinning Israelites (p. 318). The prophets, however, maintained that the Assyrians would one day have to pay for their brutality.

Winged mythical creatures adorned the palaces and temples of the Assyrians

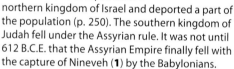

»» Oholah and Oholibah: p. 326

Figures and Stories Relevant to the Assyrians

God, see pp. 28–33

The Egyptians, see pp. 104–105

King Jehu of Israel, Vassal of the Assyrians, see the Kings of Israel, pp. 248–251

Hezekiah of Judah, see the Kings of Judah, pp. 254–257

The Babylonians, Conquerors of the Assyrians, see pp. 268–269

Isaiah, see pp. 316–319

Prophets Speaking About the Assyrians, see Jeremiah, pp. 320–323

God Saves Jerusalem The Assyrians repeatedly advanced on the borders of the Israelites in the eighth and seventh centuries B.C.E. After the downfall of the northern kingdom, the southern kingdom of Judah had to pay tributes to the Assyrians. King Hezekiah sought support from the Egyptians in order to shake off the control of the

Assyrians. Therefore, the Assyrian king Sennacherib led a retaliatory campaign against Judah in 701 B.C.E. This is also reported, along with the Bible, by a clay cylinder from the time (**3**). After Sennacherib's troops had laid waste to the country, they besieged the capital of Jerusalem (p. 256). In dire need, King Hezekiah turned to the prophet Isaiah, **3**

who cautioned him to remain peaceful and trust in God. Isaiah heralded the salvation of Jerusalem, as God would save the city. An angel of God slaughtered 185,000 soldiers in the Assyrian camp on the next night (**2**). King Sennacherib had to retreat to Nineveh, but he could not escape his fate even here, as he was killed by his own son.

The Assyrians Conquer Lachish During his military campaign against Judah in 701 B.C.E., Sennacherib conquered the Jewish city of Lachish. The inhabitants were taken prisoner by the Assyrian troops and tortured (**3**). King Hezekiah of Judah sent out messengers to Sennacherib. He informed Sennacherib that he accepted defeat and was ready to pay tributes to him. Sennacherib demanded gold and silver from Hezekiah. The Assyrians ridiculed his faith in God. As they had been able to take Lachish so easily, they considered the God of Israel to be hopeless. When Hezekiah heard of this, he put on mourning attire and prayed to God.

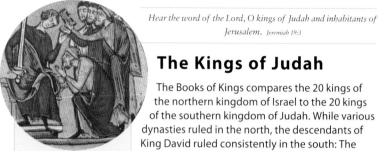

Hear the word of the Lord, O kings of Judah and inhabitants of Jerusalem. Jeremiah 19:3

The Kings of Judah

The Books of Kings compares the 20 kings of the northern kingdom of Israel to the 20 kings of the southern kingdom of Judah. While various dynasties ruled in the north, the descendants of King David ruled consistently in the south: The dictatorial claim to leadership of Solomon's son and successor Rehoboam led to the secession of 10 of the 12 Tribes of Israel (**1**) in 926 B.C.E. However, Rehoboam maintained authority over the tribes of Benjamin and Judah. Therefore God's promise to David was fulfilled, as his offspring were guaranteed sovereignty.

The kingdom of Judah was smaller and less affluent than its northern counterpart, but also contained the city of Jerusalem and the Temple of Solomon. Through a strategy of alliances, the kings of Judah tried to maintain autonomy between the powers of Egypt and Assyria, especially after the fall of the northern kingdom in 722 B.C.E. ⟩⟩

■ After the secession of the north, the dynasty of David only rules over Judah

■ The downfall of Judah and the destruction of the Temple are important events in the history of Judaism

⟩⟩ **The Family Tree of the House of David:** pp. 208–209

thaliah Is Overthrown King ehoram of Judah had married thaliah, the daughter of King hab of Israel. After the deaths f her husband and son around 45 B.C.E., Athaliah had the men in her family

killed and reigned as queen. Only Joash, the son of Ahaziah, escaped the massacre. A wet nurse rescued the infant, and one of his aunts hid him in the temple. After seven years, the reign of Queen Athaliah, which

supported foreign cults, came to an end. The priest Jehoiada showed Joash to the people and declared him king with the help of the army (**2**). Taken by surprise, Athaliah was imprisoned and then executed.

Joash Has Zechariah Killed Under the influence of Jehoiada, Joash was a devout king. After Jehoiada's death, he began to worship foreign deities. Prophet Zechariah rebuked the king, so Joash had him stoned (**4**). God punished him with an Aramaean attack under Hazael (**3**). Instead of fighting, Joash offered a tribute. The influential men of the country were outraged and killed the king.

The prophets Isaiah and Jeremiah often referred to these external threats, interpreting them as punishments for the misconduct of the kings and the people. As foretold, the kingdom of Judah fell around 587 B.C.E. when the Babylonians destroyed Jerusalem and exiled the upper class (pp. 272–273).

The Hezekiah Tunnel

As Jerusalem was faced with increasing external threats, King Hezekiah prepared the city for a siege. He had a tunnel excavated underneath the city walls that would connect a reservoir with the Gihon Spring. The building of the tunnel, mentioned in II Kings 20:20, has also been proved by archaeological finds such as inscriptions.

Hezekiah's Treasures King Hezekiah experienced the fall of the northern kingdom by the Assyrians around 722 B.C.E. This event was seen as a punishment from God for the sins of the Israelites. Therefore he had all cult images destroyed. He stood up to the Assyrians but provoked a counter campaign around 701 B.C.E. by the Assyrian king Sennacherib. Hezekiah had to pay a large tribute and hand over his treasures (**4**), as well as the gold adornments of the Temple. In spite of this, the Assyrians besieged Jerusalem. When he asked God for help, God responded by annihilating the Assyrian army (p. 253) and forcing Sennacherib to retreat.

⏵⏵ Hezekiah's Son Manasseh and the Prophet Isaiah: p. 319

(6)

Josiah's Cultural Reforms

King Josiah of Judah exclusively worshiped God. He had all idols removed and banned services to false gods. He read the laws from the books of Moses to the entire populace, including priests and prophets (**6**), making a renewed covenant with God that he and his people would follow God's laws. Josiah was less successful with his foreign policy. Around 690 B.C.E. he fell at the Battle of Megiddo against the Egyptian pharaoh Necho II (**7**) (p. 239).

Zedekiah's End After his first attack on Jerusalem around 597 B.C.E., the Babylonian king Nebuchadrezzar II placed Zedekiah on the throne. Zedekiah, however, tried to liberate the kingdom from the Babylonians. In a second campaign, Nebuchadrezzar wiped out the kingdom of Judah and Jerusalem fell after a two-year siege around 587 B.C.E. Zedekiah watched while his sons were killed (**8**). The Temple of Solomon and the whole of Jerusalem were destroyed (p. 271). The majority of the population was transported to Babylon (pp. 272–275).

(8)

≫ **Zedekiah and the Prophet Jeremiah:** p. 323

The Prophet Jeremiah Warns King Zedekiah of the Destruction of Jerusalem by the Babylonians

Jeremiah 21:7–10

7 Afterwards, says the Lord, I will give King Zedekiah of Judah, and his servants, and the people in this city—those who survive the pestilence, sword, and famine—into the hands of King Nebuchadnezzar of Babylon, into the hands of their enemies, into the hands of those who seek their lives. He shall strike them down with the edge of the sword; he shall not pity them, or spare them, or have compassion.

8 And to this people you shall say: Thus says the Lord: See, I am setting before you the way of life and the way of death.

9 Those who stay in this city shall die by the sword, by famine, and by pestilence; but those who go out and surrender to the Chaldeans who are besieging you shall live and shall have their lives as a prize of war.

10 For I have set my face against this city for evil and not for good, says the Lord: it shall be given into the hands of the king of Babylon, and he shall burn it with fire

⏵⏵ **The Prophet Jeremiah and King Zedekiah:** p. 323

From the Babylonian Captivity to the Maccabees

The Jew Esther in the court of the Persian king Ahasuerus

From the Babylonian

The Babylonian Exile

p. 279

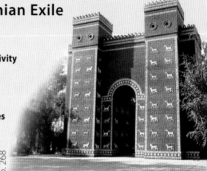

p. 268

600   550   500   450   400   350

p. 273

The Persians

p. 280

Captivity to the Maccabees

The Hellenism Era and the Dynasty of the Maccabees

p. 290

p. 290

p. 291

300	250	200	150	100	50

p. 290

p. 289

From the Babylonian Captivity to the Maccabees

After the conquest of the northern kingdom of Israel by the Assyrians in 722 B.C.E., the kings of Judah in the south sought to protect their independence through a risky strategy of alliances with the great powers. With this, however, they threatened the authority of the Babylonian king Nebuchadrezzar II. He mounted two attacks on the southern kingdom of Judah: in 597 B.C.E., when a large proportion of the population was deported to Babylon, and in 587 B.C.E., when the conquest of Judah was completed. Jerusalem and Solomon's Temple were destroyed, and the last king of the House of David, Zedekiah, was blinded and deported to Babylon. Judah became a Babylonian province ruled by a governor. Thus, Judah's political sovereignty had come to an end, along with the 400-year rule of the House of David. The Israelites' religion was also deeply affected, because the Temple was considered God's dwelling place and the people's point of encounter with him. Along with the deportation of the political and cultural elite to Babylon, the loss of the Temple as a religious focal point was a difficult test for the Israelites. The risk of losing their identity as a people was great: After all, with the destruction of the northern kingdom, ten of the 12 Tribes of Israel were lost without a trace.

Israel's experiences during this time of crisis are captured in the literature of the Bible (**1**). The songs of Lamentations and some of the Psalms record the people's grief and despair (**2**) over the Temple's destruction and the devastation experienced in Jerusalem and across their homeland. Each in its own way, the great works of the prophets Isaiah, Jeremiah and Ezekiel describe the destruction of the Temple and the following period of exile. The time in exile became a foundational experience for Judaism. On the one hand, it was a source of grievances—even today, a day of fasting is observed in memory of the Temple's destruction. At the same time, the experience of exile also led to a deeply felt longing for Zion—the place where God dwells—and the restoration of the Temple. For Jewish philosopher of religion Paul Mendes-Flohr, exile may be "the most fundamental religious idea in Judaism." Historian Ben Halpern sees in exile "the concept that is most deeply Jewish, most inherent to the Jewish people, the symbol that summarizes and spiritualizes the whole historical experience [of the Jews]."

When the Persian king Cyrus conquered Babylon in 539 B.C.E., he allowed the deported people of Judah to return home. According to the books of Ezra and Nehemiah, some 42,000 people left for Judea under the leadership of the Persian governor Sheshbazzar. In the same year, Sheshbazzar laid the cornerstone for the reconstructed Temple, although it was not completed and inaugurated until 515 B.C.E.

During the following decades, the economic situation in Judea remained weak, and religious life was also beset with difficulties. In 445/444 B.C.E., Nehemiah, a high Jewish official under the Persian king, traveled from Babylon to Jerusalem and undertook a series of reforms. He ordered the rebuilding of the city wall and reduced social tensions with a decree forgiving debtors. According to the biblical account, Ezra, a priestly scribe, also traveled from Babylon to Jerusalem to teach the people about God's laws. Like other narratives in the Bible, the books of Ezra and Nehemiah are theological interpretations of history. The prophets Haggai and Zechariah, who supported the rebuilding of the Temple, also fell within the Persian time period.

The rule of the Persians (**4**) ended in 332 B.C.E., as the military campaigns of Alexander the Great ushered in the Hellenistic age. After Alexander's death in 323 B.C.E, his empire was divided among the Diadochi (Greek for "successors"). As in earlier times, Palestine again became a bone of contention for the great powers: For two centuries, the Egyptian Ptolemies and Syrian Seleucids struggled for power in the Middle East. The Ptolemies practiced religious tolerance, and the Temple in Jerusalem enjoyed substantial autonomy. Yet in 198 B.C.E., the Seleucid Antiochus III drove the Ptolemies out of Palestine. His son, Antiochus IV, plundered the Temple in 169/168 B.C.E., desecrating it with heathen rituals. Under penalty of death, he forbade circumcision, the celebration of the Sabbath and religious festivals, and the possession of Torah scrolls. Jewish life was thus made impossible. The priest Mattathias rose up in armed rebellion against this oppression, attracting many followers. After his death, his son Judas Maccabeus assumed leadership. His first aim—recovering the Temple—was achieved in 165 B.C.E. However, political freedom was not won until 142 B.C.E., when Mattathias' youngest son, Simon, was recognized as an independent ruler.

The Jews' struggle for liberation is described in the two books of the Maccabees, which arose at the turn of the first century B.C.E. The first book focuses on the Maccabee or Hasmonean dynasty: although they were not descendants from the House of David, they show themselves as saviors of Israel. The second book of the Maccabees focuses primarily on the Temple in Jerusalem, whose rededication is commemorated by Hanukkah (**3**). The Jews won independence and restored the focal point of their religion. However, during a struggle for succession among the Hasmoneans, the Romans were called to help. They entered Jerusalem in 63 B.C.E., which heralded the Roman era in Palestine.

■ The Babylonians were a people of great religious and cultural significance

■ In the Bible, the Babylonians appear as an instrument used by God to punish the Israelites for their sins

■ The city of Babylon became a synonym for sinfulness and lust for power

II Kings 24:10 Jerusalem is besieged and conquered by the Babylonians

Isaiah 13:1–22 Isaiah promises the Israelites that God will free them from the hands of the Babylonians

II Chronicles 36:11–21 The Israelites are made captive by the Babylonians

Revelation 17 A vision speaks of Babylon as the mother of all whores and abominations on the Earth

And Babylon, the glory of kingdoms, the splendor and pride of the Chaldeans, will be like Sodom and Gomorrah. Isaiah 13:19

The Babylonians

The Neo-Babylonian Empire of the Chaldeans replaced the Assyrians as the dominant power at the turn of the sixth century B.C.E. Under the kings Nabopolassar (reigned 626–604 B.C.E.) and Nebuchadrezzar II (reigned 604–562 B.C.E.), the empire experienced its cultural and economic heyday. One generation later, internal crises such as crop failures and religious conflicts led to its downfall. In 539 B.C.E., the Persian king Cyrus II the Great defeated the last Babylonian king Nabonidus.

In the Books of Daniel and Judith, Babylon stands as an empire that presumed to rule the world and stood in competition with God.

Reconstruction of the Ishtar Gate in Babylon commissioned by Nebuchadrezzar II in current-day Iraq

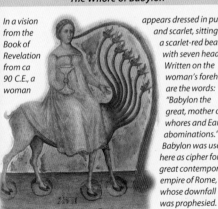

Prophecies Against Babylon In the Hebrew Bible, Babylon also appears as a tool of God. Thus, the Babylonian captivity is interpreted as God's punishment for the sins of the people of Israel. For the Bible it is clear that only God can truly rule over the heavens and Earth, and so all worldly power is subservient to him, even that of the Babylonians. Therefore, the prophet Isaiah proclaimed that the violent dominance of this superpower would also meet its end, as God would make Babylonians responsible for their actions and judge them accordingly (**1**). Then the Israelites would rejoice and possess the world in peace. Jeremiah also saw the fall of Babylon, including its gods Bel and Marduk.

Hanging Gardens Babylon was the center of a splendid civilization. Constructions such as the legendary hanging gardens (**2**), which were one of the seven wonders of antiquity, or the ornately tiled Ishtar Gate, demonstrate the capabilities of the Babylonians. In biblical texts, Babylon appears as a symbol for splendor, waste, and arrogance. Despite this, the Babylonian culture left its mark on the Bible, such as the first account of creation, because the two cultures were in close contact.

The Whore of Babylon

In a vision from the Book of Revelation from ca 90 C.E., a woman appears dressed in purple and scarlet, sitting on a scarlet-red beast with seven heads. Written on the woman's forehead are the words: "Babylon the great, mother of whores and Earth's abominations." Babylon was used here as cipher for the great contemporary empire of Rome, whose downfall was prophesied.

The Tower of Babel: pp. 58–59   **Book of Revelation:** pp. 496–497

■ Nebuchadrez-
zar II is the most im-
portant king of
the Neo-Baby-
lonian Empire

II Kings 24:10–16 The first attack by the Babylonians on Jerusalem

II Kings 25:1–21; II Chronicles 36:11–21 The second attack by the Babylonians on Jerusalem, downfall of Judah, and beginning of the captivity

Jeremiah 39:7 Nebuchadrezzar has Zedekiah's eyes gouged out and transfers him to Babylon

Daniel 2:1–45 Daniel interprets Nebuchadrezzar's dream of four world empires

Daniel 4:1–33 Nebuchadrezzar dreams of being metamorphosed by God into an animal

Nebuchadrezzar in Jerusalem
When Nebuchadrezzar be-
sieged Jerusalem in 587 B.C.E.
(**1**), King Jeconiah surrendered.
He was deported to Babylon
along with his family, officials,
and the powerful men of his
land. Nebuchadrezzar made
Zedekiah the king of Judah.

*At that time the servants of King Nebuchadrezzar of Babylon cam[e]
up to Jerusalem, and the city was besieged.* II Kings 24:10

Nebuchadrezzar II

The Neo-Babylonian Empire
reached its zenith under the
leadership of Nebuchadrezzar II
from 604 to 562 B.C.E. The king
was a successful military commander. He defeated the

The
seal of King
Nebuchadrezzar II

Egyptians and attacked the kingdom of Judah
twice, finally conquering it in 587 B.C.E. He deported the upper classes to Babylon. The destruction of Jerusalem introduced an important period in
Israel's history as the Babylonian captivity marked
the Jewish religion.

The Book of Daniel, which takes place mainly in
the court of Babylon, draws an ambivalent portrait
of Nebuchadrezzar. He appears arrogant and cruel,
but he also acknowledges the greatness of God.

treasures plundered, and the city walls broken. Zedekiah's sons were executed before him, and then he was blinded and deported to Babylon (p. 257). The conquest of Jerusalem and the destruction of the Temple were simultaneously a political and a religious catastrophe. Politically speaking, the sovereignty of Judah ended along with the 400-year-old rule of the House of David. The religion was hit at its heart, as the Temple was the residence of God (**3**). The Israelites would visit the Temple three times a

year during Passover (pp. 118–119), Sukkoth (pp. 128–129), and Shabuoth (pp. 192–193). There, they would present offerings, experience God's presence, and atone for their sins on Yom Kippur (pp. 138–139). The relationship between Israel and God was disturbed by the destruction of the Temple.

The Destruction of Jerusalem

When Zedekiah of Judah broke his pact with Nebuchadrezzar, the Babylonian king reacted with a countercampaign. He besieged Jerusalem for two years and finally stormed the city in 587 B.C.E. The royal palace and the Temple of Solomon were burnt down (**2**),

Figures and Stories Relevant to Nebuchadrezzar II

God, see pp. 28–33

Jerusalem, see pp. 226–227

The Kings of Judah, see pp. 254–257

The Babylonians, see pp. 268–269

The Babylonian Captivity, see pp. 272–273

Daniel, see pp. 336–339

Nebuchadrezzar Changes Before God

The Book of Daniel is a dispute against Nebuchadrezzar's claim to power over the earth. In Daniel 4, he dreams that a voice from heaven announces that his kingdom will be taken away and he will be driven out of the community of humankind. He was to live as an animal (**4**) until he acknowledged that God held the might of the world and could distribute this power as he wishes. As soon as Nebuchadrezzar realized God's omnipotence, he became human again.

The Babylonian Captivity

During the Babylonian captivity, in which the Israelites were exiled between ca 587 to 539 B.C.E., their religion underwent a change. As the Temple had been destroyed and the exiles had nowhere to present sacrifices to their God, prayer and study of the Torah became the focus. These were once again taken up by the rabbis after the second destruction of the Temple in 70 C.E., thus making it the foundation of Judaism. Memories of the exile play a central role in the Jewish tradition. For example, Psalm 137 is a table prayer: "By the rivers of Babylon, there we sat down and there we wept, when we remembered Zion…" (**1**).

In Exile The Babylonian captivity is interpreted by the Bible as a punishment by God for the sins of the Israelites. God punished the Israelites through Nebuchadrezzar's promotion of gentile customs. The prophet Jeremiah told the Israelites to accept their fate and to settle into their lives in Babylon. He also advised them to start families, build houses, and plant gardens, thus investing in Babylon and actively taking part in their surroundings. This way, the betterment of the city would be beneficial for its new inhabitants.

(1)

>> **The Temple in Jerusalem:** pp. 368–369   **Rabbis:** p. 456

2

The Deportation With the deportation of the upper classes of Judah, the Babylonians hoped to prevent a rebellion. This had also been implemented by the Assyrians in 722 B.C.E. during the conquest of the kingdom of Israel (**2**), and all traces of its inhabitants were lost. However, the people of Judah maintained their identity and adapted to the circumstances. Thus, a number of biblical books were composed or finalized there during the exile.

» **The Lost Tribes of the Northern Kingdom:** p. 165

The Lamentations—The Prayer of the Deepest Sorrow

Lamentations 5:1–5

¹ *Remember, O Lord, what has befallen us; look, and see our disgrace!* ² *Our inheritance has been turned over to strangers, our homes to aliens.* ³ *We have become orphans, fatherless; our mothers are like widows.*

⁴ *We must pay for the water we drink; the wood we get must be bought.* ⁵ *With a yoke on our necks we are hard driven; we are weary, we are given no rest.*

■ The bloody story of Judith and Holofernes was a beloved motif of the artists of the Renaissance

■ Judith is an example of female heroic figures in Israel

Judith 7:1–24
Holofernes, one of Nebuchadrezzar's commanders, besieges the Israelite city of Bethulia

Judith 10–11 Judith poses as a defector and enters Holofernes' camp

Judith 12–13 Judith is invited to a dinner party. When she is alone with the drunken Holofernes, she strikes off his head and flees

Judith 16:1–20 Judith thanks God and celebrates the victory

All the women of Israel gathered to see her, and blessed her, and some of them performed a dance in her honor. Judith 15:12

Judith and Holofernes

The Book of Judith was not based on historical events, but rather the story of Judith and Holofernes (**1**) serves to see who had more power: King Nebuchadrezzar II or God.

When the Babylonian king Nebuchadrezzar called the Israelites to fight with him against the Persians, they did not follow. Therefore, he sent one of his commanders, Holofernes, on a mission to punish them. When the widow

Judith learned that her city of Bethulia could barely mount a resistance to the siege, she asked God to help the Israelites, as he had done in the past. Then she dressed herself as a defector and went to Holofernes' camp. There, she praised Nebuchadrezzar's deeds and Holofernes was overcome by her beauty and intelligence. When he later threw a dinner party for his entourage, he invited her (**2**).

3

Judith Kills Holofernes

The guests at the dinner party quickly became drunk, and Judith was left alone with Holofernes. When he fell asleep, she took a sword and cut off his head (**3**), which she hid in a bag. When the body was discovered, a man present exclaimed: "One Hebrew woman has brought disgrace upon the house of King Nebuchadrezzar" (Judith 14:18). Her plan proved to be successful, as Nebuchadrezzar's troops fled and were slaughtered by the Israelites. Judith thanked God and sang a song of praise.

■ Belshazzar was the last ruler of the Babylonian Empire

■ Belshazzar's story is the foundation of numerous artistic adaptations in poetry and music

Daniel 5:1–4 Belshazzar hosts a banquet using glasses stolen from the Temple

Daniel 5:5–6 Suddenly fingers appear and write the "Mene Tekel" on the wall

Daniel 5:7–29 Belshazzar has Daniel summoned, who deciphers the words

Daniel 5:30 Belshazzar's death

You have exalted yourself against the Lord of heaven … in whose power is your very breath. Daniel 5:23

Belshazzar

According to the Bible, Belshazzar was the son of Nebuchadrezzar II and the last king of Babylon. The historical Belshazzar was probably the son and co-regent of Nabonidus, the last king of the Neo-Babylonian Empire, who was defeated by the Persians in 539 B.C.E.

The Book of Daniel reports that Belshazzar hosted a banquet and had his guests drink from the sanctified chalices that had been taken from the Temple. Suddenly, a hand appeared and wrote "Mene mene tekel u-parsin" on the wall (**1**). Terrified, Belshazzar called for someone to interpret this sign for him.

The Fall of Babylon As Daniel had prophesied, the Babylonian empire crumbled (**2**). The rulers of Babylon were symbols of human power in the Bible, who demanded unconditional fealty and clashed against God. It is clear in the Book of Daniel that God alone was the ruler of the heavens and the earth, and that no power in the world could exist if it did not correspond to his will.

Daniel Interprets the Writing on the Wall No one could explain the writing on the wall to Belshazzar (**3**). Daniel (**4**) was summoned: he said "Mene" meant that God would end Belshazzar's rule; "Tekel" meant that God had found him to be greedy; "Parsin" meant that his kingdom would be divided by the Medes and the Persians. Later that night, Belshazzar was killed and Persia took over Babylon.

■ The Persians founded the first world empire of antiquity

■ In the biblical account, the Persians play a positive role as liberators of the Jews from the Babylonian captivity

II Chronicles 36:22–23 Filled with the spirit of God, the Persian king Cyrus allows the exiles to return to Judah

Ezra 1:7 Cyrus returns the Temple implements to the Israelites

Ezra 4:1–24 Conflict arises among the people in Judah over the Temple's reconstruction

Ezra 5 Cyrus permits the rebuilding of the Temple

Isaiah 45:1 Cyrus is described as being anointed by God

Daniel 6 Daniel becomes a high official in the Persian empire but falls victim to an intrigue

Daniel 10–11 Daniel has a vision about the Persians' future

I Maccabees 1:1 Alexander the Great conquers the Persians

Thus says King Cyrus of Persia: The Lord, the God of heaven ... has charged me to build him a house at Jerusalem in Judah. Ezra 1:2

The Persians

In the sixth and fifth centuries B.C.E., the Persians (**1**) built a huge empire that stretched from Egypt to India. Its heart lay in the southwestern part of what is now Iran, with the cities of Persepolis (**2**) and Susa. In contrast to his Assyrian and Babylonian predecessors, the Persian king Cyrus II, who occupied Babylon in 539 B.C.E., allowed the conquered peoples autonomy. In the Bible, Cyrus is judged very positively and is even described as being anointed by God. He allowed the Jews to return to their homeland, permitted them to rebuild the Temple, and even returned the Temple treasures confiscated earlier by Nebuchadrezzar. A group of exiles came to Judah in 537 B.C.E.; however, their arrival was not free from difficulties. Conflicts arose over the restoration of property and the rebuilding of the Temple. The cornerstone for the construction was laid in the year of the exiles' return, but the new Temple was not inaugurated until 515 B.C.E.

②

⟫ **The Fall of the Persian Empire:** p. 288

Religious Policies of Cyrus The "Cyrus Cylinder," a clay tablet marked with cuneiform writing (**4**), describes the king's religious tolerance. According to the Bible, Cyrus supported the rebuilding of the Temple in Jerusalem (**3**). With great joy, the Jews returned from exile to begin the project. Those who remained also wanted to participate, but the governor and the high priest—both former exiles—refused. Thus, those who stayed behind attempted to hinder the rebuilding effort.

Figures and Stories Relevant to the Persians	
The Assyrians, see pp. 252–253	Captivity, see pp. 272–273
The Babylonians, see pp. 268–269	Haggai and Zechariah, see the Minor Prophets, pp. 330–333
The Babylonian	

Rebuilding the Temple After a series of delays, the reconstruction of the Temple in Jerusalem (**5**) was resumed when the Jews returning from exile gained political control. The high priest Jeschua and the prophets Haggai and Zechariah supported the Persian governor Zerubbabel, a descendant of an earlier royal family. Great hopes were placed on the reconstruction of the Temple; Haggai and Zechariah expected the Last Days of peace and harmony on earth to begin after its completion. The new Temple, dedicated in 515 B.C.E. with a great celebration, was less ornate than the previous one. It also lacked the Ark of the Covenant, the "Sea of Bronze," and the Jachin and Boaz pillars that had been in Solomon's Temple.

⟫ **The Temple in Jerusalem:** pp. 368–369

The king loved Esther more than all the other women ... so that he set the royal crown on her head and made her queen.

Esther 2:17

Esther

The events in the Book of Esther—the order to murder all of the Jews in the Persian empire and their deliverance through Esther's intervention—have not been linked to a specific historic incident. Instead, the Book of Esther describes a recurring experience for the Israelites: Finding themselves in the minority, vulnerable to persecution by seemingly invincible enemies. In this case, salvation comes via a woman. Esther managed to rescue her people at the risk of her own life. To remember the deliverance of the entire Jewish people, Mordecai and Esther instituted the festival of Purim on the day after their triumph over the Jews' enemies. Writing down what had happened, they sent the story to all the Jews in the Persian empire.

Esther and Mordecai After banishing his wife Vashti for daring to defy him, the Persian king Artaxerxes was looking for a new wife. The most beautiful young women of the empire were led to his harem. They included Esther, the cousin and adopted daughter of Mordecai (**1**), both of whom were exiled Israelites from Judah. The king was most pleased by Esther, and made her his queen.

①

▶▶ **Judith and Holofernes:** pp. 276–277

Esther Before the King Everyone was supposed to bow before Haman, the highest official. When Mordecai refused, Haman was enraged. However, taking revenge against Mordecai was not enough. Instead, he decided to murder all of the Jews in the Persian empire and confiscate their property. Mordecai asked Esther to stand up for the Jews and suggested that God had made her the Persian queen to allow her to help her people. Agreeing, she asked that all Jews fast for three days to buy time, as it was forbidden for her to approach the king without being called; she did not want to be banished for disobedience like her predecessor Vashti. Eventually Esther appeared before Artaxerxes and he was merciful (**2**).

Haman's Downfall
Esther invited the king to a banquet and asked him to bring Haman (**3**). During the meal, the king offered to grant Esther a wish. She asked him to retract the decree ordering the murder of her people. When he asked who had issued the decree, Esther pointed to Haman. The king became angry, recognizing Haman's malice. Haman was hanged on the gallows he had prepared for Mordecai (**4**). Artaxerxes canceled the decree and allowed the Jews to defend themselves from their enemies.

Purim

Purim commemorates the Jews' deliverance from their enemies in the Persian empire. The Book of Esther describes the plan of the Persian official Haman to annihilate all the Jews living in the Persian empire. The Jewish queen, Esther, was able to prevent this catastrophe by bravely speaking up before the king. As described at the end of the Book of Esther, the festival should remind people of the days wherein the Jews rested from their enemies, and their sorrow was turned to joy and their mourning to celebration

(Esther 9:22). The name of the holiday comes from the "pur," or lot, thrown by Haman to decide the date for murdering the Jews. On Purim, the Book of Esther (**4**) is read in the synagogue during the worship service. Each time Haman's name is read, the people make a commotion by stamping, hissing, and rattling (**1**). The clamor expresses their joy that Haman's plan was not carried out. On this holiday, celebrants are expressly allowed to drink vast amounts of alcohol and to feast to their hearts' content.

Purim Customs Purim is traditionally a time of much drinking and feasting (**2**). Among the special foods of this festival are "hamantashen," three-cornered pastries filled with poppy seeds and jam (**3**). Dressing up in costumes (**5**) is also a Purim custom, which may reflect the complete absence of the name of God from the Book of Esther—indicating that God steers the fate of the people involved while remaining hidden.

5

■ The priest Ezra was compared to Moses and even viewed as a second Moses

■ Ezra was a defender and protector of the Jewish identity and religion

■ Nehemiah and Ezra were the most important leadership figures at the time of the Israelites' return from the Babylonian captivity

Ezra 8:1–36 Ezra returns to Jerusalem with the Israelites

Ezra 9–10 Ezra condemns mixed marriages between Israelites and people from other ethnic groups

Nehemiah 3:1–4:17 Nehemiah oversees the rebuilding of Jerusalem's city wall

Nehemiah 8:1–12 Ezra reads the Mosaic laws out loud to the Israelites

Nehemiah 5:1–13 Nehemiah stands up for the poor, offering them relief

Nehemiah 7:69–72, 13:4–31 Nehemiah carries out religious reforms and brings in funds for the Temple

Ezra brought the law before the assembly, both men and women and all who could hear with understanding. Nehemiah 8:2

Ezra and Nehemiah

In ancient Jewish tradition, the Books of Ezra and Nehemiah are viewed as a single text. The two accounts show great linguistic and theological similarities. While Nehemiah is recorded by other sources as a historical figure, this is not the case with Ezra.

After serving the Persians as a high court official, Nehemiah arrived in Jerusalem in 445 B.C.E., where he was governor for 12 years. He ordered the rebuilding of the city walls and reduced social tensions by introducing a debt relief measure. He also carried out religious reforms. Ezra, who descended from a family of high priests, was a representative of the Persian court for Jewish religious affairs. He traveled from Babylon to Jerusalem to teach the population about God's laws.

Return From Exile The books of Ezra and Nehemiah contain lists of the returning Israelites, totaling some 42,000 people **(1)**. Since only a proportion of the returnees could settle in Jerusalem, they cast lots to decide who would live in the capital. **1**

Ezra Reads From the Torah

Ezra, whose name means "God helps," was a Persian official and a learned scholar and priest. In Jerusalem, he gathered everyone together (**2**) and recited the Torah—God's instructions—to them from daybreak to noon. Afterward, the priests and scholars interpreted the holy scriptures, helping the people understand the Torah's teachings. Finally, a great festival was held. The people promised to uphold the laws, the foundation for a life pleasing to God. The laws also included a prohibition on mixed marriages, since these could lead to idol worship. However, many marriages took place among the Israelites in exile. When Ezra heard this, he tore his clothing in mourning. During the evening prayer, Ezra confessed his people's sins to God and asked for mercy. The people were overcome with emotion, weeping and acknowledging that they had done wrong. They promised to dissolve their mixed marriages.

Nehemiah as Governor

The Persian king sent Nehemiah to Jerusalem to serve as governor (**3**). When he arrived, he found poor social and economic conditions in the city. In spite of resistance from his enemies—who envied his position and attacked Jerusalem—Nehemiah rebuilt Jerusalem's city walls (**4**). When the poor complained to Nehemiah that they had to mortgage the futures of their children to buy food, he called upon the rich to return debtors' fields, vineyards, olive groves, and homes. Nehemiah also carried out religious reforms, instituting the Sabbath and bringing in revenue for the Temple.

The Torah: pp. 130–131   Mourning Rituals: p. 346

And the king sent letters by messengers to … the towns of Judah, he directed them to follow customs strange to the land. 1 Maccabees 1:44

The Ptolemies and the Seleucids

With the conquest of the Persian Empire by Alexander the Great (**1**), Syria and Palestine also fell under Greek rule in a nearly bloodless occupation in 332 B.C.E. After Alexander's death, his empire was divided. At first, Palestine went to the Ptolemies, based in the Egyptian city of Alexandria (**2**). Yet in 198 B.C.E., the Ptolemies were pushed out by the Seleucids. While the Seleucid king Antiochus III had a liberal policy toward the Jews, his son Antiochus IV Epiphanes ruled oppressively after 175 B.C.E., raising taxes, stationing troops, and plundering the Temple. Under penalty of death, he prohibited the Jews from practicing their religion: circumcision and the keeping of the Sabbath were forbidden, and the Temple in Jerusalem was rededicated to the Greek god Zeus. These measures led to the revolt of the Maccabees. In spite of their victory, the Hel-   lenistic culture took hold, especially amidst the   upper classes.

■ The Hellenistic age began in the Middle East with the military campaign of Alexander the Great

■ Alexander's generals, the diadochi (Greek for "successors"), divided the empire among themselves after his death

■ Under Antiochus IV, the Jews experienced a period of oppression and persecution

I Maccabees 1:1–9 Shortly before his death, Alexander the Great divides his empire among his former comrades in arms

I Maccabees 1:17–28; II Maccabees 5:15–21 Antiochus IV plunders the Temple in Jerusalem

I Maccabees 1:43–64 Antiochus IV forbids the practice of the Jewish religion

I Maccabees 2:1–30 The Jewish priest Mattathias rises up against Antiochus IV's oppression

I Maccabees 13:33–42 Simon achieves full independence for Israel

II Maccabees 1:10 The Jews are mentioned in Egypt; Aristobulus, a Jew from a priestly family, is a teacher at the Ptolemaic court

Antiochus III Gives Freedom to the Jews In 198 B.C.E., when the Seleucid ruler Antiochus III took Palestine, he granted the people several privileges (**3**): he allotted funds to the Temple, exempted Jerusalem's inhabitants from tribute payments for three years, and promised to free prisoners and return their property. He stressed that they should live according to the "laws of their fathers."

Ptolemy II and the Septuagint

According to the letter of Aristeas, the Egyptian king Ptolemy II ordered the translation of the Torah into Greek in the third century B.C.E. As 72 scholars are said to have translated the Torah in 72 days, it was named the Septuagint (Latin: "seventy").

Figures and Stories Relevant to the Ptolemies and Seleucids

Antiochus IV Plunders Jerusalem

After a military campaign against Egypt, the Seleucid ruler Antiochus IV Epiphanes came to Jerusalem. Unlike his father, he showed no respect for the Jews' religion. He removed all gold and silver objects from the Temple (**4**). Later, Antiochus went even further by converting the Temple into a heathen place of worship. Horrifying scenes of desecration took place on the altar, the holy scriptures were torn, and the people were forbidden to keep the religious laws.

The Temple in Jerusalem: pp. 368–369

■ The Maccabees revolted against the Seleucids' oppression

■ The Hasmoneans founded an independent Jewish state in Palestine

I Maccabees 2:1–30 Mattathias revolts against the Seleucids and their supporters

I Maccabees 2:49–70 Judas Maccabeus is chosen to succeed his father Mattathias

I Maccabees 4:36–61 Judas Maccabeus forms an alliance with the Romans

I Maccabees 9:1–31 Judas Maccabeus falls in battle; his brother Jonathan succeeds him

I Maccabees 12–13 Jonathan is murdered and his brother Simon takes his place

I Maccabees 16:11–24 Simon is killed; his son John Hyrcanus I is appointed high priest

II Maccabees 3 The Temple's treasures are kept safe Heliodorus

II Maccabees 4:7–20 The high priest Jason promotes Greek customs

I, like my brothers, give up body and life for the laws of our ancestors, appealing to God to show mercy. II Maccabees 7:37

The Maccabees

With his brutal measures, Antiochus IV Epiphanes (p. 289) provoked resistance among religious Jews. In 166 B.C.E., the priest Mattathias from the family of the Hasmoneans led a revolt. After his death, his son Judas Maccabeus ("the Hammer") assumed leadership of the rebels, who were known as the Maccabees.

Both books of the Maccabees describe the Jews' heroic deeds and God's omnipotence. For instance, when the Seleucid Heliodor tried to loot the Temple's treasures, God sent two angels and a horseback rider to drive him away (**1**). In 164 B.C.E., Judas Maccabeus recaptured and rededicated the Temple in Jerusalem (p. 295). He and his brothers, Jonathan and Simon, continued to fight until they had driven out the Seleucids. **»**

The Hanukkah menorah commemorates the rededication of the Temple

»» The Temple in Jerusalem: pp. 368–369

Hellenism and the Jews Hellenization—the spread of Greek culture and language—began with Alexander the Great's conquest of Palestine in 332 B.C.E. The reaction of the Judeans was not negative. Hellenization was reflected in the choice of everyday language—Greek instead of Hebrew or Aramaic—and in the naming of children. It also led to the adoption of Greek educational institutions, the study of Greek literature and philosophy, and the construction of theaters and stadiums for competitions (**2**, **3**). The Jews of the diaspora actively engaged themselves with Greek ideas, as can be seen in the works of the Jewish philosopher Philo of Alexandria, who died after around 40 C.E.

Mattathias Launches an Uprising To advance the process of hellenization, Antiochus IV forced the Jews to make heathen sacrifices (pp. 288–289). When the priest Mattathias saw a Jew obeying this instruction, he became enraged and killed him along with a Seleucid official. Mattathias called upon all God-fearing people to join him (**4**). He, his five sons, and many others went underground to fight as rebels.

Martyrdom of the Seven Brothers Given the choice of eating pork or being killed, the eldest of seven brothers announced that the family would rather die than violate the Jewish laws. This answer infuriated the king, who issued an order to cut out the eldest brother's tongue, scalp him, and chop off his hands and feet. After this, he was burned alive in a frying pan. Each of the brothers remained steadfast, and one after another they were tortured and killed in this manner in front of their mother, who was later executed as well (**5**).

Finally, in 142 B.C.E., the Seleucids were forced to recognize Simon, the last surviving brother, as the high priest and autonomous ruler of the kingdom of Judah. Simon's descendants—known as the Hasmonean dynasty—reigned for a century both as high priests and kings or princes of Judah. However, they ultimately fell under the influence of the Romans, the new leading power in the western Mediterranean region. The Hasmoneans were later divided by internal struggles over the royal succession. In 37 B.C.E., Herod the Great replaced the Hasmoneans, becoming king of Judea and a vassal of the Romans.

Machaerus, a fortified palace of the Maccabees in present-day Jordan

Judas Maccabeus After his father's death, Judas Maccabeus assumed leadership of the revolt against the Seleucids. His guerrilla tactics proved successful: the Temple was reconquered in 164 B.C.E. This success was not enough, as his aim was full political autonomy for Judea. The books of the Maccabees describe his many successful battles against the Seleucids (**7**). In 161 B.C.E., the Seleucids dispatched a large number of their best soldiers (**6**) to Judea. Judas Maccabeus started with only 3,000 men, many of whom fled in the face of the powerful enemy, so that only 800 fighters remained. The battle began and Judas was killed (**8**). His brothers buried him in his father's grave in Modein. The people mourned: "How is the mighty fallen, the savior of Israel!" (I Maccabees 9:21).

Last of the Hasmoneans

Amid a conflict over succession within the Hasmonean dynasty, John Hyrcanus II called for assistance from the Romans, who had displaced the Seleucids as the leading power in the Middle East. The general Pompeius (**9**) occupied Jerusalem in 63 B.C.E. and desecrated the Temple (**10**). John Hyrcanus II had to relinquish the title of king, but remained the high priest (**11**). Meanwhile, his nephew Antigonus formed an alliance with the Parthians, archenemies of the Romans. With their help, he overthrew John Hyrcanus II, whose ear was cut

off (**12**) so that he could never again serve as high priest: a Jewish high priest could have no mutilations. Antigonus, the last Hasmonean ruler, was defeated in 37 B.C.E. by Herod the Great (**13**, a coin from Antigonus' reign).

The Nabataeans

The Nabataeans, a nomadic tribe in southeastern Palestine, founded a kingdom in the second century B.C.E. Their capital, Petra, with its buildings carved in the stone cliffs, remains an impressive sight today. They maintained close political and economic ties with their Jewish neighbors—sometimes as allies, sometimes as rivals. Herod the Great's mother was a Nabataean. They remained independent until 106 C.E., when their empire became a Roman province.

Figures and Stories Relevant to the Maccabees

God, see pp. 28–33

Angels, see pp. 42–43

The Ptolemies and the Seleucids, see pp. 288–289

The Rededication of the Temple, see Hanukkah, pp. 294–295

Herod the Great, see pp. 362–365

Herod's Descendants, see pp. 370–371

Roman Occupation, see the Romans, pp. 372–373

High Priests: p. 234

Hanukkah

Hanukkah, the Festival of Lights, which begins on the 25th day of Chislev, commemorates the rededication of the Temple in Jerusalem in 164 B.C.E. According to the Talmud, the Maccabees found only one flask of oil for the temple flame, enough for a single day. Yet the lights continued to burn for eight days. Thus, Hanukkah is celebrated for eight days and a candle is lit each day by a ninth candle named a shamesh until all are burning on the menorah (**2**). Another custom is the dreidel game.

Each side of the dreidel (**1**) is imprinted with a Hebrew letter—Nun, Gimel, Hey, or Shin. The letters stand for the words meaning "A great miracle happened there." They also represent Yiddish words—"none," "all," "half," and "put in"—referring to treats that can be won by the person spinning the dreidel.

2

▶▶ **The Temple in Jerusalem:** pp. 368–369

Rededication of the Temple

After his victory over the Seleucid generals Gorgias and Lysias, Judas Maccabeus traveled to Mount Zion (**3**). When they entered the devastated Temple, they erupted in great lamentations. The Maccabees tore their clothing and anointed their heads with ashes. Then they began cleaning up the Temple. They found priests who had remained true to the laws, carried away the altar that had been desecrated, and constructed a new altar. In 164 B.C.E., the Temple was rededicated with a great celebration. "Then Judas and his brothers and all the assembly of Israel determined that every year at that season the days of dedication of the altar should be observed with joy and gladness for eight days, beginning with the 25th day of the month of Chislev" (I Maccabees 4:59).

» **Sacrifice:** p. 45   **Mourning Rituals:** p. 346

The Prophets and the Righteous

Tobit's son Tobias was one of the righteous: Even far from his home-land, God stood by him and sent angels to help him in his work.

The Prophets and

The Major Prophets

p. 308

p. 309

1000*	950	900	850	800

L

* For some books of the Bible—such as Jonah or the book of Job—it is very difficult to allocate a definite time period. Other books, such as Daniel, were written over a long period of time and only later were ascribed to a specific author.

p. 322

p. 316

he Righteous

p. 339

p. 341

| 50 | 700 | 650 | 600 | 550 | 500 |

The Writing Prophets

p. 334

p. 330

p. 332

The Prophets and the Righteous

The word "prophet" comes from Greek. The Hebrew word is "navi," with a meaning similar to "proclaimer." According to I Samuel 9:9, the earlier term for prophet was "seer." The prophets of Israel were not a homogeneous group. They were not even all men: female prophets include Miriam, Moses' sister; the judge Deborah; and Hannah, mother of Samuel. Nevertheless, all of the prophets share one characteristic: they see themselves as proclaiming God's will. In this way, they helped shape the ethics and theology of Judaism. Most of the prophets of ancient Israel do not play a prominent role in the Bible; instead, they were regularly present at holy places and royal courts. Sometimes organized in guilds, these shrine and court prophets served as advisors for both the rulers and the common people. They were paid for their services—and they were criticized by the prophet Micah, among others, for their love of money: "Thus says the Lord concerning the prophets who lead my people astray, who cry 'Peace' when they have something to eat, but declare war against those who put nothing in their mouths" (Micah 3:5).

Much more important than these were the charismatic individual prophets. Not tied to any single place, some lived alone—at times as social outcasts—while others assembled a group of followers or disciples. Their calling usually began with an extraordinary experience in which they received a personal message from God. As the stories of the prophets make clear, these individuals chosen by God were not always pleased with their new roles and responsibilities. Many believed they were unworthy and tried to escape from the assignment. Moses pointed to his clumsy way of speaking, while

he prophet Jonah fled across the
ea in reluctance and fear.

Other than Moses—who is consid-
red by many as one of the greatest
nd most important prophet of an-
ent Israel—other prophets such as
amuel, Nathan, Elijah, and Elisha ex-
rcised great political power. Their
tories are told in the books of Samuel,
ings, and Chronicles. Starting with
mos, the scriptural prophets ap-
eared in the eighth century B.C.E. He
among the 12 minor prophets, along
ith Hosea, Joel, Obadiah, Jonah (**2**),
licah, Nahum, Habbakuk (**1**), Zepha-
iah, Haggai, Zechariah, and Malachi.
he term "minor" does not refer to
hese prophets' importance, but sim-

ly to the length of their writings. The "great" scriptural prophets are Isaiah,
eremiah, and Ezekiel. A separate book in the Bible is dedicated to each of
he scriptural prophets, although the authorship and exact dating of the texts
emains controversial among scholars. For instance, researchers divide the
ook of Isaiah into three phases, with authors designated as Isaiah, Deutero-
aiah, and Trito-Isaiah.

The work of a prophet is often erroneously compared to that of a soothsayer.
mong the prophets, however, there was less emphasis on prophesying in the
ense of predicting the future. More accurately, the prophets were truth-
ellers: individuals who uncover and proclaim the truth. With this aim, the
rophets often made themselves unpopular among the people as well as the
ulers. The prophets' statements did not usually coincide with public opinion;
nstead, they called attention to deficiencies in society and people's behavior.
n fact, the prophets often mercilessly criticized their contemporaries.

This criticism of social conditions played an important role among the prophets before the Babylonian captivity, such as Amos, Hosea, Isaiah, and Jeremiah. They also harshly condemned the worship of foreign gods. Warning of God's judgment in the form of natural catastrophes and military defeats, they demanded that the people make a radical break with their sinful ways.

The prophets' blunt criticism of society often made them outcasts. In this way, the rulers—and the people—sought to weaken their unwelcome messages. The prophets were socially shunned or accused of being mentally ill. This can be seen in the biblical account of the prophet Ezekiel. When Ezekiel received another parable from God, he at first refused to relate the story to the people. Ezekiel found the parable too obscure; he feared that he would lose credibility and be thought of as insane. The prophets of the exile and post-exile periods, including Deutero-Isaiah, Ezekiel, Trito-Isaiah, Haggai, Zechariah, and Malachi, were closely involved in the development and systemization of Jewish monotheism. At the same time, they awakened hopes for salvation and a future era of peace and harmony. Linked to this are apocalyptic visions of God's Final Judgment, as seen, for example, in parts of Daniel.

While the Christian tradition places Daniel just behind the three great prophets, he is not considered a prophet in the Hebrew Bible. For Jews, figures such as Daniel and Job (**4**) belong to the group of the righteous. The prophet Ezekiel said that even if both were present when God punished a sinful land: "they would save only their own lives by their righteousness" (Ezekiel 14:14). The stories of the righteous, such as that of Tobit and his son in the diaspora, are aimed at providing a model for readers: even far from their homelands and through tribulations, the righteous hold fast to God. From a Christian perspective, Jesus of Nazareth fulfills the visions of the Old Testament prophets (**3**, Isaiah at Christ's Ascension into heaven). John the Baptist, who prepared the way for Jesus, is viewed by many Christians as the last of the prophets.

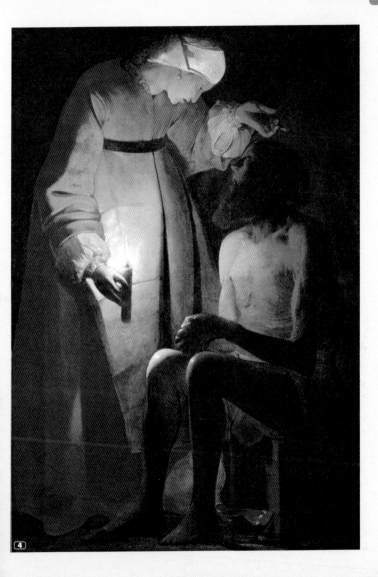

■ Nathan is the first historically verifiable Israelite prophet

■ Nathan exercised large influence on the court of David

II Samuel 7:3–17 Nathan delivers God's promise to David

II Samuel 12:1–12 Nathan's reprimand of David

I Kings 1:11–14 Nathan supports Bathsheba and Solomon

I Kings 1:38 Solomon anointed

Nathan said to David, "Do all that you have in mind, for God is with you." 1 Chronicles 17:2

Nathan

Nathan is the oldest prophet from the Hebrew Bible to be historically dated with accuracy. He was active during the rule of King David in the first half of the tenth century B.C.E. He received his prophecies directly from God. Nathan delivered one of the few original prophetic utterances: In II Samuel 7:8–16 Nathan pronounces to King David the lasting legacy of his kingship and dynasty. Researchers believe that the biblical text was formulated for the first time after Solomon's death and revised later. At its core, however, the words of the prophet still have validity as a testimony from the time of David.

For Nathan, moral stipulations were established by the will of God and were thus incontestable. He believed that even a king must live according to the laws of God, as is shown by his criticism of David's adultery with Bathsheba.

Prophecy and Kingship

Earlier prophets, such as Elijah and Elisha, mostly aimed their criticisms at kings, whereas later prophets, such as Isaiah and Jeremiah, mainly addressed their prophecies to the whole population of Israel. The prophets were involved with politics and often passed judgment on rulers for their crimes and abuses of power. Elijah and Elisha in particular set themselves against the increasing power of outside influences. They campaigned vigorously for the preservation of the original social and economic culture. Due to their critical, often negative prophecies, many prophets formed a niche outside of society. This made it possible for them to simultaneously scorn others' faults, while fighting to conserve old norms.

Nathan's Reprimand After his deplorable affair with Bathsheba, Nathan criticized the king (**1**) with the parable of a poor and a rich man. The rich man held a banquet, but rather than killing his own cattle, he slaughtered the sheep of the poor man. Rebuking the rich man, David was told by Nathan that he, David, is the rich man. Thus, the king repented to God.

Figures and Stories Relevant to Nathan

David, see pp. 216–221

Zadok, see pp. 234–235

Solomon, David's Heir, see pp. 238–241

Bathsheba, David's Wife, see pp. 228–229

Adonijah, see David's Children, pp. 230–231

Nathan and Zadok Anoint Solomon King In the conflicts over the succession to the throne of King David, Nathan went against the old king's elder son Adonijah. With Nathan's assistance and counsel, Bathsheba was able to assert her son Solomon's claim to the throne. When Nathan heard of Adonijah's plans to assume the kingship, he reported them to Bathsheba. Altering their tactics, they managed to persuade David to confirm Solomon as his successor from his deathbed. Along with Zadok the priest and the military commander Benajah, Nathan was given the task of anointing Solomon king (**2**) (p. 235).

Anointment: p. 196

■ The prophet Elijah fought against the veneration of foreign deities

■ He came into conflict with the rulers of Israel

I Kings 17:1 Elijah prophesies a drought to King Ahab of Israel as a punishment from God

I Kings 17:6 Ravens provide Elijah with nourishment

I Kings 17:19–24 Elijah brings a dead child back to life

I Kings 18:1–40 On Mount Carmel Elijah wins in a challenge against the prophets of Baal

I Kings 18:40 Elijah kills the fallen prophets of Baal

I Kings 19:1–4 Elijah flees from the wrath of Jezebel into the desert

I Kings 19:5–7 An angel appears to Elijah twice

I Kings 19:11–18 Elijah encounters God on Mount Horeb

I Kings 19:19 Elijah meets Elisha, his new companion

II Kings 2:12 Elijah does not die, but rather travels to heaven in a fiery chariot

II Kings 2:13–15 Elisha takes Elijah's mantle and becomes his successor

Elijah said to them, "Seize the prophets of Baal; do not let one of them escape." Then they seized them ... and killed them there.

I Kings 18:40

Elijah

Elijah embodied the model of the wandering prophet. He appeared at the time of the Israelite kings Ahab and Ahaziah from around 871 to 851 B.C.E. In I Kings 17–19, Elijah is presented as a new Moses. There is a parallel in their tales as they both experience theophany, an appearance by God: Similarly with Moses, God appeared to Elijah on Mount Horeb. As God fed Moses in the desert with quail and manna, ravens (**1**) gave Elijah bread and meat. ▷▷

Elijah was sustained by ravens on Mount Horeb

▷▷ **Moses:** pp. 110–115 and 120–125

Elijah and the Angel Elijah's fight against the Baal cult brought him into conflict with Queen Jezebel, who supported Baal's priests. Out of fear, Elijah fled into the desert. Exhausted and despondent, he wished to die and eventually fell asleep. However, God stood by his prophet and Elijah was twice woken by an angel (**2**). On the first occasion Elijah was given bread and water, on the second he was told to go to Mount Horeb. There, God appeared and ordered him to anoint Jehu as the new king of Israel and proclaimed a swift death of all followers of Baal: They were to fall by Jehu's sword (p. 250).

Prophetic Healing

Powers of healing were one of the basic tools of a prophet. As reported by Elijah, he once brought the son of a widow back to life by lying three times over the boy and asking God to send him back to the living. Such religious acts of healing called for certain rituals like the laying of a hand or the intoning of set phrases. It is in this respect that such healing is not so far removed from current-day medicine: the waiting room itself or the use of a technical language comprehensible only to the "initiated" lends the

doctor a certain "aura." For modern medicine as well as for religiously staged healings, a firm belief in the effectiveness of the treatment is important for its success. Even Jesus required faith for his healing powers to be effective, and in Matthew 17:19–20 he criticized those of little faith.

Miracles of Jesus: pp. 406–407   **Appearances of God:** p. 317

Elijah's goal was to enforce the worship of a single God. However, the Canaanite deity Baal, whose worship was promoted by Queen Jezebel, was gaining increasing support. Elijah declared that only the God of Israel, and not Baal, could give humanity the gifts of rain and fertility. To prove his claim, Elijah met with 450 Baal prophets on Mount Carmel (**5**). Elijah and the prophets of Baal both asked their God for fire through the sacrifice of a bull. Whichever God responded with fire would officially become the one true God. The prophets of Baal limped to their altar, cried out loud, and lacerated themselves with knives, but Baal did not produce any fire. Elijah mocked them before asking his own God for fire. God answered directly and sent fire from heaven, proving the God of Israel as the one true God. Elijah killed the defeated Baal prophets (**3,4**).

The Carmelite Order

During the Crusades in the mid-12th century, a group of Christian settlers, the Carmelites, lived on Mount Carmel. The rules of the order, first composed in 1209, stipulated poverty, solitude, and the forsaking of meat. They focus on contemplative prayer and mission work. The mystics Teresa of Ávela and Juan de la Cruz accomplished a reform in the 16th century, which led to the founding of the discalced Carmelites. As a sign of their particular abstinence, they wear no shoes and so are commonly called the "barefoot."

Elijah's Ascension to Heaven
As Elijah's death was approaching, God sent him to three different places. Elijah repeatedly asked his pupil Elisha to leave him, but he stayed with Elijah. At each place, the prophet's followers warned Elisha of Elijah's imminent rapture. At Jordan, Elijah granted Elisha a last wish—a portion of Elijah's spirit. A fiery chariot then appeared, picked up Elijah, and took him to heaven (**6**). Elisha took Elijah's mantle that had fallen to the ground. Seeing this, they knew that his spirit resided in Elisha.

6

The Prophet's Mantle: p. 314

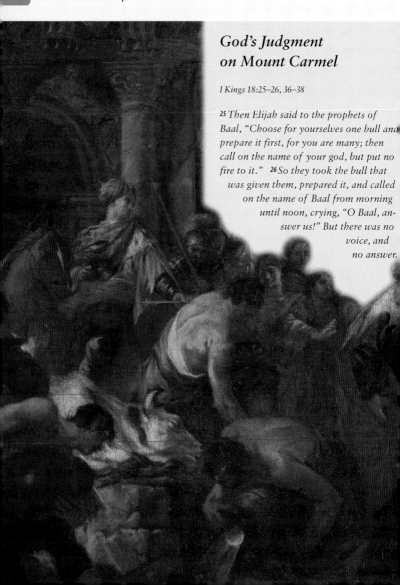

God's Judgment on Mount Carmel

I Kings 18:25–26, 36–38

25 Then Elijah said to the prophets of Baal, "Choose for yourselves one bull and prepare it first, for you are many; then call on the name of your god, but put no fire to it." **26** So they took the bull that was given them, prepared it, and called on the name of Baal from morning until noon, crying, "O Baal, answer us!" But there was no voice, and no answer.

They limped about the altar that they had made. ...
³⁶ *At the time of the offering of the oblation, the prophet Elijah came near and said, "O Lord, God of Abraham, Isaac, and Israel, let it be known this day that you are God in Israel, that I am your servant, and that I have done all these things at your bidding.* ³⁷ *Answer me, O Lord, answer me, so that this people may know that you, O Lord, are God, and that you have turned their hearts back."* ³⁸ *Then the fire of the Lord fell and consumed the burnt-offering, the wood, the stones, and the dust, and even licked up the water that was in the trench.*

The Bible and Music

The *Elijah* oratorio by Felix Mendelssohn had its premiere performances in England in 1846 and 1847, which were received with enthusiasm by the audience. Referencing the stories of Elijah, Mendelssohn compared Prince Albert to a prophetic artist-priest, who fought against the false deities of art. The libretto, with its numerous quotations from the Old Testament, is theatrically poetic in its conception, and a paradigm of such works. The exhilarating texts describing Elijah's fight against polytheism do not need any scenic portrayal to clarify their dramatic appeal. To this day, *Elijah* remains one of the oratorios staged most often. In 19th- and 20th-century England, Handel's *Messiah* was also comparably popular.

German composer Felix Mendelssohn-Bartholdy

The score to the Messiah personally written by Handel

Christmas Oratorio Johann Sebastian Bach's *Christmas Oratorio* is based on verbatim biblical quotations from Christmas stories from the Gospels of Luke and Mark, as well as on newly composed texts. The content of oratorios is mostly spiritual and so they are performed in

>> Messiah: p. 404

concerts without stage scenery or costumes (**1**). The name "oratorio" is assumed to have derived from the devotional practices of the Oratorians, a society of priests in Rome. They recited popular, hymnlike songs with moral content, frequently in the form of a dialogue.

Handel's *Messiah* George Frederick Handel was responsible for the revival of the oratorio form. His oratorios were meant, unconventionally, to be staged theatrically, but this incurred the opposition of the Anglican Church. However, even without the stage, he still managed to enrich the biblical content through his scoring, such as the *Messiah* (**2**) of 1742.

MESSIAH

AN

Oratorio

IN SCORE

As it was Originally Perform'd.

Composed by

Mr HANDEL

To which are added

His additional Alterations.

London. *Printed by* Mess.rs Randall & Abell *Successors to the late* Mr J. Walsh *in Catharine Street in the Strand — of whom may be had the compleat Scores of* Samson, Alexander's Feast, *and* Acis & Galatea.

2

■ Elisha had great political influence in northern Israel

■ There are many stories about the miracles of Elisha

I Kings 19:19–21 Elisha joins up with the prophet Elijah

II Kings 2:12–14 Elisha becomes Elijah's successor

II Kings 4:1–7 Elisha increases the oil of the widow

II Kings 4:8–37; 8:1–6 Elisha and the Shunemite woman

II Kings 9:1–6 Elisha has Jehu anointed as king

But Elisha said, "Hear the word of the Lord."

II Kings 7:1

Elisha

Elisha, a rich farmer, was confirmed by Elijah as his successor. In contrast to Elijah, Elisha gathered a great number of followers around him and attained great political influence in the northern kingdom of Israel. Thus his prophecies were at

The bears in the story of Elisha were probably Syrian brown bears.

the disposal of the kings, and he even accompanied them on campaigns against the Moabites. Elisha promoted the rise to power of Jehu against the royal house of Omri, as Jehu, as the new king, would stamp out the followers of Baal. Of special note are the many miracles of Elisha, but also the ambivalence of his nature, as pointed out in II Kings 2:23–25. Here, he curses some children who mocked his bald head. He stands by as 42 of the children are mauled to death by two bears.

The Prophet's Mantle

The mantles (or cloaks) of the prophets are a major theme. As Elijah ascended to heaven, he left his mantle to Elisha, thus confirming him as his successor. The mantle empowered Elisha with powers, such as splitting the waters of the Jordan. In the New Testament, the mantle appears in the story of John the Baptist, whom Christians view as Elijah's successor.

» **John the Baptist:** pp. 378–381

Elisha and the Shunemite Woman

In Shunem, a rich woman housed Elisha in a guest room specially built for him. One day, Elisha asked her what she desired in return for her hospitality. The Shunemite said that she wanted no repayment, but Elisha's servant Gehazi knew that she was childless. Elisha promised her a child and, one year later, she had a child. When the child died, she turned to Elisha (**1**). He prayed to God and leaned over the lifeless body of the child, bringing him back to life. Elisha later warned the woman of a coming famine, which saved the lives of her and her family.

Elisha Increases the Oil of the Widow

Along with having the power to heal, Elisha was able to multiply food. The wife of a deceased follower of Elisha begged the prophet for help as she was in debt and her creditor wanted to sell her children as slaves. She had used all of her provisions and owned only one remaining jug of oil. Elisha multiplied the oil so that the woman needed of many receptacles to accommodate it all (**2**). The widow sold some of the oil to pay off her debts, and was able to live with her children from the remaining profits.

Figures and Stories Relevant to Elisha

The Moabites, see The Neighboring Peoples of Israel, pp. 166–167

The Cult of Baal, see pp. 168–169

Jehu, see the Kings of Israel, pp. 248–251

Elijah, Elisha's Predecessor, see pp. 306–309

》 **Prophetic Healing:** p. 307

■ Isaiah was a prophet, adviser, and politician under the rulers of the kingdom of Judah

■ For Christians, Isaiah's prophecies foretell the coming of Jesus

Isaiah 5:1–7 The song of the infertile vineyard

Isaiah 6 God appears to Isaiah and calls him to be a prophet

Isaiah 9:1–6 Isaiah foretells the coming of the Prince of Peace

Isaiah 11 Isaiah promises the Messiah and his realm of peace

Isaiah 13–23, 34 God's tribunal over Israelite enemies

Isaiah 24–27 God's trial of the world and the salvation of Israel

Isaiah 30:1–7; 31:1–3 Premonitions of an alliance with the Egyptians

Isaiah 30:27–33; 31:4–9 God's trial of the Assyrians

Isaiah 36–37 God saves Hezekiah and the kingdom of Judah from the Assyrians

Isaiah 39 Isaiah tells King Hezekiah of the threat of defeat at the hands of the Babylonians

Isaiah 40–55 People of Israel displaced into exile

They will look to the earth, but will see only distress and darkness, the gloom of anguish. Isaiah 8:22

Isaiah

Current-day research posits that the works of many authors were compiled together in the Book of Isaiah, with at least five centuries lying between the earliest and the latest parts of the book. The names of the authors remain unknown, but they are distinguished from the actual Isaiah (**2**) as Deutero-Isaiah (second Isaiah) and Trito-Isaiah (third Isaiah). Each author professed his own message, which had a specific historical context. Along with further fragments of biblical texts, excavations around the area of Khirbet Qumran near the Dead Sea led to the discovery of a 23-foot scroll (**1**) of the Book of Isaiah from the first century C.E. ≫

≫ **The Qumran:** pp. 379

God in the Wind

*Prophets Moses, Elijah, and Isaiah experienced similar appearances of God: At first, God announced his coming with thunder, lightning (**4**), storms, and quakes. Then, he appeared in the stillness that followed this natural chaos. God showed himself to Elijah in a calm, soft wind and, although God's exhibition to Isaiah was introduced with smoke and noise, Isaiah actually saw him sitting in peace upon a throne. This illustrates the conditions in which contact with God is possible. God did not appear in a storm, which would frighten people, as only in peace do humans feel secure and ready for new encounters.*

An Angel Touches Isaiah

Isaiah's vocation as a prophet came to him as a vision in which he saw God enthroned. He was surrounded by numerous seraphim—angels with six wings. Isaiah was afraid that he might die for having seen God because he was impure and sinful. However, an angel flew to him and touched glowing coal to his lips (**3**) and declared him free from all sin. Then God turned to Isaiah and asked him who he should make his messenger. Isaiah offered himself up for this task and was charged by God to speak to the people and to proclaim the threat of a disaster to Judah.

◗ **Moses:** pp. 110–115 and 120–125   **Elijah:** pp. 306–309

When Isaiah spoke of the contemporary political situation, he showed himself to be pessimistic and at the same time full of faith in God. He saw the ascendancy of the Assyrians over Judah as a justified punishment for the sinful conduct of the Judeans. Isaiah was hopeful that God would soon put an end to this foreign rule and strive for peace.

Isaiah's vision details the coming of a "Prince of Peace," a descendant of King David. This Prince of Peace was later equated with the Messiah (p. 220). Christians consider this as an allusion to the arrival of Jesus. In order to correspond to this prophecy, Jesus' family tree (**6**) was traced to King David.

Isaiah and the Assyrians

Isaiah foretold a time of oppression for the kingdoms of Israel and Judah. He was alluding to the military campaigns of the Assyrians in the second half of the eighth century B.C.E. (**5**, Assyrians with two Jewish prisoners). Isaiah interpreted the defeat of his people as punishment for their lack of faith, but attested that God would punish the enemies of Israel later as he stands against nonbelievers.

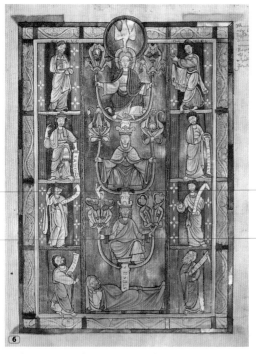

Figures and Stories Relevant to Isaiah

God, see pp. 28–33

The Seraphim, see Angels, pp. 42–43

God's Covenant With Israel, see pp. 142–143

David, see pp. 216–221

The Assyrians, see pp. 252–253

Hezekiah and Manasseh, see the Kings of Judah, pp. 254–257

▷▷ **The Family Tree of the House of David:** pp. 208–209

Isaiah's Martyrdom The Babylonian Talmud (p. 503) reports on the martyrdom of Isaiah. After the death of the pious King Hezekiah, his son Manasseh became king. He did not follow the faith and commands of his father for long, but rather worshiped the demon Beliar. When Isaiah heard of Manasseh's worship of false idols, his prostitution, and his decline from the true faith, he criticized him and prophesied renewed troubles for Jerusalem. Manasseh responded by having the prophet captured and brutally killed: Isaiah was cut in two with a pruning saw (**7**). During his execution, Isaiah saw God and was able to suffer these torments without a single cry of pain.

References to Jesus

In Christian interpretations, parts of the Hebrew Scripture are references to Jesus as the future Messiah. This is reflected in the ordering of the books of the Christian Old Testament: The books of history, the Exodus from Egypt, the time of the kings, and the exile and the return from Babylonian imprisonment are followed by the books of the prophets. These form a bridge into the reports of Jesus in the Gospels of the New Testament. The Christian understanding of the Old Testament prophecies can be seen in the interpretation of the prophets' words in the Gospels. For instance, the birth of Jesus from a virgin's womb relates to a literal translation of Isaiah 7:14, which states that the future savior of Israel was to be born of an almah, translated as "virgin" or "young woman."

Jesus as the Messiah: p. 404   Virgin Birth: p. 388

■ Jeremiah announced the downfall of Jerusalem as a punishment from God and was tortured by his people as a result of his message

■ Jeremiah seemed melancholic and full of self-despair

Thus says the Lord of hosts, the God of Israel: Amend your ways and your doings, and let me dwell with you in this place. Jeremiah 7:3

Jeremiah

Jeremiah (**2**) lived in the seventh century B.C.E., when the kingdom of Judah was increasingly beset by its enemies. Jeremiah did not just predict this growing threat, but he also viewed it as a justified punishment from God. God communicated with him through images, such as a blossoming branch (**1**) and an over-boiling pot, which was a symbol of impending disaster.

Jeremiah's Vision of the Boiling Pot When Jeremiah was called up to be a prophet he saw a pot that was boiling over from the north. God explained that this was a symbol for the actual disaster emanating from the north. God proclaimed that he would judge the people of Judah, who had started to pray to foreign gods. Therefore the kingdoms of the north as well as those of the Assyrians and Babylonians were called upon to lay siege to Jerusalem. The image of the boiling pot was taken up again during the time of the Reformation (**3**). Very much in the style of Reformist criticism, God was supposed to have pointed to the pope, the clerics, the princes, and the Turks as the instigators of an impending catastrophe.

Jeremiah's Lamentations

For a long time, Jeremiah was considered to be the author of the Book of Lamentations. Today it is assumed to be the work of many authors. These lamentations are five complexly constructed, evocative poems about the fate of Judah, and Jerusalem after its destruction around 587 B.C.E. The lamentations describe the hardships with which God punished his people for their sins; however, they also contain hope for grace and salvation. They aim to be universal in their themes of repentance and reflection. The texts were presumably performed at religious services, in which the faithful came together in a spirit of mourning, sadness, and repentance for the destruction of the Temple. Such services probably took place around the ruins of Solomon's Temple (pp. 274–275).

The contrast between the prophet's own wishes and the will of God was shown more clearly with Jeremiah (**4**) than in the other prophets. Even though he did not want to listen, the word of God forced itself upon him more and more. Jeremiah spoke of this inward struggle openly and doubted whether he could bear it. But the sacrifices that he made, including his celibacy and isolation, were directly linked with his prophetic existence. He acted as God's witness with his being, not just as a transmitter of God's words.

Jeremiah and Nebuchadrezzar The Babylonian king, Nebuchadrezzar II, expanded the reach of his power in the Middle East and made the kingdom of Judah pay him tribute. In Jeremiah's eyes, Nebuchadrezzar was sent by God to punish the people of Judah for their sins. He not only predicted the destruction of Jerusalem, but even welcomed it. The inhabitants, however, did not take this news well and locked Jeremiah up. When they were defeated by the Babylonians in 597 B.C.E., which Jeremiah had prophesied, he was set free by King Nebuchadrezzar (**5**). The Babylonians made Zedekiah the new king of Judah, and, although warned against it by Jeremiah, he revolted against the Babylonian occupation. Because of this, Jerusalem was conquered and destroyed in 587 B.C.E. Jeremiah fled to Egypt, but most of the inhabitants were taken to Babylon (p. 257).

Figures and Stories Relevant to Jeremiah

God, see pp. 28–33

Jerusalem, see pp. 226–227

The Assyrians, see pp. 252–253

Zedekiah, see the Kings of Judah, pp. 254–257

The Fall of Jerusalem, see pp. 258–259

The Babylonians, see pp. 268–269

Nebuchadrezzar II, the Babylonian King, see pp. 270–271

Jeremiah in the Cistern

Jeremiah's prophecies about the threat of disaster made him highly unpopular. As Jerusalem was besieged by the Babylonians (**8**), the heads of the city feared that panic would break out among the common people. To keep Jeremiah contained, he was imprisoned within a highly uncomfortable cistern (**6**). Yet, Zedekiah had sympathy for Jeremiah and so freed him. Jeremiah spoke again to the king and told him that he could not escape the punishment God had set for him. He would fall into the hands of his enemies and Jerusalem would be destroyed. In spite of these prophecies, Zedekiah did not punish Jeremiah. For his own protection, Jeremiah remained under the custody of Zedekiah. It was here that he awaited Jerusalem's ruin (**7**).

The Babylonian Captivity: pp. 272–273

■ Ezekiel lived in exile among the Jews captured by Nebuchadrezzar II

■ Ezekiel had experiences in which he felt as if he was floating, or that he could not move or speak

Ezekiel 1–2 Ezekiel is called by God to be a prophet and witnesses God's glory

Ezekiel 3: 12–21 God names Ezekiel as Israel's "watchman"

Ezekiel 5:5–17 God tells Ezekiel of the future judgment over the people of Israel

Ezekiel 7 Ezekiel receives a detailed account of God's impending destruction of Israel

Ezekiel 8:8–18 God shows Ezekiel the idols in the Temple

Ezekiel 11:5–13 God punishes the leaders of the people

Ezekiel 20:45–48 God tells Ezekiel the parable of the forest fire

Ezekiel 23 Ezekiel relates the parable of the sisters Oholah and Oholibah as an analogy for Israel's alliances with neighboring peoples

Ezekiel 37:1–14 Ezekiel sees Israel as a valley of dry bones

But if you warn the wicked, and they do not turn from their wickedness ... they shall die for their iniquity. Ezekiel 3:19

Ezekiel

In 597 B.C.E., Ezekiel, the son of a priest, lived among the Jews deported to Mesopotamia by Nebuchadrezzar II (pp. 256–257). In Jewish tradition, he is sometimes seen as the son of his elder contemporary Jeremiah.

A trumpet blast would warn the people of the coming destruction proclaimed by God

The elders responsible for the community in exile asked Ezekiel for advice and divine instruction (**1**). God defined his prophet's duty as that of a watchman: he should warn the people of the predicted destruction. At the same time, Ezekiel gave the exiled believers new hope: God would restore their home, unify the Israelites, and protect them.

»» The Babylonian Captivity: pp. 272–273

Ezekiel Witnesses the Glory of God In his first vision, Ezekiel witnessed God's glory. He saw a storm approaching from the north, with a tremendous cloud and flickering flames. Within the fire, four human-like figures appeared, each with four faces, four wings, metallic hooves, and human hands among their wings. Thanks to their four faces, they could run in any direction without turning. The faces were all different: In front, they appeared human, on the right they looked like lions, on the left like steers, and in the back like eagles. The figures touched wings and formed a circle. A fire burned at the center with lightning bolts emerging from it. Each of the figures was standing on a wheel that had eyes on its rims. The sky above their heads looked like a crystal canopy. Here, Ezekiel saw a throne where a figure sat surrounded by fire and blinding brilliance: the glory of the Lord (**2**).

2

3

Vileness of Idol Worship In another vision, God brought Ezekiel to the Temple in Jerusalem. He told Ezekiel to break a hole in the wall, and he witnessed the horrors of idol worship: people were burning incense and bowing down to the sun and hideous images of animals (**3**). Because of their rejection of him, God announced further tribulations for the people of Judah until they worshiped God alone.

⯈ **God's Covenant With Israel:** pp. 142–143

Oholah and Oholibah With the parable of the immoral sisters Oholah and Oholibah (**4**), Ezekiel criticized the sinfulness of the kings of Judah. Oholah and Oholibah were unfaithful, taking many lovers and acting like harlots. This behavior symbolized Judah's alliances with foreign powers such as Egypt and Assyria. As punishment, the sisters' lovers—or the foreign powers—would rise up against them. This prophecy of destruction was aimed at ending the immorality and providing a warning to the next generation.

Figures and Stories Relevant to Ezekiel

God, see pp. 28–33

The Egyptians, see pp. 104–105

The Assyrians, see pp. 252–253

The Kings of Judah, see pp. 254–257

Nebuchadrezzar II, see pp. 270–271

Jeremiah, Contemporary Prophet, see pp. 320–323

Parable of the Forest Fire With the parable of the forest fire (**5**), Ezekiel announced God's judgment over the southern kingdom of Judah. He prophesied an unstoppable fire in the "Forest of the South" that would consume everything, including the trees, land, and people. Although God interpreted these complex parables for Ezekiel, he was still afraid that he would be seen as crazy.

The Vision of the Boneyard

In his vision of the boneyard (pp. 328–329), the prophet Ezekiel was led by God to a field strewn with dry human bones. God commanded Ezekiel to prophesy that they would be brought back to life. Ezekiel did as he was told, and he soon began to hear a rustling sound. The lifeless bones had begun to move—the skeletons reassembled themselves and began growing tendons, flesh, and skin. Finally, God filled them with breath, and an army of people stood before Ezekiel (**6**). God interpreted the vision for him: the skeletons represented the Israelites. They were dry and withered due to the inhumane conditions they were living in during exile. Yet, the awakening of the dead represented the future revival and reunification of Israel. After the downfall of Jerusalem and the end of the Israelites' time in exile, God would proclaim a new future for his people. He wanted to do what seemed impossible at the time: lead them back into their promised homeland.

The Spiritual "Dry Bones"

Spirituals are religious songs that arose among African-American slaves in the American South. Through music, they were able to express their desire for liberation using religious metaphors. Ezekiel's vision of the reawakening of the dead provided the material for the spiritual "Dry Bones."

⟩ **The Bible and Music:** pp. 312–313

Parable of the Boneyard—God Breathes New Life into Israel, the Valley of the Dead

Ezekiel 37:1–2, 8–11

1 *The hand of the Lord came upon me, and he brought me out by the spirit of the Lord and set me down in the middle of a valley; it was full of bones.* 2 *He led me all round them; there were very many lying in the valley, and they were very dry. …* 7 *So I prophesied as I had been commanded; and as I prophesied, suddenly there was a noise, a rattling, and the bones came together, bone to its bone.* 8 *I looked, and there were sinews on them, and flesh had come*

upon them, and skin had covered them; but there was no breath in them. **9** *Then he said to me, "Prophesy to the breath, prophesy, mortal, and say to the breath: Thus says the Lord God: Come from the four winds, O breath, and breathe upon these slain, that they may live."* **10** *I prophesied as he commanded me, and the breath came into them, and they lived, and stood on their feet, a vast multitude.* **11** *Then he said to me, "Mortal, these bones are the whole house of Israel." They say, "Our bones are dried up, and our hope is lost; we are cut off completely."*

■ The shortest books of the prophets are considered together as the Book of the Minor Prophets

Hosea 1–9 God commands Hosea to marry a harlot

Joel 2 Joel calls upon the people to repent, foretelling the coming of an army

Amos 7–9 In five visions, Amos witnesses Israel's destruction

Obadiah 1 Obadiah prophesies against the Edomites

Jonah 1–2 Jonah is told to proclaim the coming destruction of Nineveh

Micah 2–3 Micah speaks out against social injustice

Nahum 1–2 Nahum prophesies the destruction of Nineveh

Habbakuk 1–2 Habbakuk denounces the unjust social conditions in Israel

Zephaniah 3:1–6 Zephaniah warns against the godless

Haggai 1:1–2:19 Haggai calls for the rebuilding of the Temple

Zechariah 1:1–6:8 Zechariah has eight symbolic visions about the Messiah and a new world

Malachi 3 Malachi talks about the Messiah

Then everyone who calls on the name of the Lord shall be saved.

Joel 2:32

The Minor Prophets

The minor or "12" prophets include Hosea, Joel, Amos, Obadiah, Jonah, Micah, Nahum, Habbakuk, Zephaniah, Haggai, Zechariah, and Malachi (**1**). The term "minor prophets" refers to the shortness of the books, not their importance. The number 12 is also often associated with the 12 Tribes of Israel.

Aside from the Book of Joel, the books of the minor prophets are time-specific documents. The prophets criticized failings, such as the exploitation of the people or violations of divine commands. They warned of God's retribution through natural catastrophes or military defeat. Yet, the minor prophets also provided a message of hope for a future era of peace, when God would vanquish Israel's enemies. Thus, Israel's history is a drama in which the people either turn toward or away from God.

Hosea Hosea arose as a prophet in the eighth century B.C.E. in the northern kingdom of Israel. God commanded him to marry the prostitute Gomer (**2**). This marriage symbolized Israel's idolatrous "whoring" with other gods. Hosea and Gomer had three children, whose names were given by God as symbols of the

2

Israelites' fate. The first son was called Jezreel, after the place where the Omride dynasty was destroyed by King Jehu (p. 251). Hosea's daughter was named Lo-ruhamah, or "no pity," since God had no sense of pity for Israel. The youngest son was Lo-ammi, "not my people," as God no longer viewed the unfaithful Israelites as his people.

Joel The Book of Joel, of un-certain date, prophesies God's justice on Judgment Day. He claimed a powerful people, the "enemy from the north," would attack Israel like locusts (**3**) and lay waste to the land. However, he claimed God's people should not give up hope, but repent and atone, as whoever "calls on the name of the Lord" will be saved, God will judge the enemies of his people and peace will reign.

3

Jonah God commanded Jonah to go to Nineveh and preach against its inhabitants. Unwilling to obey, Jonah fled on a ship (**4**). God unleashed a storm and the sailors, believing Jonah was responsible, threw him overboard. Jonah was swallowed by a gigantic fish (pp. 334–335). For three days, Jonah remained in the belly of the fish until God commanded it to spit him out. Jonah agreed to go to Nineveh and prophesy about God's judgment. The people admitted their guilt and repented. When God spared the city, Jonah was furious and feared that no one would believe him. He settled down outside the city, angry with God's actions. God raised a vine that sheltered Jonah from the sun, but withered again the next day. Again, Jonah was furious. But God explained that just as Jonah cared about the vine, which he enjoyed only for a day, God cared about Nineveh with its inhabitants, "who could not tell their right hand from their left."

4

Micah The prophet Micah was active in the late eighth century B.C.E., and thus was a contemporary of Amos, Hosea, and Isaiah. Like them, he criticized the prevailing social and religious conditions. Micah denounced the greed of the upper class and gave a warning to the leaders of Judah, including the prophets and priests. At the same time, he spoke of God's mercy for the people and his coming reign of peace. From a Christian perspective, Micah's prophecies are especially important (**5**), as he said that the future king of Israel would come from Bethlehem. For Christians, Jesus' birth in Bethlehem suggests he is the foretold bringer of peace.

Social Injustice—A Violation of God's Commands

The criticism of society and government lies at the very heart of the Book of the 12 Prophets. The prophet Amos harshly condemned the luxurious life of the upper class and the exploitation of the poor. He made clear that these extreme social disparities violated God's will, and that the rich would one day be punished for their arrogance. Even today, religious groups working toward fairer social conditions refer to the biblical prophets. For example, the "Open Church," a German left-liberal religious organization, has presented an award called the Amos Prize since 2001. The award recognizes civic courage within the church and society.

» **References to Jesus in the Old Testament:** p. 319

Nahum Living under the Assyrians at the turn of the seventh century B.C.E., the prophet Nahum vividly prophesied the impending destruction of the Assyrian capital, the "great whore Nineveh." His oracle claimed: armed riders will enter the city, killing until the streets are covered with corpses, a great fire will rage (**6**), and Nineveh's damage will be "beyond measure," as the wounds inflicted will never heal. Those who hear of it will applaud, as they have suffered from the Assyrians' cruelty.

Haggai and Zechariah The post-exile prophets, such as Haggai, Zechariah (**7**), and Malachi, proclaimed that an imminent time of harmony and reign of peace would be arranged by God. They pointed to the reconstruction of the Temple in Jerusalem as the first sign of this new beginning (pp. 280–281). Haggai criticized the Israelites for only being concerned with their own homes after returning from exile, initially leaving God's house in ruin. For this, God punished the people with a drought (**8**). Repeatedly, the prophets warned the people of God's retribution in the form of storms or raging fires. The forces of nature directly represented God's power, since the natural order was his creation.

◗ **The Whore of Babylon:** p. 269

Jonah's Prayer—Inside the Belly of a Fish

Jonah 2:1–10

1 Then Jonah prayed to the Lord his God from the belly of the fish, 2 saying, "I called to the Lord out of my distress, and he answered me; out of the belly of Sheol I cried, and you heard my voice.

3 You cast me into the deep, into the heart of the seas, and the flood surrounded me; all your waves and your billows passed over me. 4 Then I said, 'I am driven away from your sight; how shall I look again upon your holy temple?' 5 The waters closed in over me; the deep surrounded me; weeds were wrapped around my head 6 at the roots of the mountains. I went down to the land whose bars closed upon me for ever; yet you brought up my life

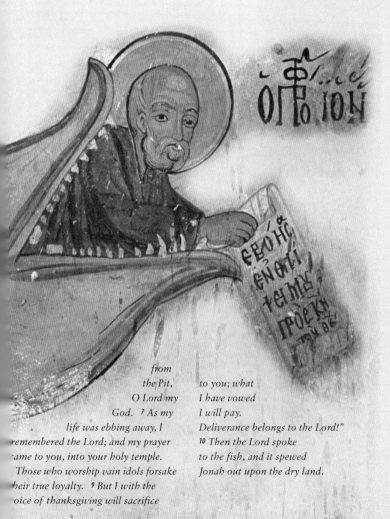

from
the Pit,
O Lord my
God. **7** As my
life was ebbing away, I
remembered the Lord; and my prayer
came to you, into your holy temple.
Those who worship vain idols forsake
their true loyalty. **9** But I with the
voice of thanksgiving will sacrifice

to you; what
I have vowed
I will pay.
Deliverance belongs to the Lord!"
10 Then the Lord spoke
to the fish, and it spewed
Jonah out upon the dry land.

■ Daniel was an especially talented Israelite in exile, who won respect for himself and God

■ The Book of Daniel's scope and significance are evaluated differently by Jews, Catholics, and Protestants

He delivers and rescues ... for he has saved Daniel from the power of the lions. Daniel 6:27

Daniel

Daniel lived during the time of Babylonian exile, at the court of King Nebuchadrezzar II and his successors. In numerous situations—for instance, in the lions' den (**1**) and the fiery furnace— Daniel and his friends demonstrated their unshakable belief in the God of Israel. Daniel's special abilities included the interpretation of dreams. Nebuchadrezzar II was tormented by fearsome nightmares, but none of his soothsayers could interpret them. Only Daniel, with God's help, could explain the king's visions (**2**).

Some scholars theorize that the Book of Daniel first appeared under the Maccabees in the second century B.C.E. In this context, Daniel's visions and dream interpretations referred to the Jews' conflicts with the Seleucid rulers (pp. 290–291). Prophecies dating back into the past were proved true in the present, while also raising hopes for a better future.

Three Men in the Fiery Furnace

Daniel's three friends Shadrach, Meshach, and Abednego were thrown into a fiery furnace as punishment when they refused to pray to an idol that had been erected by King Nebuchadrezzar (**3**). In the furnace, Nebuchadrezzar saw four men, not three. He called them back out, and they climbed out completely untouched—an angel of God protected them against the flames.

Figures and Stories Relevant to Daniel

God, see pp. 28–33

Angels, see pp. 42–43

The Babylonians, see pp. 268–269

Nebuchadrezzar II, see pp. 270–271

Belshazzar, see pp. 278–279

The Persians, see pp. 280–281

The Maccabees, see pp. 290–293

Dream of the Four Empires

In a dream, King Nebuchadrezzar saw a figure made of gold, silver, copper, and iron, standing on feet of clay (**4**). The figure was shattered by a stone falling from heaven. The stone soon grew into a mountain that filled the entire world. According to Daniel's interpretation, the figure's gold head represented Nebuchadrezzar's realm. The other parts of the figure foretold future empires, but these would be crushed by God's kingdom, symbolized by the stone falling from heaven.

Dreams and Their Meanings: p. 101

Vision of the Four Beasts Daniel dreamed of four monsters rising from the sea (**5**), interpreted as four kingdoms that would reign one after another. The fourth animal had ten horns, and when it grew a new horn, three other horns fell off. The interpreter read the ten horns as ten kings and claimed that a new king would follow and depose three others.

The interpreter foretold that the new king would blaspheme against God and alter the laws, but that this king's rule would not last, as God would ascend his throne on Judgment Day. Afterward, God would give his people sovereignty over the world.

Daniel in the Lions' Den As Daniel predicted to Belshazzar, the son of Nebuchadrezzar (pp. 278–279), his empire was conquered by the Persians. The Persian king, Darius, named Daniel one of his governors. However, when Daniel disobeyed King Darius' prohibition, praying openly to God, he was thrown into a den of lions (**6**). Plagued by his conscience, the king went directly to the lions' den the next morning. Daniel was still alive, since God had sent an angel to shut the lions' mouths. Darius now recognized that Daniel's God was the living God allowed the worship of Him in the empire.

6

Daniel Kills the Dragon The Book of Daniel has several additional narratives in the Extended Book of Daniel. These include the account of Susanna in the bath, as well as two stories detailing Daniel's reluctance to worship foreign gods. The Babylonians tried to force Daniel to pray to their god Bel (Marduk), in the form of the deity's symbolic animal, a dragon. In both accounts, Daniel exposed the idolatrous cults as frauds. The food offerings presented to Bel were not consumed by the idol, but were carried away by the priests. Finally, Daniel killed the supposedly divine dragon by throwing an indigestible cake made of tar, fat, and hair into its mouth (**7**). In the dragon story, Daniel was also thrown into a lions' den and survived.

Susanna in the Bath Two older men saw Susanna in her home. When she was alone in the bath, the two men came and harassed her (**8**). They threatened to accuse her of adultery with a young man if she did not do what they wanted. Afraid, she called out for help, but the two old men followed through with their false accusation. She was sentenced to death, but shortly before her execution, Daniel demanded a new trial. He exposed the truth by questioning them separately. While one reported seeing Susanna with the young man under an oak, the other said it was a mastic tree.

Daniel in the Lions' Den

Daniel 6:17–23

¹⁷ A stone was brought and laid on the mouth of the den, and the king sealed it with his own signet and with the signet of his lords, so that nothing might be changed concerning Daniel. ¹⁸ Then the king went to his palace and spent the night fasting; no food was brought to him, and sleep fled from him. ¹⁹ Then, at break of day, the king got up and hurried to the den of lions. ²⁰ When he came near the den where Daniel was, he cried out anxiously to Daniel, "O Daniel, servant of the living God, has your God whom you faithfully serve been able to deliver you from the lions?"

²¹ Daniel then said to the king,
"O king, live for ever!
²² My God sent his angel and shut
the lions' mouths so that they would
not hurt me, because I was found
blameless before him; and also before
you, O king, I have done no wrong."
²³ Then the king was exceedingly glad
and commanded that Daniel be taken
up out of the den. So Daniel was
taken up out of the den, and no
kind of harm was found on
him, because he had
trusted in his God.

■ The story of Tobit and his son Tobias illustrates God's concern for his people

Tobit 2:7–10 Tobit becomes blind

Tobit 5:1–22 Tobias sets out on a journey, accompanied by the angel Raphael

Tobit 6:1–9 Tobias catches a fish

Tobit 7:9–16 Tobias marries his cousin Sarah

Tobit 11 Tobias heals his father's blindness

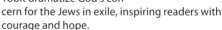

Revere the Lord all your days, my son, and refuse to sin or to transgress his commandments. Tobit 4:5

Tobit

The Book of Tobit was written by an unknown author, most likely in the second century B.C.E. Among Protestants, it is placed among the Apocrypha (p. 500). The stories about Tobit dramatize God's concern for the Jews in exile, inspiring readers with courage and hope.

Tobit was among the Jews led into exile by the Assyrians after the conquest of the northern kingdom of Israel (p. 259). He settled in the Assyrian capital of Nineveh with his son Tobias. In contrast to many exiles, he continued to obey God's commands. Tobit and his son are models of love and faithfulness. They were rewarded by God, who sent an angel to accompany them in the foreign land (**1**).

Tobit Becomes Blind The Assyrian king had forbidden the exiled Israelites from burying their dead. Yet Tobit "feared God more than the king" and secretly interred the dead at night. When Tobit once again came home tired, he lay down to sleep in the shadow of a wall, and a swallow's droppings fell on his eyes (**2**). When he awoke, he found that he was blind. His relatives taunted him, because his many good deeds seemed to have been of no use. Yet like Job (pp. 346–349), Tobit held fast to his faith in spite of his misfortune.

Tobias and the Angel Raphael On the orders of his father, the young Tobias set out on a journey. He was joined by a muscular young man, who was eventually revealed to be the archangel Raphael. When the pair reached the Tigris River, Tobias was afraid of a large fish. His companion advised him to catch the fish and keep its viscera to use as medicine (**3**). Later, Tobias was able to use the fish's liver to free his cousin Sarah—who later became his wife—from the clutches of an evil spirit.

Figures and Stories Relevant to Tobit

God, see pp. 23–28

Raphael, see Angels, pp. 42–43

The Assyrians, see pp. 252–253

Job, see pp. 346–349

Tobias Heals His Father With his wife Sarah, Tobias returned to Nineveh, where his parents were eagerly waiting for him. In accordance with the advice given to him by the archangel Raphael, Tobias anointed his father's eyes with bile from the fish, restoring his sight (**4**). The father and son wanted to give the traveler—whom they still took for a young man—a generous reward. But Raphael revealed himself as an angel of God, and the two men knelt in awe. Before the angel departed, he praised the deeds of Tobit.

Job's Fate—God and Satan Make a Bet

Job 2:3–10

3 The Lord said to Satan, "Have you considered my servant Job? There is no one like him on the earth, a blameless and upright man who fears God and turns away from evil. He still persists in his integrity, although you incited me against him, to destroy him for no reason." **4** Then Satan answered the Lord, "Skin for skin! All that people have they will give to save their lives. **5** But stretch out your hand now and touch his bone and his flesh, and he will curse you to your face."

6 The Lord said to Satan, "Very well, he is in your power; only spare his life." **7** So Satan went out from the presence of the Lord, and inflicted loathsome sores on Job from the sole of his foot to the crown of his head.

8 Job took a potsherd with which to scrape himself, and sat among the ashes. **9** Then his wife said to him, "Do you still persist in your integrity? Curse God, and die." **10** But he said to her, "You speak as any foolish woman would speak. Shall we receive the good at the hand of God, and not receive the bad?" In all this Job did not sin with his lips.

■ Job became the object of a bet between God and the devil

■ Job's fate became exemplary for the question of whether God is just

Job 1:6–12 God and Satan make a deal to put Job's faith to the test

Job 1:13–19 Job's children, servants, and animals are killed

Job 1:22 Job does not lose his faith or charge God with doing wrong

Job 2:4–6 God allows Satan to further test Job by harming his body

Job 2:7–3:26 Job becomes ill and curses the day of his birth

Job 2:9–10 Job's wife questions his persistant faith in God

Job 4–37 Job's friends mourn with him and then give him their opinions

Job 38–42:6 Job turns directly to God in his suffering

Job 38–41 God speaks to Job

Job 42:7–9 God justifies Job and his complaints to Job's friends

Job 42:10–17 Job is blessed by God and receives his wealth back doubled

The Lord gave, and the Lord has taken away; blessed be the name of the Lord. Job 1:21

Job

The legend of the pious but sorely tested Job is an exemplary story in literature exploring the nature of morality. Traditional oriental wisdom is based on the belief in the connection between actions and their moral consequences. The Book of Job turns this assumption on its head in that happiness and riches are not always the result of pious behavior, and misfortune and poverty are not necessarily linked to any godless actions of the individual.

As a result of a bet between God and Satan, Job suffered greatly, despite his piety, severing the link between actions and a karmic result. The situation of those who suffer unjustly necessitates a new explanation. The Book of Job offers various solutions without clearing it up completely: how can an inherently benevolent God allow suffering? Therein lie the roots of the theodicean dilemma, the question of whether God is just (French: "théodicée," from Greek: "theós," or God, and "dike," or justice). ⟩⟩

Rituals of Mourning

When Job learned of the death of his children, he performed the traditional rituals of mourning. He tore his clothing, shaved his head, and covered himself in ashes. The tearing of his clothes represented the destruction of the evil spirits inhabiting them, and shaving his head symbolized human sacrifice. Covering himself with ashes served two purposes: as a disguise from the vengeful dead and as a symbolic burial.

⟩⟩ **Is God Just?:** p. 30 **Wisdom Literature:** pp. 242–243

God and Satan God asked Satan what he thought of Job (**1**). Satan confirmed Job's piety, but claimed that he did not honor God for his own sake, but rather that he did not doubt because his life was a happy one. Otherwise, Satan claimed, Job would lose his faith. However, God was confident in Job and let Satan interfere in his life in order to test him.

Job's Wife After the devil received God's permission to cause harm to Job, he was subjected to a series of catastrophes. First, he lost his animals (**3**) along with his servants.

Thereafter, all his children died at a celebration and finally he became incurably ill. All that was left him was his wife, although it is unclear whether this is a further punishment.

Although she looked after her sick and desperate husband (**2**), his firm hold on his faith provoked criticism from her. She advised her husband to turn away from God and end his life.

The issue of the suffering of innocents has always been a common theological problem. The biblical tale of Job is based upon an older folk story. This version, which survives to the present day, was repeatedly manipulated and probably appeared between the fifth and third centuries B.C.E.

Linguistically, the dialogues and speeches in the Book of Job are similar to the poetry of the Psalms. The Book of Job is artistically composed and counts as one of the most important stories of world literature. The power of the text lies in the vivid narrative of Job's existential suffering. The texts show his pain to the reader and force him to identify with Job.

Job's Friends Job's friends initially showed solidarity with him, and took a vow of silence with him for seven days and nights (**5**). After that, each of them presented his own explanation for Job's suffering (**4**). Elifas mentioned the link between action and consequence, saying that God does not let the just suffer, thus laying the blame on Job himself. Bildad tried to extract a lesson from the experience of suffering. Zofar reminded Job that life was a mystery and the search for an explanation was in vain. Elihu praised God and told Job to remember his power.

The Figure of Job in Literaure

The story of Job has been re-worked many times in history, as the question of the reasons for suffering has presented itself anew to every generation. In 16th century German theater, the didactic element of the story was emphasized, i.e., the dialogue between God and Satan, Job's praise of God, and the miraculous restoration of what Job had lost. In Voltaire's Candide, the titular character experienced the same suffering

JOSEPH ROTH
HIOB
ROMAN EINES EINFACHEN MANNES   20. TAUSEND

STEFAN ZWEIG IN DER KÖLNISCHEN ZEITUNG: Man erlebt, statt zu lesen. Und man schämt sich nicht, endlich auch einmal von einem wirklichen Kunstwerk ganz sentimentalisch erschüttert zu sein.
NEUE BADISCHE LANDESZEITUNG: Dieser Hiob ist eine unvergeßliche Figur, so deutlich wie die Figuren des Märchens. Es entstehen Szenen, die von der Kraft biblischer oder homerischer Szenen sind.
KARTONIERT RM 3.50 • GANZLEINEN RM 5.—
GUSTAV KIEPENHEUER VERLAG
Prospekt für die 2. Auflage des Romans „Hiob". DLA, Prospektsammlung.

as Job, allowing Voltaire to offer sharp criticism of Leibniz' theory that the present world is the best of all possible ones. From this, a passionate discussion developed, focusing on the theodicean question of whether God is just. In the 1920s, Joseph Roth again re-worked the story of Job. Job's desperate complaints to God were investigated by a Jewish teacher, who saw in this destiny the path to existentialism.

Job Receives His Riches Back Doubled Since Job received no comfort from the advice of his friends, he turned directly to God, who appeared before him in a storm. God noted his own supremacy through evidence of the creation. However, Job's questions as to the reasons for his suffering remained unanswered. He received an indirect answer in the very appearance of God, which demonstrated God's trust in him. The story of Job confirms the absence of a causal link between actions and moral consequences. In the end, he returned to health and his wealth was restored to him doubled (**6**).

Figures and Stories Relevant to Job

God, see pp. 28–33

Wisdom Literature, see pp. 242–243

Satan, see pp. 350–351

6

The Psalms: pp. 222–223   God in the Winds: p. 317

Satan

As the belief in a single God gained prominence, evil also became ascribed to this all-encompassing deity. The source of the negative aspect of God's nature is his anger at the disloyalty of man, and thus Satan (**1**) is a dark and destructive personification of divine wrath.

In the New Testament, Satan appears as the opponent of God; he is ruler over all demons (**4**) and can cause harm to man both physically and spiritually. Jesus' cures free people from demons and the power of the devil (p. 406). In biblical terms, the victory of God over Satan is already complete, but Satan is left a certain sphere of influence through which he tries to cause as much damage as possible. Safety from his clutches lies in faith, and through his faith, the believer places himself under the influence of God, safe from the power of the devil.

Temptation of Christ In the New Testament, Jesus was tempted by Satan, who wanted to prevent Jesus' life and death from inaugurating the rule of God. After Jesus had fasted in the desert for 40 days and nights (p. 404), Satan came to him to try and capitalize on his weakness (**2**). He told Jesus to turn rocks into bread and prove he was the son of God. Thereafter, he led Jesus to a temple and told him to throw himself from it to demonstrate his powers. Finally, he led Jesus to a high mountain and offered him all he could see as his kingdom. Jesus resisted these temptations, answering with reference to the supremacy of God. Jesus put his trust in God, who would care for him even in his hour of greatest need.

Hajj The Hajj, the pilgrimage to Mecca, is one of the five central pillars of Islam and is the duty of every Muslim. Part of the Hajj ritual is the symbolic killing of the devil, in which the pilgrims throw stones at the pillars that represent the devil (**3**). Thereafter, many pilgrims cut their hair to symbolize the start of a new life without sin.

⏩ **God:** pp. 28–33

The New Testament

The New Testament is the second part of the Christian Bible. It contains 27 different texts written between 50 and 130 C.E. in the Greek language: four Gospels, 21 Epistles, the Acts of the Apostles, and the Book of Revelation. At the center of the New Testament is Jesus, a traveling Jewish preacher, who was crucified on the Cross by the Romans around 30 C.E. The central theme of his proclamation was the coming "Kingdom of God." After the Crucifixion, however, the focus changed and the proclaimer himself became the central theme, but as the crucified and risen Messiah—the Son of God. The New Testament texts detail the life, ministry, and death of Jesus in many forms and from different perspectives.

According to the New Testament, Jesus Christ will judge those who are raised from the dead on Judgment Day.

The Life
of Jesus
# of Nazareth

Jesus of Nazareth came into the world in the most humble of ways.

The Life of Jesus

p. 393

Jesus and His Surroundings

| 40 | 30 | 20 | 10 | 0 | 10 | 20 | 30 | 40 |

The Romans and the Jewish Elite

p. 463

# of Nazareth

p. 404

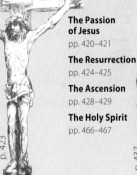

p. 423

p. 437

50   60   70   80   90   100

The Disciples of Jesus

p. 444

The Life of Jesus of Nazareth

Outside of Christian Greco-Roman literature, other sources prove the historical existence of Jesus; however, these texts do not say anything about the content of his teachings. Only the Gospels of the New Testament give detailed information about the life and ministry of Jesus, which centered around Galilee.

The son of Mary (**1**) and Joseph began as a follower of John the Baptist, who baptized him (**2**). Jesus shared John the Baptist's belief that the end of the world was near and that people could only save themselves from the judgment of God through change. Jesus differed from John in that he did not baptize his followers. Instead, he focused on his ministry, which was centered on anticipating the "Kingdom of God." Jesus agreed with the foundational Jewish beliefs, such as monotheism in God and that he would prevail over all evil and the sins of humanity. Jesus proclaimed the Kingdom of God not only through his preaching, but also through his acts. His miracles proved the reality of God's dominion. He showed this most clearly through the expulsion of demons, as it is a part of the Jewish doomsday prophecy that with the advent of God's reign demons would be disempowered.

For instance, when Jesus appeared before those possessed in Capernaum, he restored their original nature as sinless beings. The Gospels also say that Jesus had healing powers. In the New Testament, belief was not the effect but rather the precondition for Jesus' miracles. In this way, he differed from many miracle workers that were living at the time. He often performed his healings with the phrase: "Your belief helped you." In contrast to the contemporary miracle workers, Jesus included the healed person in the act.

①

Jesus often preached to his followers through parables, which were used to break down large concepts into a simple story using elements from daily life. For example, through the parable of the seed Jesus talked about seeds, fields, and harvest in order to make clear the hidden growth of God's rule. The ethics of Jesus were made most clear in the Beatitudes during the Sermon on the Mount. In this, Jesus showed himself as an advocate of the poor, the hungry, and the afflicted, and promised them the Kingdom of God. In the close

but not yet reached Kingdom of God, they would receive justice, as different standards would apply there from the world of men. The ethics of Jesus also include the love of one's enemy and non-violence. However, the very radical demands of Jesus should be understood in the context of his prophecy. In the first and last instance, Jesus spoke of a God who accepts people unconditionally and it is the choice of the people to be accepting of this love. Rather than for selfish reasons, people should turn to God and reflect his love unto

others through exercising pacifist qualities like turning the other cheek.

One of the best documented facts in the New Testament is Jesus' violent death. Sources estimate that Jesus died around 30 C.E. and sometime close to the Jewish celebration of Passover. The Jewish priestly aristocracy had him arrested and handed over to the Romans. Pontius Pilate condemned him to death on the Cross (**3**), an especially cruel manner of execution that Romans reserved for political insurrectionists. The catalyst for Jesus' condemnation was the fact that, after his prophetic appearance in Galilee, he wanted to take the message of the coming of the Kingdom of God to the Holy City of Jerusalem. Within pious Jewish circles, there was the expectation that, at the end of days, God would focus his lordship on the holy city. With his claim that the rule of God was bound to one person, Jesus inevitably provoked a confrontation with the priestly aristocracy. His prophecies about the destruction of the Temple and the expulsion of the moneylenders from the Temple were possibl

Jesus' last attempts to prepare Jerusalem for the advent of God's Kingdom. According to the accounts of the Gospels, Jesus was convinced that his message would be implemented. It is less clear how he could have imagined this implementation in more detail. According to some scholars, the prophecy of suffering in the Gospels is regarded as a subsequent construction.

The Passion and the Paschal narratives in the New Testament do not merely replay the suffering and death of Jesus, but rather interpret these occurrences theologically. In this way, the Gospels revisit this theme in the Old Testament tradition, which is particularly pronounced within the prophet Isaiah's "Servant poems." Delivery was found in Jesus, pictured as God's servant who suffered for "the many" in their place, and therefore the disgraceful execution of Jesus on Good Friday appeared in a new light. With this in mind, the crucified and risen Jesus took the center stage in Early Christian beliefs. However, there are also multiple interpretations of Jesus' Resurrection in the texts of the New Testament. On one hand, the Gospels underline the reawakening of Jesus and thereby the active role of God. The four Evangelists also emphasize that it was Jesus' metamorphosed body that enabled the disciples to recognize the risen Christ. On the other side, according to Paul, Jesus was dually a human being who died on the Cross, as well as the Christ (Greek: "kyrios") (**4**), which he achieved through his Resurrection. It was through his death and later Resurrection that Jesus gave salvation to all people. However, all of the New Testament writings consistently say that God's salvation had found its ultimate realization in Jesus.

■ Herod the Great dethroned the Hasmoneans and founded a dynasty that would last until the end of the first century C.E.

■ Despite his political achievements, Herod was unpopular

Matthew 2:1 Herod learns of Jesus' birth

Matthew 2:16–18 Herod has all the newborn children of Bethlehem killed

Matthew 2:19–22 Herod's death; division of his kingdom

When Herod saw that he had been tricked ... he sent and killed all the children in and around Bethlehem. Matthew 2:16

Herod the Great

Ruling ca 38–4 B.C.E., Herod was one of the most important rulers of ancient Israel. He mainly owed his sobriquet "the Great" to his impressive building works (**1**, aqueduct by Caesarea Maritima) and economic growth that accompanied his reign. In spite of this,

After the suicides of Cleopatra and Mark Antony, Herod became a loyal ally of Octavian, later known as Caesar Augustus.

the image of Herod made by the ensuing ages was negative. He was unpopular among his subjects, and in the Bible he appears as a brutal militarist.

Herod's father was Antipater the Idumaean, who made his career serving the last of the Hasmonean rulers. The Idumaeans were forced to support Judaism as early as the second century B.C.E. Moreover, Herod's mother was a Nabataean. Hence, according to his opponents, Herod was little more than a "half-Jew." Like his father, Herod stood on the side of the Romans, the new power in the Middle East. ⏩

⏩ **David:** pp. 216–221   **Solomon:** pp. 238–241

(2)

Murder of Aristobulus When Herod became king he named, at the request of his wife Mariamne, her 17-year-old brother Aristobulus III as the new high priest. Fearing that Aristobulus, who was the last of the royal house of the Hasmoneans, could challenge his position of power, Herod had him drowned in the pool of his palace (**2**). He mourned for his brother-in-law and declared his death to be an accident. Later, he had his wife and several of his sons murdered.

Empire of Herod the Great After his victory over Antigonus in 37 B.C.E., Herod successfully expanded his region of control. To this end he challenged the Egyptian queen Cleopatra (**3**), who wanted to reclaim regions of the Ptolemaic Empire, including the whole of Palestine. Finally Octavian, the future Caesar Augustus, rewarded Herod for his loyalty by expanding his lands. After his death in 4 B.C.E., Herod's empire was divided among three of his sons (p. 370).

In 40 B.C.E. the Parthians, rivals of the Romans, installed the Hasmonean Antigonus as leader of Jerusalem. Herod fled to Rome and was made the king of Judah by the Senate. With the help of the Romans, he returned and defeated Antigonus. After Octavian's victory over Mark Antony at Actium around 31 B.C.E., Herod placed himself on the side of the victor and was rewarded with an expansion of his domain. Through his marriage to the Hasmonean Mariamne, Herod tried to give

The three wise men from the Orient before King Herod the Great

his leadership a touch of legitimacy. However, to the Jews he remained a foreign intruder and a representative of the Roman garrison. He suppressed all dissenters of Rome and he even killed his relatives from the royal house of the Hasmoneans.

Jesus of Nazareth was allegedly born in the last years of Herod's rule. According to many researchers, Herod was unfairly judged by his family tragedy and reports of infanticide in Bethlehem. Although resistance to his politics increased toward the end, an almost 30-year-long peace is associated with his rule.

Herod's Construction Program

Herod promoted the culture and economy of his empire through construction projects. He strove to develop Jerusalem (**4**), especially the Temple, which was considered one of the most beautiful buildings of antiquity. He had palaces erected across the land, such as in Jericho and Masada, a cliff-top fortress by the Dead Sea. With his founding of the port Caesarea Maritima, he could enjoy the amenities of the Hellenistic-Roman culture without being exposed to the criticism of the religious Jews in Jerusalem.

⟩⟩ **The Temple in Jerusalem:** pp. 368–369

Infanticide in Bethlehem According to Matthew 2, Herod learned about the birth of Jesus from the magi (pp. 394–395). When the magi asked about the newborn king of the Jews, scribes named Bethlehem as the birthplace of the Messiah. Acting as a false friend, Herod gave them the task of reporting news of the child to him so that he could pay homage. When the wise men did not return from Bethlehem due to a dream in which God warned them against it, Herod had all children aged two years and younger murdered (**5**). Historical-critical exegesis (p. 501) suggests that the biblical story is not a report of historical facts but an echo of Herod's brutality. He had all challengers, including his own sons, executed.

The Herodium At the end of his life Herod was suffering from persecution complex. He had a fortress, the Herodium, built on a bank (**6**) in the desert near Bethlehem as an asylum. A palace is located at the foot of the fortress, which contains a mausoleum where the sarcophagus of Herod has recently been discovered.

Figures and Stories Relevant to Herod the Great

Idumeans, the Successors of the Edomites, see the Neighboring Peoples of Israel, pp. 166–167

Queen Cleopatra of Egypt, see Ptolemies and Seleucids, pp. 288–289

The Hasmoneans, see the Maccabees, pp. 290–293

Herod's Descendants, see pp. 370–371

The Romans, pp. 372–373

The Three Wise Men, see pp. 394–395

Jesus of Nazareth, see pp. 402–409; 414–419

The Infanticide of Bethlehem, see pp. 366–367

The Infanticide of Bethlehem

Matthew 2:16–18

16 *When Herod saw that he had been tricked by the wise men, he was infuriated, and he sent and killed all the children in and around Bethlehem who were two years old or under, according to the time that he had learned from the wise men.* 17 *Then was fulfilled what had been spoken through the prophet Jeremiah (Jeremiah 31:15):* 18 *"A voice was heard in Ramah, wailing and loud lamentation, Rachel weeping for her children; she refused to be consoled, because they are no more."*

The Temple in Jerusalem

In biblical times there were three temple sites in Jerusalem. The Temple of Solomon (p. 240) was destroyed by Nebuchadrezzar and rebuilt in the post-exile era (pp. 286–287). Herod actually only renovated this Temple; however, the expansions he made were so extensive that they resembled a new construction. Herod, who saw himself as the new Solomon, deemed it was his mission to bring Solomon's Temple back to its full greatness (**2**,**4**). At the same time he was able to realize the Hellenistic-Roman ideal of a city center and to form the Temple of Jerusalem into one of the wonders of the ancient world. The western wall of the Temple, revered by Jews from all over the world, the Wailing Wall (**1**), is only a small part of the originally formidable construction. Nothing is left of the halls of columns, which surrounded the Temple's square.

The Temple was a domain specified for the practices of the sacral cult. The Court of the Gentiles could be accessed by going through a gateway. The Court of the Women was to be found farther inward and was separated from the Court of the Priests. In the center of the Temple, the holiest spot, the Ark of the Covenant was kept safe. Only the high priests could enter this room on the Day of Atonement—Yom Kippur.

Temples and Synagogues After the destruction of the Temple by the Romans in 70 C.E., the Torah superseded the sacrificial cult as the means of communication with God. The synagogues (**3**) became places of congregation for prayers, services, and Torah instruction. The center of every synagogue to this day is the shrine of the Torah. Intrinsic aspects of services are prayers, such as the "Hear, O Israel!" (pp. 144–145), the blessings from the rabbis, and readings from the Torah and the prophets.

▷▷ **High Priests:** p. 234   **Yom Kippur:** pp. 138–139

When Herod saw Jesus, he was very glad ... because he had heard about him. Luke 23:8

Herod's Descendants

Herod the Great bequeathed his kingdom to his sons Herod Archelaus, Herod Antipas, and Herod Philip (p. 363). The Romans soon overthrew Archelaus and annexed Judea. Herod

The ruins of Machaerus, a fortress of Herod Antipas

Antipas, the sovereign of Galilee and Perea, was known for the killing of John the Baptist (**1**) and for his encounter with Jesus. He had his political savvy to thank for the length of his rule, which went on until 37 C.E. A nephew of Herod Antipas, Herod Agrippa I was a close friend of the Romans and so was given practically all of Herod the Great's sovereign lands. In order to gain popularity with the conservative Jews, he had the Christians in Jerusalem, including the Apostles James and Peter, tortured.

■ Herod's descendants rule as vassals for Rome in various places in Palestine

Matthew 2:22 Archelaus rules as the king of Judea

Mark 6:18 John the Baptist criticizes Herod Antipas

Matthew 14:1–12; Mark 6:21–29 Herod Antipas has John the Baptist beheaded

Luke 23:6–12 Jesus before Herod Antipas

Acts 12 Herod Agrippa I has James killed and Peter taken prisoner

Jesus Before Herod Antipas

Herod Antipas was the ruler of Galilee, the home of Jesus. According to the Passion tale in the Gospel of Luke, Jesus, as one of Herod Antipas' subjects, was sent as a prisoner to him by Pilate (**2**). To begin with, Herod was pleased to be able to meet Jesus and hoped to see a miracle. When Jesus kept silent when asked the last question, however, the high priest and scribes began to taunt him.

Herod also showed Jesus his disdain and had him sent back to Pilate wrapped in a grandiose robe. Jesus' appearance before Herod evidently had no decisive meaning for the outcome of the trial against him. The theological essence of the tale of Herod is that it underscores the innocence of Jesus, as neither Pilate nor Herod Antipas could prove that he had committed any wrongdoing.

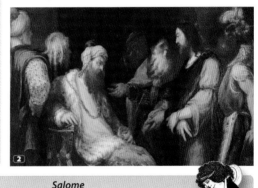

2

Salome

Salome, as recounted by Flavius Josephus, is identified in the New Testament as the daughter of Herodias, the wife of Herod Antipas. She danced before the guests at the birthday celebrations of her stepfather, Herod Antipas. When she was granted one wish, she demanded, at the behest of her mother, John the Baptist's head on a plate. Herod fulfilled this wish and had John executed (p. 381). This story, from Mark's Gospel, has been repeatedly reworked in art and literature. In the opera Salome by Richard Strauss, which premiered in Dresden in 1905, Herod is so disgusted by the behavior of his stepdaughter that he has her killed. In Oscar Wilde's play of the same name, it is Salome who wants to see John dead, as he had spurned her kiss.

■ At the time of the New Testament, the Romans were the ruling power in the Middle East

■ Because Christians refused the cult of the Roman emperor, they were persecuted

Maccabees 8:1–32 The Maccabees forge an alliance with Rome

Luke 2:1–3 The Roman emperor Augustus conducts a census of the people

Matthew 27:1–14; Mark 15:1–5; Luke 23:1–4; John 18:28–38 Jesus is taken before the Roman governor Pontius Pilate and judged

Acts 22:27 The Apostle Paul holds Roman citizenship

Acts 28:17–31 Paul is taken to Rome

In those days a decree went out from Emperor Augustus that all the world should be registered. Luke 2:1

The Romans

Judaism and Christianity were under the influence of the Roman Empire in the early first century C.E. Ultimately, even the Maccabees sought an alliance with the Romans (**1**) (pp. 290–293), and King Herod and his descendants sustained this political strategy (pp. 362–371). For the majority of the Jews, however, the Roman ruling authority would remain a foreign body. In the Great Jewish Revolt between 66 and 70 C.E., the future emperor Titus was temporarily able to break the Jewish resistance by destroying Jerusalem and its Temple (**2**).

Jesus was born under the rule of Emperor Augustus and crucified by the governor Pontius Pilate. Christianity spread rapidly through the Roman Empire due to the empire's uniform language, its relatively calm political situation ("Pax Romana"), and its intellectual unity. The cult of the emperor, as a sign of the Roman lust for power, presented the Christians with a problem, as it went against their religious creed.

⊃⊃ The Temple in Jerusalem: pp. 368–369   **Roman Occupation:** p. 461

Destruction of Jerusalem In the year 6 C.E., the Romans deposed Herod Archelaus, son of Herod the Great, and placed Judea under the regime of a Roman governor. The lack of caution in the Romans' leadership and the appalling execution of the office of the governor provoked growing resistance from the people of Jerusalem in 66 C.E. The religious practices of the Roman garrison helped to eventually escalate these mounting tensions into the First Jewish-Roman War. The ensuing siege of Jerusalem dragged on as a bloody stalemate until the city's walled defenses were broken in 70 C.E. during a final assault led by the future Roman emperor Titus Flavius. The Temple of Jerusalem was destroyed (**3**), and the cult objects were led through Rome in a victory parade.

In Front of a Roman Court The high priest, who was appointed by the Romans and the High Council (pp. 462–463), regulated the internal affairs of the Jews. Both the Romans and the High Council were also responsible for the lower jurisdiction. Life-and-death decisions, however, were made by the governors, as was the case with Jesus. He was accused of treason and insurgency and so brought before Pontius Pilate (**4**).

Flavius Josephus

The Jewish military commander and historian Flavius Josephus (died ca 100 C.E.) was the most important Hellenistic author dealing with contemporary events related to the New Testament. As the son of a Jewish aristocratic family, he took part in the Great Jewish Revolt against the Romans. However, he later changed sides and received Roman citizenship and the surname of the Flavian emperors Vespasian and Titus, who had promoted him. He authored many works, such as The Jewish War and The Jewish Antiquities, an account of Jewish history from creation to the Great Revolt. Both texts remain priceless today for interpreting and historically contextualizing New Testament texts.

Figures and Stories Relevant to the Romans

The Hasmoneans, see the Maccabees, pp. 290–293

Herod the Great, see pp. 362–365

Pontius Pilate, see pp. 460–461

The Early Christians, see pp. 480–481

Paul, Citizen of Rome, see pp. 488–491

■ Elizabeth and Zechariah were the parents of John the Baptist

Luke 1:5–25 An angel announces the birth of John the Baptist to Zechariah

Luke 1:39–45 Pregnant Mary visits pregnant Elizabeth

Luke 1:57–66 Elizabeth gives birth to John the Baptist

> *But the angel said to him, "Do not be afraid, Zechariah, for your prayer has been heard. Your wife Elizabeth will bear you a son, and you will name him John."* Luke 1:13

Elizabeth and Zechariah

Elizabeth, like her husband Zechariah, was a descendant of the lineage of Aaron the priest. According to the infancy narrative in the Gospel of Luke, they had both reached a very high age, were just in the eyes of God, and were childless due to Elizabeth's infertility. God heard their prayers and the angel Gabriel promised them the birth of a child. Six months before her cousin Mary, Elizabeth brought a son into the world, John the Baptist. Both families (**1**) stayed in close contact and later Jesus was baptized by John (p. 404).

The motif of childlessness and motherhood has its echoes in the Old Testament: Sarah and Rebekah also became pregnant by the grace of God.

❯❯ Sarah: pp. 68–69   Rebekah: pp. 82–83

The Announcement of the Birth of John The archangel Gabriel announced the birth of John to Zechariah during a sacrifice in the temple (**2**). As Zechariah would not believe without a sign, the angel struck him dumb. When John was born, and had been given a name at his circumcision on the eighth day after the birth, the still speechless Zechariah wrote it down on a little tablet (**3**). Shortly after this, to the amazement of all, he could speak again and praised God. In his Gospel, Luke artfully forms these words of praise into a prophetic hymn. This carries the Latin name *Benedictus* (pp. 376–377) after the first words that Zechariah spoke.

Mary and Elizabeth The story of Mary and Elizabeth in the Gospel of Luke is composed as a parallel tale: Both have the birth of a son prophesied and both sons play a great role in the New Testament. After the archangel Gabriel had promised the birth of Jesus to Mary, she met with her cousin Elizabeth. With the two pregnant women (**4**) meeting, the two strands of the story join together. Entering Elizabeth's house, Mary greeted Elizabeth, to which the child in Elizabeth's womb reacted by moving. When Elizabeth spoke a glorification for Mary and her child, she answered with the hymn "My soul magnifies the Lord." This hymn, the *Magnificat* (pp. 384–385), was put to music by Johann Sebastian Bach, which is named after its opening word in Latin.

Figures and Stories Relevant to Elizabeth and Zechariah

God, see pp. 28–33

Angels, see pp. 42–43

John the Baptist, Son of Elizabeth and Zechariah, see pp. 378–381

Mary, Cousin of Elizabeth, see pp. 386–389

Jesus of Nazareth, see pp. 402–409 and 414–419

Annunciation of Jesus, see Mary, p. 387

Benedictus– The Song of Zechariah

Luke 1:68–79

68 Blessed be the Lord God of Israel, for he has looked favorably on his people and redeemed them.
69 He has raised up a mighty savior for us in the house of his servant David,
70 as he spoke through the mouth of his holy prophets from of old,
71 that we would be saved from our enemies and from the hand of all who hate us.
72 Thus he has shown the mercy promised to our ancestors, and has remembered his holy covenant,
73 the oath that he swore to our ancestor Abraham, to grant us
74 that we, being rescued from the hands of our enemies, might serve him without fear,
75 in holiness and righteousness before him all our days.
76 And you, child, will be called the prophet of the Most High; for you will go before the Lord to prepare his ways,
77 to give knowledge of salvation to his people by the forgiveness of their sins.
78 By the tender mercy of our God, the dawn from on high will break upon us,
79 to give light to those who sit in darkness and in the shadow of death, to guide our feet into the way of peace.

■ John baptizes Jesus in the River Jordan

■ John introduces water baptism

■ John is the second most important saint after Mary

Luke 1:57–66 John is the son of Elizabeth and Zechariah

Matthew 3:1–3; Mark 1:1–3; Luke 3:1–6; John 1:19–28 John announces the coming of Jesus, the Messiah

Matthew 3:1–12; Mark 1:1–5; Luke 3:1–18 John calls upon people to change their sinful ways. As a sign of their repentance, he baptizes them in the River Jordan

Matthew 3:13–17; Mark 1:9–11; Luke 3:21–22; John 1:29–34 John baptizes Jesus in the Jordan

Matthew 14:1–12; Mark 6:14–29; Luke 3:19–20 John is seized by Herod Antipas and beheaded at the wish of Herodias

John 3:25–30 John attracts many followers and is revered up to the present day

You yourselves are my witnesses that I said, "I am not the Messiah, but I have been sent ahead of him." John 3:28

John the Baptist

John the Baptist is one of the great figures of early Christian literature. His name is mentioned most frequently in the New Testament besides Jesus and Paul. Wearing a simple garment made from camel's hair (**1**), the son of Elizabeth and Zechariah appeared, preaching repentance. Like earlier prophets, he spoke of the coming kingdom of God and urged people to undergo a spiritual transformation. As a sign of their repentance, they should be baptized.

Jesus was among the people baptized by John in the River Jordan (**2**); however, it is doubtful whether he was one of John's followers. In any case, some of them later joined the movement surrounding Jesus, bringing the practice of baptism into the Christian churches. After Jesus' death, baptism was practiced by his followers, as a symbol of entry into the Christian community. ⏩

⏩ **Baptism:** pp. 382–383

John Meets Jesus When John the Baptist was asked who he was, he answered that he was neither the Messiah nor a prophet. Instead, he indicated Jesus (**3**) and said: "Behold the lamb of God, who takes away the sin of the world!" With this metaphor, the New Testament references the symbol of the sacrificial lamb. Standing at the center of the Jewish feast of Passover (pp. 118–119), the lamb represents the liberation of the Israelites from bondage in Egypt. Thus, when John called Jesus the lamb of God (p. 426), he was presaging Christ's future Crucifixion. In Christianity, Jesus on the Cross took the sins of the world and they were forgiven. God's Son was sacrificed to liberate people from their sinful nature. This connection between John and Jesus is seen most clearly in the Gospel of John. The first three Gospels, in contrast, tend to emphasize John's work.

3

The Essenes and Qumran

In 1947, at Khirbet Qumran on the Dead Sea, clay jars were found with scrolls sealed inside them. These "Dead Sea scrolls" may date back to the Jewish community of the Essenes. According to the historian Flavius Josephus, the Essenes rejected the rites of the temple, preferring to study scriptures in isolated communities. Many commonalities between John's followers and the Essenes have been identified. Whether John was a member of the sect remains controversial. For instance, the baptism practiced by John as a sign of the forgiveness is not comparable with the Essenes' ritual ablutions.

⟩ **The Passion of Jesus:** pp. 420–421

From a Christian point of view, John is considered to be the forerunner of Jesus (**4**). For the Evangelists, John fulfills prophecies from the Old Testament. According to Mark, when Jesus was baptized the Holy Spirit descended in the form of a dove (**5**), and a voice from heaven said: "You are my Son, the Beloved; with you I am well pleased." This sentence combines references from Genesis, the Psalms, and the Book of Isaiah. Thus, at Jesus' baptism, his fate can already be interpreted according to the Old Testament: Jesus will be a new Isaac, a son who is willing to be sacrificed (p. 78); he will be a new David, a savior who redeems the world (p. 220).

▶▶ **References to Jesus in the Old Testament:** p. 319

Herodias and John the Baptist's Head According to the Gospel of Mark, John the Baptist was beheaded. The people responsible for his death were Herodias—wife of King Herod Antipas—and her daughter Salome, although the latter's name does not appear in the New Testament. As Herod watches his stepdaughter dance for him at a feast, the king becomes so pleased with Salome that he promises to grant her a wish. On her mother's instructions, Salome demands John the Baptist's head on a platter. Herodias hated John because he publicly criticized her marriage with her brother-in-law Herod. Since Herod had given his pledge before the assembled guests, he reluctantly fulfilled Salome's wish: He ordered the execution of John the Baptist and presented his head on a platter (**6**).

John in the Qur'an

The Qur'an describes John the Baptist as a prophet, along with Jesus and Muhammad. He is known for his devotion to God and his obedience to his parents (Surah 19:12–14). He is also described as an ascetic. Both Muslims and Christians pay homage at his tomb in the Umayyad Mosque of Damascus.

Baptism

Baptism in Christianity has its roots in the Jewish laws on cleanliness. Through repeated ritual washings, or ablutions, people can be washed clean of impurities produced by guilt or disease. As practiced by John the Baptist (**2**), baptism was linked to repentance and the forgiveness of sins, and carried out only once, in contrast to the Jewish cleanliness rituals. Baptism with water and the Holy Spirit is a sacrament in major Christian churches, signifying the baptized person's entry into a particular community (**1**,**4**).

The trinitarian baptismal formula—"In the name of the Father, the Son, and the Holy Spirit"—refers to Jesus' command to his disciples to be baptized, found in the Gospel of Matthew. In other church communities, baptism through immersion is used to provide a physical experience symbolizing Christ's death and Resurrection.

②

Adult Baptism In many churches, the baptism of children is common practice. However, many independent denominations—Baptists, Pentecostals, and Adventists—view the person's confession of faith as a key component. Consequently, baptism is practiced on adults who have prepared themselves spiritually. Following the example of the Bible, Baptists are baptized through full immersion (**3**, Baptists at the River Jordan).

③

» The Church: pp. 454–455

The Sanctus of Mary— The Magnificat

Luke 1:46–55

46 *And Mary said, "My soul magnifies the Lord,* 47 *and my spirit rejoices in God my Savior,* 48 *for he has looked with favour on the lowliness of his servant. Surely, from now on all generations will call me blessed;* 49 *for the Mighty One has done great things for me, and holy is his name.* 50 *His mercy is for those who fear him from generation to generation.* 51 *He has shown strength with his arm; he has scattered the proud in the thoughts of their hearts.* 52 *He has brought down the powerful from their thrones, and lifted up the lowly;* 53 *he has filled the hungry with good things, and sent the rich away empty.* 54 *He has helped his servant Israel, in remembrance of his mercy,* 55 *according to the promise he made to our ancestors, to Abraham and to his descendants for ever."*

■ Mary, the mother of Jesus of Nazareth, is still venerated today in Islam and Christianity

■ Depictions of Mary are the second most common theme of Christian art, after those of Jesus

Luke 1:26–38 An angel tells Mary that Jesus will be born

Luke 1:39–45 Mary visits her cousin Elizabeth

Luke 1:46–55 Mary thanks God with a song of praise

Luke 2:1–5 Mary and Joseph travel to Bethlehem for the census

Luke 2:1–21; Matthew 1:18–25 Mary gives birth to Jesus in Bethlehem

Luke 2:22–38 Mary and Joseph bring Jesus to the Temple

John 2:1–12 Jesus and Mary attend the wedding at Cana

Matthew 27:55–56; Mark 15:40–41; John 19:25–27 Mary grieves for Jesus at his Crucifixion

Acts 1:14 Mary among the disciples

The angel said to her, "Do not be afraid, Mary, for you have found favor with God." Luke 1:30

Mary

Mary, the mother of Jesus, was from Nazareth in Galilee. She was married to the carpenter Joseph, a descendant of King David. In the New Testament, Mary plays a central role in the narratives of Jesus' birth and childhood. According to the Gospel of Luke, she conceived a son through the Holy Spirit and gave birth to him in a stable in Bethlehem. Theologically, these events are recognized as the fulfillment of Old Testament prophecies. Besides the Bible's references to Mary, there are many stories about her in non-biblical texts. Modern-day believers continue to be moved by the theme of the loving and suffering mother, standing by her son until death. Theologians have also intensively studied the figure of Mary. As the Mother of God, she plays an especially important role in Catholicism. ▷▷

Anne, Mother of Mary

The apocryphal Protoevangelium of James (p. 447) names Anne and Joachim as Mary's parents. Through God's mercy, Anne becomes pregnant after years of childlessness. According to the Catholic doctrine of the Immaculate Conception, her daughter Mary is born without original sin (p. 40). Thus, as the bearer of the Mother of God, Anne played a role in God's plan for the world's salvation. In Christian art, she is often depicted in an "Anna Selbdritt," a three-figure representation in which she appears behind Mary and Jesus.

▷▷ **Jesus as the Messiah:** p. 404

The Annunciation and the Birth of Jesus The angel Gabriel appeared to Mary and told her of the coming birth of Jesus (**2**). He called her "blessed among women," since her son was the prophesied Messiah. But Mary was confused: How could she be pregnant when she had not yet slept with a man? The angel explained that she would conceive God's son through the Holy Spirit. For God, nothing is impossible: Mary's cousin Elizabeth, believed to be barren, was also pregnant (pp. 374–375). The announcement of Jesus' birth overshadowed that of John the Baptist. While John came from a family of priests, Jesus was a descendent of King David. Nevertheless, Jesus' birth in Bethlehem (p. 402) took place in humble surroundings. Weak and helpless, he was laid in a feeding trough (**1**). The Son of God shared the fate of those to whom God's message was directed: the poor, the weak, and the needy.

The Virgin Birth

In the ancient Middle East, a term meaning "virgin" was used for a virgin girl, who was eligible for marriage. The reference in the Gospel of Matthew to the "Virgin Mary" giving birth to Jesus is tied to a prophecy from Isaiah. According to him, the savior of the last days would be born to a "maiden." The Hebrew original, however, does not use the word for "virgin" in the sense of an "untouched girl" (Hebrew: betula), but the term for "young woman" (Hebrew: alma). However, the Greek translation of the Old Testament, called the Septuagint (p. 289), preferred a term meaning "untouched woman." Since the New Testament authors drew their Old Testament references from the Septuagint, they continued to use the word meaning "untouched woman."

Pietà Mary witnessed her son's Crucifixion (**4**). Jesus commended his mother to the disciple John, asking them to support each other as if they were mother and son. The theme of the suffering mother cradling Jesus' body in her arms after it had been taken from the Cross (**5**) has found expression in the Pietà (Italian: "compassion").

⏩ **References to Jesus in the Old Testament:** p. 319

Mary's Assumption

Very little is known about Mary's fate after the death of her son. According to the Gospels, Mary at first remained in the company of the disciples and Jesus' female followers. In the teachings of the Catholic Church, Mary's body and soul were taken up to heaven after her death (**6**). As the "Queen of Heaven," she shares the heavenly majesty of her son.

Mary's House at Ephesus

According to Christian tradition, after Jesus' death, Mary accompanied the disciple John to Ephesus, on the Aegean coast of Asia Minor, where there was a large Jewish community. In the year 431, the Third Ecumenical Council of the period was held there. At this "Council of Ephesus," Mary was proclaimed to be the "God-bearer" (Greek: theotokos). Even today, the house in which Mary and John are said to have lived can be seen: "The House of Mother Mary" (Turkish: "Meryem Ana evi") near Ephesus. The identi-fication of this house goes back to the visions of German nun Anna Katharina Emmerick, who died in 1824. She is said to have described Mary's house so precisely that French priests were later able to find it. As Mary also appears in the Qur'an, the "Meryem Ana evi" is revered by Muslims.

The Veneration of Mary

A tradition of intense veneration of Jesus' mother developed in the course of Christianity, and is reflected in literature, music, and art (**2**), as well as spiritual expressions, mysticism, and devout rituals (**3**). This veneration is also evident at shrines such as those at Lourdes, Fatima, Czestochova, and Altötting.

Some theological assertions about Mary—for instance, her immaculate conception—are not always supported by the New Testament. Thus, Biblical exegesis and Church teachings face the challenge of illuminating God's interactions with Mary, using sources both within and outside of the Bible.

Many have criticized some of the consequences of traditional views of Mary, since they proved detrimental to the image—and self-image—of women. Comparisons between Mary and Eve set up the dichotomy of the "seductress" and the "virgin." Today, Mary is taking on meaning as a "sister in faith." The New Testament describes the greatness, as well as the doubt, involved in her path to belief.

2

⏩ **Saints and Martyrs:** pp. 484–485

The Rosary An expression of devotion to Mary in the Catholic Church is the recitation of the rosary. The rosary (**1**) is a string of prayer beads with a cross attached. The beads are organized into five groups of ten small beads and one large bead. Prayer begins at the Cross, with the believer making the sign of the Cross, professing his or her faith, and asking for an increase of the three heavenly virtues: faith, hope, and charity. Then, the Lord's Prayer is said for each large bead, and the Hail Mary prayer is said for each small one. The prayers are dedicated to a particular set of "mysteries"; a meditation on each theme is added to the Hail Mary prayer in five groups of ten. According to the occasion, a believer may meditate on the joyful, sorrowful, or glorious mysteries.

■ Joseph, a carpenter, was Jesus' legal father

Jacob the father of Joseph the husband of Mary, of whom Jesus was born, who is called the Messiah. Matthew 1:16

Joseph

The New Testament appears interested in Joseph only with regard to his importance for Jesus' heritage. According to Old Testament prophecies, the Messiah must not only be born in Bethlehem, but must also be a descendant of King David (p. 220). Yet Joseph's portrayal in the Gospels remains ambiguous.

Matthew 1:19 Hearing Mary is pregnant, Joseph considers leaving her

Matthew 1:20–25 An angel tells Joseph of Mary's conception through the Holy Spirit

Luke 2:1–5 Joseph and Mary travel to Bethlehem

Matthew 2:1–12 Wise men visit Joseph, Mary, and Jesus

Matthew 2:13–14 An angel warns Joseph to flee to Egypt

① The Gospel of Matthew points to Joseph as Mary's husband; at the same time, Jesus' divine origin must be established. Thus, Matthew interrupts Jesus' family tree, with Jesus being conceived by the Holy Spirit. Later, Joseph once again appears in the role of legitimate father (**1**) when he gives Jesus his name. Thus, for theological reasons, the legal recognition of Jesus as Joseph's son in the New Testament appears to be more significant than his biological origin.

Josephite Marriage

Joseph's sketchy portrayal in the Gospels stimulated the imagination of early Christian writers. Thus, the apocryphal Protoevangelion of James (p. 447) from 150 C.E. describes God performing a miracle to show the high priests that the Virgin Mary and the carpenter Joseph from Galilee will be brought together in marriage. According to the Christian tradition, Joseph and Mary never

had sex, even after Jesus' birth. Marriages such as these have now come to be referred to as a "Josephite marriage." However, brothers and sisters of Jesus are mentioned in various parts of the New Testament. According to non-biblical texts, these are Jesus' half-siblings, the children of Joseph from an earlier marriage. Some Christian traditions see them not as literal siblings, but as close relatives.

References to Jesus in the Old Testament: p. 319 **The Virgin Birth:** p. 388

Life of a Carpenter The most detailed depiction of Joseph is found in the "Story of Joseph the Carpenter," which appeared around 400 C.E. In it, Jesus describes the life of Joseph to his disciples. According to this account, Joseph, a widower, already had six children from an earlier marriage when he was chosen by priests to become engaged to Mary. Joseph remained vigorous to an advanced age, teaching Jesus the profession of carpentry (**2**). Most of the text consists of a description of Joseph's death among his family (**4**).

The Flight to Egypt
According to the Gospel of Matthew, an angel appeared to Joseph and warned him about King Herod's plan to kill all newborn children in Bethlehem (p. 365). That same night, Joseph led his family to safety, fleeing with them to Egypt (**3**). After Herod's death, Joseph was visited again by an angel in a dream, who told him to return to his homeland. As commanded by God, Joseph settled in Nazareth, a town in Galilee.

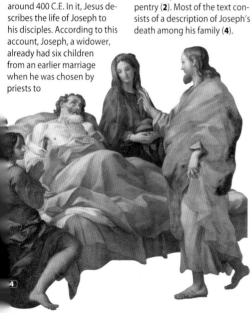

■ The three wise men appear in the Bible from the Orient

■ The three wise men were probably astrologers

Matthew 2:1–10 The three wise men follow a star to the birth of Jesus

Matthew 2:7–8 Herod the Great tries to learn something about Jesus from the three wise men

Matthew 2:11 The three wise men give gold, frankincense, and myrrh to Jesus

Wise men from the East came to Jerusalem, asking, "Where is the child who has been born king of the Jews?" Matthew 2:1-2

The Three Wise Men

The story that the three wise men, or "magi" (**1**), came from the East to Bethlehem to pay homage to Christ is only told in Matthew's Gospel. They were probably astrologers from Babylon, a stronghold of astronomy. At the start of the third century, the Church writer Tertullian deduced from a prophecy by the prophet Isaiah that they were kings. Later, the theologian Origen assumed from the giving of gold, frankincense, and myrrh that there were three of them. In the ninth century they were given

The word "magi" comes from the Greek name "magoi" for Persian pries

the names Caspar, Melchior, and Balthazar, probably derived from the Latin house blessing "Christus Mansionem Benedicat" ("Christ bless this house").

Figures and Stories Relevant to the Three Wise Men

Angels, see pp. 42–43

David, see pp. 216–221

Isaiah, see pp. 316–319

Herod the Great, see pp. 362–365

Mary, the Mother of Jesus, see pp. 386–389

Joseph of Nazareth, see pp. 392–393

Jesus of Nazareth, see pp. 402–409 and 414–419

The Evangelists, see pp. 430–433

①

The Search for the New King of the Jews The magi from the East followed a star and arrived in Jerusalem. When they asked about the newly born king of the Jews, King Herod became curious. He gave the magi the task of searching for this king on his behalf (**2**) (p. 365). The magi continued to follow the star into Bethlehem. Here, they found Jesus in a crib (**3**), paid homage, and gave him gifts. In a dream, God ordered them to return to their own country without reporting anything about the child to Herod. For most researchers the story has a theological significance, as the end of days was supposed to

begin with the birth of Jesus. According to a prophecy by Isaiah, this can be recognized by a time when the people come to Jerusalem to pray to God. They are represented by the magi, who come to pay homage to Jesus.

The Star-Singers and the Shrine to the Three Kings

A wealth of traditions surrounds the magi, such as the shrine to the Three Kings in the Cologne Cathedral. It is said that the shrine holds the magi's bones, which were brought to Cologne in the fourth century. In German-speaking regions there are the "star-singers," in which children dress up as the Three Kings and collect money for charity.

Star of Bethlehem

There were many early attempts to scientifically explain the appearance of the star mentioned in the Gospel of Matthew. In the early 14th century, the astronomer Johannes Kepler proved that a great celestial conjunction of Jupiter and Saturn had occurred in 7 B.C.E., around the time of Christ's birth. Such rare star constellations could be clues to explaining the biblical "Star of Bethlehem."

Alongside scientific explanations, there are theological interpretations of the star. In antiquity, phenomena in the heavens, such as comets or eclipses, were harbingers for special events. Ancient legends link the appearances of stars together with the births of famous personalities such as Alexander the Great, Julius Caesar, and Emperor Augustus. In this sense, the star of Bethlehem also announces the birth of a king (**1**), as Jesus was considered to be the newborn king of the Jews, the long-awaited Messiah and savior. The Gospel of Matthew is again bound to Old Testament prophecies, as it says in Numbers 24:17, "A star shall come out of Jacob, and a scepter shall rise out of Israel."

②

▶▶ **References to Jesus in the Old Testament:** p. 319

3

omet Theory The theory has een espoused many times that ne star of Bethlehem could ave been a celestial body dentical to Halley's Comet (**2**). his has its origins in the history of art. Giotto di Bondone painted the star as a comet in his fresco *The Three Kings* (**3**) around 1303/1305, as he had seen Halley's Comet himself a few years earlier. However, as comets were predominantly considered to be bringers of disaster in ancient times, the comet theory as an interpretation of the star of Bethlehem is probably not applicable.

The Story of Christmas— Birth of Jesus

Luke 2:1–14

1 *In those days a decree went out from Emperor Augustus that all the world should be registered.* 2 *This was the first registration and was taken while Quirinius was governor of Syria.* 3 *All went to their own towns to be registered.* 4 *Joseph also went from the town of Nazareth in Galilee to*

Judea, to the city of David called Bethlehem, because he was descended from the house and family of David. **5** He went to be registered with Mary, to whom he was engaged and who was expecting a child. **6** While they were there, the time came for her to deliver her child. **7** And she gave birth to her firstborn son and wrapped him in bands of cloth, and laid him in a manger, because there was no place for them in the inn.

8 In that region there were shepherds living in the fields, keeping watch over their flock by **9** then an angel of the Lord stood before them, and the glory of the Lord shone around them, and they were terrified. **10** But the angel said to them, "Do not be afraid; for see—I am bringing you good news of great joy for all the people: **11** to you is born this day in the city of David a Savior, who is the Messiah, the Lord. **12** This will be a sign for you: you will find a child wrapped in bands of cloth and lying in a manger." **13** And suddenly there was with the angel a multitude of the heavenly host, praising God and saying, **14** "Glory to God in the highest heaven,   and on earth peace among those whom he favors!"

Christmas

Christmas is one of the most important festivals in Christianity along with Easter and Pentecost. The incarnation of God in Jesus is celebrated on this day. The New Testament does not mention a birth date for Jesus. The first recorded celebration of Christmas on December 25th stems from 336 C.E. This date was originally connected with the winter solstice, upon which games were held in the Roman Empire for the glorification of the Sol Invictus, the sun god.

The Gospel of Luke tells the story of Jesus' birth an event of historical importance. The Evangelist related the events in context of the Roman emperor Augustus, the Syrian governor Quirinius, and a tax assessment in the Roman Empire. The references to secular history are a theological illustration that the birth of Jesus (**3**) is something that touches the entire world. For Luke, Bethlehem stood as the central point of the world (**2**, church of the birth in Bethlehem), as it was here in the City of David that the Messiah and savior was born.

①

②

Father Christmas The image of Father Christmas as an old man with a white bushy beard and a red, fur-lined coat (**1**) is a combination of several different cultural traditions. One contribution to this image was the folk character "Belznickel" created by the German-American caricaturist Thomas Nast in 1881. Known as "Santa Claus" in the U.S., the fervor surrounding him and the giving of presents has displaced the celebration of Jesus's birth.

≫ The Messiah: p. 404

3

To you is born this day in the city of David a Savior, who is the Messiah, the Lord. Luke 2:11

Jesus of Nazareth

Birth and Childhood

In the New Testament, Luke wrote the most about Jesus' birth and childhood in his "infancy narratives" (**1**). According to him, Jesus was brought humbly into the world in a stable. Luke shared the theological view that the Messiah would take part in the fate of his contemporaries in Palestine from the very beginning. The shepherds (**2**), who were the first to come to the child in Bethlehem, are representative of the poor of Palestine, to whom the proclamation of Jesus is first and foremost directed. After they had prayed to the child, they told people what they had seen and heard with enthusiasm. In contrast to the disciples, however, the shepherds were not called to missionary service, but rather returned to their flock.

◾ Jesus was the son of God

◾ The four Evangelists wrote about Jesus' life and ministry

Luke 2:1–21 Jesus is born in a stable in Bethlehem

Luke 2:22–40 Simeon and Anna recognize the Messiah in Jesus

Luke 2:41–52 The 12-year-old Jesus has discussions in the Temple

Matthew 3:13–17; Luke 3:21–22; Mark 1:9–11 Jesus is baptized by John in the Jordan

Mark 4; Luke 8:4–18 Jesus' parables

Matthew 14:34–36; Mark 6:53–56; Luke 5:12–26; John 5:1–18 Jesus' healing miracles

Matthew 19:13–15; Mark 10:13–16; Luke 18:15–17 Jesus blesses the children

Luke 19:1–10 Jesus converts the tax-official Zacchaeus

Matthew 14:13–21; Mark 6:30–44; Luke 9:10–17; John 6:1–13 Jesus feeds 5,000 people with only five loaves and two fish

p.414 ⟫

2

⟫ Annunciation and Birth of Jesus: p. 387

Simeon and Anna A lesser-known section from the childhood tale of Luke is the story of Simeon and Hannah. According to Jewish custom, Jesus was circumcised on the eighth day after his birth in the Temple of Jerusalem. During this ceremony, Simeon, an old man, came by, to whom God had revealed that he would see the Messiah before his death. He took the child into his arms and sang a song of praise (**3**), the *Nunc Dimittis*. Simeon attested that God had fulfilled his promise and he spoke prophetically of the imminent fate of Jesus and his mother Mary. Jesus was identified as a light for the gentiles and as "a sign that will be opposed." Hannah, an 84-year-old prophetess, who spent her time fasting and praying in the Temple, also sang a song of praise for Jesus as the savior of Israel.

The 12-Year-Old in the Temple A biographical episode from Jesus' youth in the Bible is of Jesus at 12 years old in the Temple. Jesus went on a pilgrimage with his parents to Jerusalem at Passover. When Mary and Joseph were searching for him on the return journey, they found him in the Temple, discussing matters with the scribes and astounding them with insightful questions (**4**). This tale is supposed to demonstrate that, even at an early age, Jesus was endowed with divine authority.

⊃ **Passover:** pp. 118–119

Baptism and Preaching

According to three of the Evangelists, Jesus' ministry began with his baptism. The wandering preacher John baptized him in the River Jordan (p. 380). Jesus did not become one of John's disciples, but rather retreated into the desert for 40 days. Here, he fought off the temptations of the devil (p. 350). Jesus returned convinced of his divine mission. He chose disciples in Galilee and began to preach. Thereby he sought out the simple populace and social outcasts.

Jesus' Baptism During Jesus' baptism in the River Jordan by John, the heavens opened up and the Holy Spirit descended in the form of a dove (**2**) as a voice spoke: "You are my son, the Beloved; with you I am well pleased"

(p. 380). In the Gospels, John the Baptist believed he would only prepare the way for Jesus. In the Gospel of John, he pointed to Jesus and declared: "Here is the Lamb of God who takes away the sins of the world" (**1**).

The Messiah

The hope for the Messiah (Hebrew: "the anointed") in Judaism is substantiated by the prophesied Messiah-King from the House of David (p. 220). As this desire remained unfulfilled, the Israelites awaited the Messiah as a savior and bringer of the end of days sent by God. Another aspect of this Messiah was understood as being more secular, for instance, as the liberator of the Jews from Roman dominion. All of the expectations of the Messiah from the Old Testament run together in the New Testament. The portrait of Jesus in the Gospels unifies the figures of king, prophet, and priest. In the Greek translation, the title of the Messiah ("Christus") became another name for Jesus. This fact points toward the vitality of the Messianic anticipation that thrived in Palestine at this historical turning point.

≫ References to Jesus in the Old Testament: p. 319   **Anointment:** p. 196

Figures and Stories Relevant to Jesus

God, see pp. 28–33

David, see pp. 216–221

John the Baptist, see pp. 378–381

Mary, see pp. 386–389

Joseph, see pp. 392–393

Matthew, Mark, Luke, John, see the Evangelists, pp. 430–433

The Holy Spirit, see pp. 466–467

p.419 »

Jesus and the Children According to the first three Gospels, Jesus' preaching was directed mainly at the simple folk, and also at children. Mark and Luke report that the disciples prevented a group of children from approaching Jesus. However, Jesus called them to him and blessed them (**3**). He encouraged his disciples to accept the Kingdom of God with the humility of a child. This was later used as an argument for the baptism of children.

Zacchaeus In order to see Jesus as he entered Jericho, the short tax-official Zacchaeus climbed a tree (**4**). Tax-officials were hated for levying excessive amounts on people. Thus Jesus faced outrage when he visited Zacchaeus' house. However, he converted Zacchaeus, and the tax-official repaid what he had falsely exacted many times over.

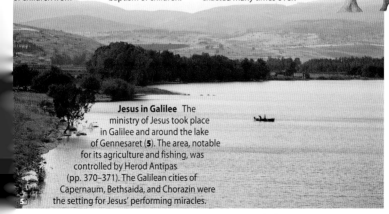

Jesus in Galilee The ministry of Jesus took place in Galilee and around the lake of Gennesaret (**5**). The area, notable for its agriculture and fishing, was controlled by Herod Antipas (pp. 370–371). The Galilean cities of Capernaum, Bethsaida, and Chorazin were the setting for Jesus' performing miracles.

Miracles and Healing

The New Testament reports on about 30 miracles performed by Jesus, including the healing of the sick, natural wonders, exorcism of demons, and the waking of the dead. They are not to be understood in terms of natural science, but rather in terms of theology. Biblical tales of miracles are stories of faith and therefore signs of the coming Kingdom of God. They are not meant to be proofs of faith in Jesus Christ, but rather presuppose faith in him. Therefore, they stand in the ancient tradition in which miracles are understood as extraordinary occurrences that point to the workings of higher powers. The ways in which these miracles are described are founded as much upon Hellenistic-Greek motives as on Old Testament-Jewish writings.

At a sermon by Jesus, his throng of listeners grew hungry. Jesus took some bread and fish and blessed them so that over 5,000 people could feast on them and be full.

The Healing of a Blind Man
Jesus healed a blind beggar in Jericho. At first, the man could not get close to Jesus due to the mass of people. When he cried "Jesus, son of David, have mercy on me!" he was healed because of his faith in Jesus. Afterward, he stood up and followed Jesus (**1**).

Through the exorcism of demons, Jesus brought some people back to their original state

The Wedding at Cana

According to John, Jesus performed his first miracle at a wedding in Cana, which he went to with his mother. When the wine had run out, Jesus had six jugs filled with water (**2**). When the cellarmaster took a sip, the water had turned into wine. The Gospel of John closely links the life of Jesus with the resurrected Christ. In this sense, the miracle of the wine is the first sign of his divinity.

The Healing of the Lame Once Jesus entered into a house, some people wanted to bring a man on a stretcher to him to be healed. As a crowd of people was blocking the entrance, they took him to the roof, dislodged some of the bricks, and lowered him down to Jesus (**3**). When Jesus saw the faith of the lame man, he spoke an absolution for his sins. The scribes and Pharisees saw this as a blasphemous act and said: "Who can forgive sins but God alone?" Then the lame man stood up and walked.

Calming of the Storm One evening, Jesus sailed with his disciples over the lake at Gennesaret. Even though a storm raged and the waves grew higher (**4**), Jesus slept soundly in the rear of the boat. Fearing for their lives, the disciples awoke him and Jesus brought the storm to a standstill. Jesus scolded his disciples for their lack of faith and told them that in future situations they should have less fear and more faith in God.

⟐ **Prophetic Healing:** p. 307

Parables

In his preaching to the people, Jesus often employed parables, as they could present complex
ideas through simple images. The images Jesus
used derived mainly from nature, the surroundings, and the everyday life of his home in Galilee,
such as the parables of the sower, of the mustard
seed, or of the treasure in the field. Along with this,
metaphors from the Jewish tradition played a very
large role: father, king, shepherd, and host as representations of God, the vine as the picture of Israel,
the harvest for the Last Judgment, or a wedding
feast for an imminent time of peace. All of Jesus'
parables were the same in the sense that they
all refer to the coming Kingdom
of God.

*Jesus compares faith with a mustard
seed: Something great can grow out
of something small.*

Lost Sheep

When criti-
cized for asso-
ciating with
sinners, Jesus
used the
parable of the
lost sheep (**1**)
(Luke 15:1–7):
A good shep-
herd is pre-
pared to
leave his
flock in jeopardy in order to
rescue one lost sheep. God is far
more pleased with a repentant
sinner than with a
group of already right-
eous people.

The image
of the good
shepherd
resurfaces in
the New Testa-
ment. A shep-
herd's crook (**3**)
is the symbol of
a bishop, who is
supposed to
look after
fellow Christi-
ans as a
3 shepherd.

The Prodigal Son Luke
15:11–32 tells of a man and his
son. The son has his inheritance
paid out to him and wastes
everything that he has. When
he returns, his father forgives
him and takes him in again
(**2**). God is ready to re-accept
anyone showing remorse in
the same way (p. 32).

» **Representations of God:** p. 32

The Good Samaritan The most well known parable in the New Testament (Luke 10:25–37) tells of a man who is ambushed and mugged in the desert. A priest and a Levite passed by him without doing anything. Then a Samaritan came along who tended to the attacked man's wounds (**5**) and found him lodging. The parable is an example of how an outsider helps while those who would be expected to do something fail. This parable is also appreciated by those who are not religious due to its moral content.

The Wise and the Foolish Bridesmaids Matthew 25:1–13 tells of ten bridesmaids who go to meet the bridegroom before the wedding. The wise bridesmaids took extra oil for their lamps (**7**). As the bridegroom was late, their lamps went out. While the foolish bridesmaids were out buying more oil for their lamps, the bridegroom arrived and took the wise bridesmaids into the wedding (**6**). When the foolish bridesmaids returned, they found the door shut. Thus humans should be ready for the coming of the Kingdom of God like the wise bridesmaids.

The Samaritans

The Samaritans were shunned by devout Jews as a mixed Jewish-gentile race. The Samaritans only consider the five books of Moses, the Torah, to be sacred and accepted Moses as their prophet. As they were not allowed to assist with the re-building of the Temple in Jerusalem after the Babylonian captivity, they built their own place of worship on Mt. Gerizim. They celebrate their own holidays at this site, according to their own calendar, to this day. This background makes it clear just how controversial Jesus' parable of the good Samaritan must have been: Jesus presented the story to his Jewish listeners using a member of a group despised for its religion as an ethical model for behavior.

Sermon on the Mount

The Sermon on the Mount is at the heart of Matthew's Gospel (chapters 5–7). As mountains were associated with closeness to God in the Bible, Matthew chose a mountain (**3**) as a site for a proclamation by Jesus (**4**). In this way, it is reminiscent of Mount Sinai and the revelation of Moses. The Sermon on the Mount is not an actual discourse by Jesus, but rather a collection of the various things he had said. It begins with the blessing of the poor in spirit (pp. 412–413), in which people oriented to a particular set of values are promised the Kingdom of God. The Beatitudes followed metaphors and counter-propositions ("antitheses") as examples of correct behavior. Jesus' prayer the "Our Father" (**2**) stands in connection with three warnings on true piety. The Sermon on the Mount has been interpreted in many ways over the years. Today, most theologians believe that Jesus did not want to devalue the laws of Moses, but rather sought to bring them back to their original worth.

①

Our Father The "Our Father" is the most important prayer (**1**) in Christianity. It is the only prayer that Jesus taught his disciples. Matthew presents it in a longer form than in Luke's Gospel. The personal address, "Our Father," stands in Jewish tradition. The coming of the Kingdom of God is expressed in the use of "your." Prayers with "we pray" articulate the everyday cares of those praying. The (later devised) closing "For thine is the kingdom…" expresses the closeness of God.

②

③

≫ **God Gives Moses His Commandments:** pp. 121–122   **The Ten Commandments:** pp. 126–127

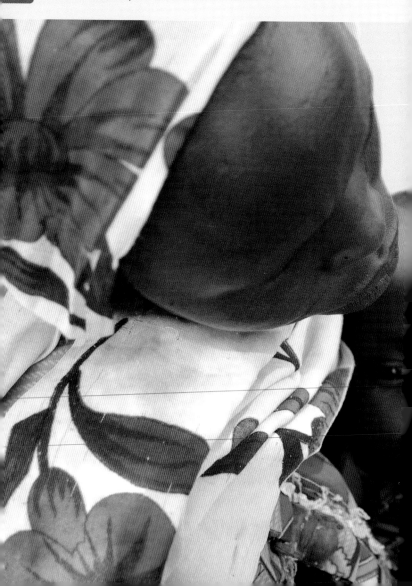

The Beatitudes

Matthew 5:1–12

1 *When Jesus saw the crowds, he went up the mountain; and after he sat down, his disciples came to him.* 2 *Then he began to speak, and taught them, saying:* 3 *"Blessed are the poor in spirit, for theirs is the kingdom of heaven.* 4 *Blessed are those who mourn, for they will be comforted.* 5 *Blessed are the meek, for they will inherit the earth.* 6 *Blessed are those who hunger and thirst for righteousness, for they will be filled.* 7 *Blessed are the merciful, for they will receive mercy.* 8 *Blessed are the pure in heart, for they will see God.* 9 *Blessed are the peacemakers, for they will be called children of God.* 10 *Blessed are those who are persecuted for righteousness' sake, for theirs is the kingdom of heaven.* 11 *Blessed are you when people revile you and persecute you and utter all kinds of evil against you falsely on my account.* 12 *Rejoice and be glad, for your reward is great in heaven, for in the same way they persecuted the prophets who were before you."*

« p.402

■ Jesus was a faithful Jew

■ Jesus saw himself as a prophet

Matthew 21:12–17; Mark 11:15–19; Luke 19:45–48; John 2:13–16 Jesus casts the moneylenders out of the Temple

Luke 22:7–23 Jesus has a final meal with his disciples

Matthew 26:47–56; Mark 14:43–52; Luke 22:47–53; John 18:1–11 Jesus is betrayed by Judas and taken prisoner in the garden of Gethsemane

Matthew 27:1–14; Mark 15:1–5; Luke 23:1–5; John 18:28–40 Jesus is brought before the governor Pontius Pilate and sentenced to death

Matthew 27:31–56; Mark 15:21–41; Luke 23:32–49; John 19:17–37 Jesus' Crucifixion

Matthew 28:1–15; Mark 16:1–18; Luke 24:1–49; John 21:1–14 The resurrected Jesus appears to the disciples

Mark 16:19–20; Luke 24:50–53 Jesus' ascension

Jesus in Jerusalem

Even though Jesus' ministry was mainly concentrated around Galilee, he reached his pinnacle and his end in Jerusalem. It was here that he had confrontations with the Jewish religious leaders

When Jesus entered Jerusalem, he was received like a king

and the Roman occupying power. Jesus came to Jerusalem with his supporters for a great pilgrimage festival, which took place every year for Passover. He arrived in the city from the Mount of Olives like a king, riding on a donkey. This corresponds to the words of the prophet Zechariah in Zechariah 9:9: "O daughter Zion! … Lo, your king comes to you; triumphant and victorious is he, humble and riding on a donkey." His purification of the Temple was also a prophetic sign: When Jesus saw the merchants and moneylenders in the Temple's court, he pushed their tables over, as they were desecrating the house of God (**1**).

①

»» **References to Jesus in the Old Testament:** p. 319

The Last Supper Shortly before his death, Jesus celebrated a final meal with his disciples (**2**), which is described in the first three Gospels as a Passover meal. The festive meal, at which the tale of the liberation from Egypt is retold, is the opening and also the highpoint of Passover. With his words, "This is my body, this is my blood," Jesus symbolically indicated the bread and wine at the feast as his own flesh and blood. This acted as a proclamation of his forthcoming death. As the Second Coming of Jesus would be delayed, the Apostle Paul added the supplement: "Do this in remembrance of me."

The Supper

The biblical supper, known as the Eucharist (Greek: "saying of thanks"), was an important liturgical celebration for the early Christians. Since the Reformation, the Eucharist has been regarded by both Catholics and Protestants. However, due to theological issues concerning the station of the priest, there is still no common celebration of the Eucharist between them.

Jesus on the Mount of Olives According to the first three Evangelists, Jesus went to pray on the Mount of Olives in the garden of Gethsemane (**3**) the night before his Crucifixion. Filled with fear, he implored God to let the cup of his suffering pass from him. This is a theologically significant location, as the visions of the prophets Ezekiel and Zechariah saw the Messiah coming into Jerusalem from the Mount of Olives to establish the rule of God. Jesus on the Mount of Olives has two sides. When he speaks of the destruction of the Temple, he appears as the Messiah. On the other hand, his prayer displays his humanity.

⊃ **Passover:** pp. 118–119

The Crown of Thorns In the Gospels of Mark, Matthew, and John, the Roman soldiers mocked

Jesus as the false "King of the Jews." They placed a crown of thorns (**1**) on his head and covered him in a purple robe, a color normally reserved for those of high bearing. The crown of thorns acted above all as a parody of a king's crown. The thorns possibly came from a plant later known as "Christ Plant," which grows long, pointed barbs.

Capture and Sentencing

The Jewish Temple guard captured Jesus in the Garden of Gethsemane, beyond the Kidron Valley east of Jerusalem. Judas, one of the 12 disciples, greeted Jesus with the exclamation "Rabbi!" and kissed him. He had agreed upon this sign with the guards (p. 439), who grabbed Jesus and led him away (**2**). Jesus was taken to an interrogation in front of the High Council, the highest Jewish court in the palace of the high priests in the upper city of Jerusalem. At first, they found no reason for conviction (pp. 462–463); however, when Jesus said that he could tear down the Temple and build it again in three days, and, moreover, answered that he was indeed the Messiah, the High Council accused him of blasphemy. As the High Council was not allowed to impose a death sentence, it referred Jesus to the governor Pontius Pilate. Jesus said little during this trial and he was sentenced to death (pp. 460–461).

▷▷ **The Romans:** pp. 372–373 **The High Council:** p. 463

The Flagellation of Jesus

Jesus was flagellated before his Crucifixion (**4**). Such flagellation, which usually did not lead to death, was used to punish slaves. The Romans employed it as a means of torture or as a supplementary punishment for crucifixion. It was implemented with bundled straps, which were fastened with pieces of bone or lead. The condemned were tied to a column and whipped. The Gospel of Mark interprets Jesus' castigation as the redemptive suffering of the servant of God foreseen by Isaiah.

Jesus Before Pilate

Jesus' ultimate death sentence was made by Pontius Pilate (**3**). At the trial, the Evangelists describe Pilate as being conflicted. While he did sentence Jesus to death, he, according to the Gospel of Matthew, washed his hands of guilt and passed responsibility to the Jewish authorities. In the Gospel of John, Pilate poses the famous question "What is truth?"

Stations of the Cross

The Stations of the Cross were introduced by the Franciscans in the 14th century. Since then, a procession has wound through the Via Dolorosa (Latin: "way of sorrow") in Jerusalem (**6**) every Friday. Along the route, which leads from the residence of Pontius Pilate to Mount Golgotha, Jesus' suffering is recalled (**5**).

⧉ **The Passion of Jesus:** pp. 420–421

Death and Resurrection

According to the Gospels, Jesus was crucified as a political agitator by the Romans, possibly on April 7th in 30 C.E. He probably hung on the post naked during this agonizing punishment, which was usually reserved for political criminals. His hands and feet were bound to the wood with rope or nails and a tablet was positioned on the top of the Cross, which specified the crime of the condemned. Jesus' Cross read "I.N.R.I." (**1**) for "Iesus Nazarenus Rex Iudaeorum" (Latin: "Jesus of Nazareth, King of the Jews"). According to the Gospels' reports, Jesus died relatively quickly. Death usually occurred after several days through the breakdown of the bodily functions. The burial of Jesus' corpse by Joseph of Arimathea (pp. 464–465) was an exception: Normally the condemned stayed on the cross until decomposed.

The Resurrection Shortly after his death by Crucifixion (**2**), the Jesus movement, under the leadership of Peter, professed that Jesus had been resurrected from the dead. How the Resurrection actually transpired is not detailed in the New Testament. However, what is reported is that a special event gave the disciples certainty that Jesus had returned to them. "Cross" and "revival" stand for two separate levels of reality. While "died" is historically verifiable, "resurrected" is a statement of faith. In the formulation "God revived him on the third day," the faith of Easter is a statement about God and his power to conquer death (pp. 426–427).

» **Resurrection:** pp. 424–425 **Easter:** pp. 426–427

Ascension After the death and Resurrection of Jesus, the story of his ascension to heaven in the Gospel of Luke depicts his visible departure. Jesus took his disciples to Bethany near the Mount of Olives. He was taken up to heaven as he blessed them (**3**). In the stories of the Apostles, Jesus was taken up by a cloud, and two men in white garments explained this occurrence to the disciples. It could be said that Luke played on the Old Testament story of the ascension of the prophet Elijah (p. 309) in both of his accounts of Jesus' Ascension. On the other hand, he told the story in a way similar to how the Greek and Roman authors described the apotheoses (deifications) of their heroes.

Figures and Stories Relevant to Jesus

God, see pp. 28–33

Angels, see pp. 42–43

Matthew, Mark, Luke, John, see The Evangelists, pp. 430–433

Judas Iscariot, see pp. 438–439

Jesus' Disciples, see the Apostles, pp. 442–449

Jesus' Female Disciples, see Mary Magdalene, pp. 436–437

Peter, see pp. 450–453

Nicodemus, see pp. 456–457

Pontius Pilate, see pp. 460–461

High Priests, see Annas and Caiaphas, pp. 462–463

Joseph of Arimathea, see pp. 464–465

≪ p.405

Jesus' Tomb Jesus' corpse was allegedly set in a tomb near the site of his Crucifixion in Golgotha. Today, the Church of the Holy Sepulcher stands at this place (**4**). When women came to Jesus' tomb some days later, they found it empty. Angels announced the Easter message to them that Jesus had risen.

The Symbol of the Cross

The Cross, as an instrument for a style of execution, is a shocking reality. As Jesus' death by Crucifixion cannot be separated in Christian faith from his Resurrection, the Cross underwent a change in meaning to a symbol of Christian faith. As a sign of hope it has become widespread in art and culture across the globe.

Crosses are found by the sides of roads, on church towers, and on mountain summits, as well as on jewelry chains. The horizontal one of the two beams of the Cross is often seen as a symbol for unity among humans, whereas the vertical represents humankind's relationship to God.

≫ **Ascension:** pp. 428–429

The Passion of Jesus

Stories of Jesus' Passion are the oldest part of the New Testament. The central beliefs of the death and Resurrection of Jesus were in circulation predominantly among the first Christians. They formed the basis of the Gospels, which were written later. The Gospel of Mark, considered the oldest Gospel by most scholars, was known as "The Passion with an extended introduction."

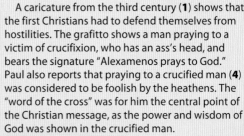

A caricature from the third century (**1**) shows that the first Christians had to defend themselves from hostilities. The grafitto shows a man praying to a victim of crucifixion, who has an ass's head, and bears the signature "Alexamenos prays to God." Paul also reports that praying to a crucified man (**4**) was considered to be foolish by the heathens. The "word of the cross" was for him the central point of the Christian message, as the power and wisdom of God was shown in the crucified man.

Passion Rituals In Spain and the Philippines, there is a tradition of holding Passion rituals during Holy Week. Self-castigations and staged crucifixions (**3**) draw in thousands of spectators each year. Participants take part in the ritualized visualization of Christ's suffering (**2**) in order to fulfill a vow. As humanity has already been redeemed through the suffering of Christ, the Passion rituals have no biblical foundation. Today the medial staging of human suffering is at the forefront.

>> The Early Christians: pp. 480–481

4

 423

Jesus' Last Words

1. *Then Jesus said, "Father, forgive them; for they do not know what they are doing." (Luke 23:34)*

2. *"Truly I tell you, today you will be with me in Paradise." (Luke 23:43)*

3. *"Woman, here is your son." / "Here is your mother." (John 19:26–27)*

4. *"My God, my God, why have you forsaken me?" (Mark 15:34)*

5. *"I am thirsty." (John 19:28)*

6. *"It is finished." (John 19:30)*

7. *"Father, into your hands I commend my spirit." (Luke 23:46)*

The Resurrection

Belief in the Resurrection is central to Christian faith. Its significance is based on the fact that the Resurrection of Jesus (**1**) is understood in anticipation of the Resurrection of all humankind. This faith has its origins in the avowals of the first Christians.

After Jesus' death on the Cross, the Gospel movement initially seemed to have failed. However, it was bound together by the belief in the resurrected Jesus. With his Resurrection, Jesus became an object of proclamation. Today, faith in the Resurrection is a special challenge, particularly from an intellectual point of view, as it demands a personal willingness to be devotedly engaged with an intangible reality.

Resurrection of the Dead
The Resurrection of Jesus is associated with the resurrection of all dead people on Doomsday, the day of Christ's second coming when he will judge humanity as the savior of the world (Latin: salvator mundi) and establish an eternal kingdom of peace (**4**). One image, which is rooted in Ezekiel's visions in the Old Testament, describes how the dead will rise from their graves.

Women at the Tomb On Easter morning, women came to Jesus' tomb and saw that the stone had been rolled away. They went inside and met an angel (**3**), who said that Jesus had risen (p. 437).

The Tomb of Jesus At the time of Jesus, it was common in Palestine to be housed inside a cave (**2**). These caves had several rooms with niches in the walls to place the dead. They were closed by large stones, which could be rolled along furrows in the ground.

>> **The Death and Resurrection of Jesus:** pp. 418–419 **Parable of the Boneyard:** pp. 328–329

4

Easter

As the celebration of the Resurrection of Jesus, Easter is the most important holy day in Christianity. It follows the Holy Week, during which time the Passion of Jesus is contemplated (**3**). As Jesus woke on the first day of this week, Easter is celebrated on a Sunday. Catholic and Orthodox Christians begin their Easter services with the Easter Vigil, as the New Testament reports that the Resurrection occurred in the early morning. Then the Easter candles are lit by the Easter fire and people call out: "Christ, the light."

The holiday is closely linked with the Jewish festival of Passover because Jesus was in Jerusalem for Passover when he was arrested. According to the Gospel of John, Jesus was killed simultaneously with the Passover lambs in the Temple, which refers to a symbolic representation of Jesus, called "the lamb of God" by John the Baptist, who carries the sins of the world (p. 379). Passover and Easter are both festivals of liberation: just as Jews celebrate God's liberation of the enslaved Israelites from Egypt on Passover, Christians contemplate their freedom from death through the Resurrection of Jesus.

Eggs are traditionally given at Easter, which are painted with ornamental or Christian motifs (**1**). Another tradition is the Easter Laugh (Latin: risus paschalis), which expresses joy at the Easter miracle.

Passover: pp. 118–119

Religious Festivals

Easter Lamb The Easter lamb is a symbol for the resurrected Christ in much of Christian art, as he was viewed as the new Passover lamb. In many depictions, its blood is poured into a chalice as a symbol of Jesus' Crucifixion and of the sacrament of the Last Supper. In memory of his victory over death, the lamb is often shown with a flag bearing a cross. This led to the custom of making a lamb from sweet baked dough (**2**) to be eaten after the fast of Lent.

The Ascension

In the New Testament, the Evangelist Luke narrates the ascension of Jesus to heaven, at the end of his Gospel and the beginning of his Acts of the Apostles. In the first version, Jesus led his disciples to Bethany on the Mount of Olives opposite Jerusalem (**3**). When they got there, he raised his hands up and while blessing them, was taken up to heaven (**1**). The disciples returned to Jerusalem full of joy and went into the Temple. In Acts, the Ascension occurs 40 days after the Resurrection. Two angels explained to the disciples that Jesus would soon return (**4**). This portrayal tries to show that Jesus fulfills the Old Testament prophecies of Zechariah (p. 333), according to which the Mount of Olives will be the place where the feet of the Lord will stand at the end of days (Zechariah 14:4). In the Chapel of the Ascension on the Mount of Olives, footprints can be seen to this day, which were supposedly left by Jesus when he ascended to heaven (**2**). As the Qur'an also reports on the ascension of Jesus, the Chapel of the Ascension is as much a sacred site for Muslims as it is for Christians.

1

2

3

>> **References to Jesus in the Old Testament:** p. 319

■ The four Gospels report on the life of Jesus

■ The Evangelists have individual symbols: a human for Matthew, the lion for Mark, the bull for Luke, and the eagle for John

■ The liturgical book of the Gospels is sometimes called the evangelistary

Ezekiel 1:10 The visions of the prophet Ezekiel are the guidelines for the Evangelist symbols

Matthew 1:1; Mark1:1; Luke 1:1–4 The Evangelists understand themselves as being biographers for Jesus

Matthew 1:1 The Gospel of Matthew is strongly marked as Judeo-Christian, as he introduces Jesus as the son of David

Mark 4 The Gospel of Mark contains many parables

Luke 1:1–4 The Evangelist Luke thinks of himself as a historian

John 1:29–34 John emphasizes that Jesus was simultaneously human and the Son of God

The beginning of the good news of Jesus Christ, the Son of God.
Mark 1:1

The Evangelists

The term Gospel or "god-spell" is an Old English translation of the Greek word "euangelion," meaning "good news." The Gospels are the first four books of the New Testament, which portray the life and ministry of Jesus. The term for the authors of these texts, the Evangelists, is derived more directly from "euangelion." The Evangelists did not seek to provide historically exact information, but rather a theologically focused biography of Jesus' life.

In spite of this, the main features of his message and the years of his ministry can be reconstructed from the Gospels. The Gospels are named according to their authors: Matthew, Mark, Luke, and John. In the early Church, it was assumed that the Gospels were written by some of Jesus' disciples as eyewitness reports of the Crucifixion and the Resurrrection.

Gospel Readings Two or three biblical readings are usually presented during Christian services (2). After a reading from the Old or New Testament, an extract is read from the Gospels. On special occasions, verses are read from Gospel editions adorned with jewels (1).

The Evangelist Symbols The early Christian theologian and church father Jerome assigned four symbols to the Evangelists in the fourth century C.E., which have since been utilized frequently in artistic depictions of the Evangelists (**3**). As the Gospel of Matthew starts with a detailed description of Jesus' human lineage, his symbol is a man. The Gospel of Mark begins with a description of John the Baptist as the "roarer in the desert," and so he received the symbol of a lion. The Gospel of Luke opens with the sacrifice of the aged Zechariah in the Temple, which is typified by a bull. The patterns of thought in the Gospel of John can be described as flights of spirituality and so are represented by the eagle. These four figures, which originally derived from images of God's glory in a vision of the prophet Ezekiel (p. 325), can also be seen as symbols for Jesus' incarnation, sacrificial death, Resurrection, and Ascension. The symbolism of Ezekiel was taken up again in the Revelation of John 4:6–8: Four beings in the forms of a lion, a bull, a man, and an eagle sit around the heavenly throne worshiping the Lord.

3

Animals in the Bible: p. 140

Today's scholars think that the story of Jesus' story was initially transmitted orally and later transcribed. The names of the Evangelists were added in the second century during the compilation of the New Testament. The first three Gospels are known as the synoptic Gospels (p. 503).

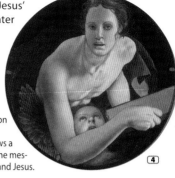

Matthew The Gospel of Matthew (**4**) was authored around 80 C.E. It has a distinct Judeo-Christian leaning and presents Jesus as the son of David and the Messiah of Israel (p. 404). The account of the Sermon on the Mount (pp. 410–411) draws a parallel between the message of the Torah and Jesus.

Mark The Gospel of Mark was written after 70 C.E. during the Roman destruction of the Temple of Jerusalem (p. 373). The Gospel is directed towards a gentile-Christian readership, which is shown by the emphasizing of gentile figures, such as the possessed man from Gerasenes and the captain of Capernaum, to whom Jesus revealed himself as the Son of God. Some attention is given to Jesus' parables, such as the comparison between the Kingdom of God and a mustard seed (pp. 408–409). Mark emphasized the stories of Jesus' miracles, such as the healing of the possessed or sick, the calming of the storm on the lake, or the feeding of the five thousand, show Jesus at the height of his power and glory (pp. 406–407). Mark's lion later became the heraldic animal for the city of Venice (**5**).

Coptic Christians

The Coptic Church of Egypt traces its origins to the Evangelist Mark. He is supposed to have traveled to Alexandria with the Egyptians, who witnessed the Pentecost miracle, and founded the Coptic Church. Mark supposedly had a martyr's death in Alexandria around 68 C.E. The current Coptic patriarch, Pope Shenouda III, is considered to be the 117th successor of Mark. Since the Council of Chalcedon in 451, the Coptics have asserted that Jesus had one nature as entirely divine.

▷▷ Judeo-Christians and Pagan-Christians: pp. 501 and 502

Luke An old legend states that Luke was a painter (**6**). This is true in the metaphorical sense, as Luke "painted" masterful texts with biblical motifs. Around 80 C.E., he wrote his two volumes: his Gospel, which tells the biography of Jesus as a history of salvation, and his book of Acts, which describes the early history of the Church. Both are directed at a predominantly Hellenistic readership. Luke saw himself as a historian, as he was well-versed in the works of classical historians.

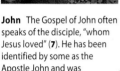

John The Gospel of John often speaks of the disciple, "whom Jesus loved" (**7**). He has been identified by some as the Apostle John and was credited as being the author of this Gospel until as late as the second century C.E. He was supposed to have written it at the end of the first century in Asia Minor; however, this has been widely disputed. It is accepted that the Gospel was written around 90 C.E. The Gospel of John was obviously written during a time of sharp conflict between Jews and Judeo-Christians, as is shown in the polemic use of "Jews" to describe those hostile to Christianity. Nevertheless, the Gospel still has strong Jewish influences, and thus could have stemmed from Judeo-Christian circles. John depicts Jesus as the Son of God more explicitly than the other Gospels. Jesus reveals himself as the Son sent by God while his miracles are proofs of his magnificence. He is identified above all as the Son, who completes his task according to the will of God.

Icons

A tradition of painting icons developed in eastern churches from a legend that the Evangelist Luke painted a portrait of Mary. The icons are intended to create a spiritual connection between the observer and the figure represented.

■ Mary and Martha were Lazarus' sisters and friends of Jesus

■ Mary and Martha were symbolic female archetypes

■ Lazarus was brought back to life by Jesus, even though he had been dead for four days

Luke 10:38–42 When Jesus visits Mary and Martha, Mary listens to him, while Martha fulfills the role of the hostess

John 11:1–2 Mary anoints Jesus' feet

John 11:32–45 Jesus reawakens the dead Lazarus, the brother of Martha and Mary

Jesus said to her, "I am the resurrection and the life. Those who believe in me, even though they die, will live." John 11:25

Lazarus, Mary, and Martha

The sisters of Lazarus, Mary and Martha, lived in Bethany on the edge of the Mount of Olives in front of the gates of Jerusalem. According to the Gospel of John, Jesus loved all three siblings, the eldest of which was Martha. It was also to Martha that Jesus directed the words that present a quintessence for the whole story of the resurrection of Lazarus: "I am the resurrection and the life." Mary is portrayed as being highly emotional. She fell at Jesus' feet and wept, but she also expresses her faith: if Jesus had been there earlier, Lazarus would have survived. Jesus also cried by Lazarus' tomb (**1**).

Mary and Martha In the Gospel of Luke, Jesus visited the sisters Mary and Martha in Bethany. Mary listened to Jesus, while Martha acted as hostess (**2**). When Martha complained to Jesus that Mary was not helping her, Jesus defended her, as she had chosen "the better part." In the Gospel of John, Mary anointed Jesus' feet with nard oil. This is often seen as Jesus' symbolic anointment as the king of the Jews before his entrance into Jerusalem.

⏩ **The Miracles of Jesus:** pp. 406–407

Resurrection of Lazarus

The Gospel of John tells how Lazarus, the brother of Mary and Martha, was suffering from a serious illness. The sisters called for Jesus, but when he arrived Lazarus had already been dead for four days. However, Jesus awoke Lazarus and he stepped out of his tomb, still wrapped in burial cloth (**3**). The resurrection of Lazarus is the greatest miracle that Jesus performs in the New Testament. The pivotal point from a theological perspective is expressed in Jesus' words to Martha: He was both the resurrection and the life.

> *Figures and Stories Relevant to Lazarus, Mary, and Martha*
>
> **God**, see pp. 28–33
>
> **Jesus of Nazareth**, see pp. 402–409 and 414–419
>
> **The Evangelists**, see pp. 430–433
>
> **The Resurrection**, see pp. 424–425

Mary and Martha as Role Models

In later interpretations, Martha and Mary are viewed typologically. In the third century C.E., the Church author Origen compared the roles of Martha with the "active life" (Latin: vita activa) and Mary's with the "contemplative life" (Latin: vita contemplativa). While the mystic Meister Eckhart attributed a closeness to God to the lifestyle of Martha, the Reformation movement criticized Martha's behavior in an attempt to justify herself with her actions. In terms of cloister life, there is still a difference between active and contemplative orders.

⟩ Jesus and Women: p. 436

■ Mary Magdalene was one of Jesus' disciples

■ Mary Magdalene was an affluent woman, who financially supported Jesus

■ Jesus appeared to Mary Magdalene after the Resurrection

Luke 7:36–50 A female sinner, later named as Mary Magdalene, anoints Jesus' feet

Luke 8:2 Mary Magdalene is healed by spirits

John 19:25 Mary Magdalene stands with Mary, the mother of Jesus, at the Cross

John 20:11–18 The resurrected Jesus appears to Mary Magdalene

After the sabbath, as the first day of the week was dawning, Mary Magdalene and the other Mary went to see the tomb. Matthew 28:1

Mary Magdalene

Seven women in the New Testament bear the common forename of Mary (Hebrew: Mirjam). The sobriquet "Magdelene" is a reference to Mary's origin from the town of Magdala, which lay on the west coast of the lake of Gennesaret. She was a wealthy woman in the circle of Jesus' most trusted disciples. As she has been associated with the woman who anointed Jesus, she is usually depicted with an ointment (**1**). Luke states that she was already associated with Jesus in Galilee, whereas she is not mentioned in the other Gospels until Jesus' death. In the Gospel of John, she stands at the Cross next to Jesus' mother, with Mary, the wife of Clopas, and Jesus' favorite disciple. It is also significant that Mary Magdalene was one of the women who were the first witnesses to Jesus' Resurrection.

Jesus and Women

In the New Testament, Jesus does not treat women as subordinates like the majority of his contemporaries. The Gospel of Luke explains that women such as Johanna, Susanna, Mary, the mother of James and John, and Mary Magdalene were female disciples—a part of Jesus' ministry and companions on his journey. Other affluent women were also mentioned as supporting Jesus and spreading the Gospel. The Epistles state that women were colleagues in the commune.

Mary Magdalene as a Sinner In the Christian tradition, Mary Magdalene is often identified with the figure of the sinner who dried Jesus' feet with her hair as reported by Luke (**3**). This led to the erroneous idea that Mary Magdalene converted to Jesus after a life of sexual debauchery and thereafter led a life of repentance.

Noli Me Tangere According to the first three Gospels, Mary Magdalene and other women arrived at Jesus' tomb, where an angel appeared to them and announced the Easter message (**2**). In the Gospel of John, Mary Magdalene first went alone to the grave on Easter morning. When she found it open, she summoned Peter and Jesus' favorite disciple. After they had left, Mary Magdalene stayed there alone and cried, and then two angels appeared. Jesus appeared, but she thought it was the gardener. When she later recognized him, Jesus forbade her to hold him (**4**)—which was later translated as "not to touch" under the initial Latin translation ("noli me tangere"). Mary Magdalene immediately conveyed the Easter message to the disciples and thus became the first proclaimer of the Resurrection.

> *Figures and Stories Relevant to Mary Magdalene*
>
> Angels, see pp. 42–43
>
> Jesus of Nazareth, see pp. 402–409 and 414–419
>
> The Evangelists, see pp. 430–433
>
> The Disciples of Jesus, see the Apostles, pp. 442–447
>
> Peter, see pp. 450–453

The Resurrection: pp. 424–425   **Easter:** pp. 426–427

■ Judas betrayed Jesus to the high priests and scribes

■ Jesus was betrayed by Judas in the Gospels of Matthew, Mark, and Luke; however, according to John, Jesus implicated himself

Matthew 26:14–50; Mark 14:10–46; Luke 22:2–48 Jesus is betrayed by Judas in the Garden of Gethsemane

Matthew 26:15; Mark 14:11; Luke 22:5 Judas gets money from the high priests

Matthew 27:3–5 Judas commits suicide

Judas, is it with a kiss that you are betraying the Son of Man?

Luke 22:48

Judas Iscariot

Judas, one of the 12 disciples, carries the sobriquet "Iscariot" that might be a reference to the city of Karioth, which was a center for radical zealots who fought against the Roman occupation (p. 446). This leant credence to the theory that Judas himself was a zealot, who became disillusioned, as Jesus had not proven himself to be the Messiah in terms of a political liberator, and so sold him to the high priests for money (**1**,**2**).

Judas is usually known as a "betrayer." The New Testament itself speaks of the "delivery." This expression makes the historically and theologically problematic figure of Judas apparent: God saved the world by delivering his son to his death, but this was simultaneously the free action of a human.

>> Jesus as the Messiah: p. 404

Kiss of Judas Before his Crucifixion, Jesus prayed in the Garden of Gethsemane (pp. 415–416). Judas delivered Jesus to the high priests' guards in this garden. The Gospel of Mark attests that greed for money was not his primary motive, as the authorities promised Judas a reward only after he had decided to hand over Jesus. The threat made against Judas—"It would have been better for humankind if he had never been born"—reserves judgment for God. Ultimately, Jesus' suffering and death corresponded to God's will. Only the first three Gospels speak of Judas' kiss (**3**). He reproduces a motif from the Old Testament and reflected the possibility of betrayal among friends. In the Gospel of John, Judas led the guards to Jesus before he implicated himself by answering "It's me" when the guards asked who they were searching for.

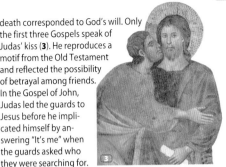

Judas' Death The Gospel of Matthew reports that Judas committed suicide out of despair (**4**). Before doing so, he threw the 30 pieces of silver, which had been his payment, into the Temple. The Gospel of Luke says that Judas died from a fall. The early Christian bishop Papias of Hierapolis further imagined details of Judas' death in the second century: The site where Judas hanged himself became uninhabitable for eternity. Allegedly, no one could walk over this spot without holding their nose.

Figures and Stories Relevant to Judas Iscariot

The Kiss of Judas—Judas Betrays Jesus to His Enemies

Matthew 26:47–50

47 While he was still speaking, Judas, one of the twelve, arrived; with him was a large crowd with swords and clubs, from the chief priests and the elders of the people.

48 Now the betrayer had given them a sign, saying, "The one I will kiss is the man; arrest him."

49 At once he came up to Jesus and said, "Greetings, Rabbi!" and kissed him.

50 Jesus said to him, "Friend, do what you are here to do." Then they came and laid hands on Jesus and arrested him.

■ In the Gospels, the 12 disciples gathered by Jesus were
called as the Apostles

■ The number 12 stands for
the 12 Tribes

**Matthew 4:18–22; Mark
1:16–20; Luke 5:1–11; John
1:35–42** The first disciples
called up by Jesus are fishermen
from Galilee

**Matthew 10:1–4; Mark
3:13–19; Luke 6:12–16** The 12
disciples are given their vocation
by Jesus

John 13:1–20 Jesus washes the
disciples' feet

**Matthew 26:17–30; Mark
14:12–25; Luke 22:7–38; John
13:21–30** The Last Supper

Luke 24:36–49 Jesus appears
to two disciples in Emmaus

John 20:24–31 Thomas doubts
Jesus' Resurrection

Acts 8:26–40 The deacon
Phillip baptizes a high official
from Ethiopia

Luke 6:15 Simon probably
belonged to a group of zealots
before his vocation

Revelation 21:14 The 12
stones of the wall of the New
Jerusalem are designated by
the Apostles

*And Jesus said to them, "Follow me and I will make you fish for
people."* Mark 1:17

The Apostles

Initially, the Apostles (Greek: "the sent") were only
the 12 disciples, who were given their vocation by
Jesus. The first three Gospels report that Jesus selected 12 men from his disciples. He sent them out
in pairs to announce the coming of the Kingdom of
God. These 12 were also his companions. According
to the Gospel of Matthew, Jesus told them to make
all nations their own disciples.

The number 12 has a symbolic significance, as
the 12 Apostles correspond to the 12 Tribes of Israel.
The central importance of the number 12 is shown
in the fact that after Judas' death, Matthias was
voted into the group in his stead. The Gospels do
not use the term "Apostle" as a job title. The Apostles were first and foremost only those men who
Jesus called upon to spread his message. Paul insisted that he should also be considered an Apostle,
as he also had seen the resurrected Christ.

**Vocation of the First
Disciples** At the start of his
public ministry, Jesus collected
a group of supporters. The first
he found were two fishermen
by his home of Galilee by Lake
Gennesaret, Simon (Peter) and
Andrew (**1**). When Jesus asked
them to follow him, they immediately dropped their nets.
Jesus metaphorically said they
were to be fishers of men.

» **The 12 Tribes of Israel:** pp. 162–165

Vocation of Zebedee's Children

The two fishermen James and John were the sons of Zebedee (**2**). As two of Jesus' favorite disciples, they approached Jesus with the request to sit at his right and left sides in the Kingdom of Heaven. They were, along with Peter, witnesses to Jesus' transfiguration. The Gospel of Matthew also mentions that James and John's mother was one of the women who followed Jesus and served him faithfully until his Crucifixion.

Washing of the Feet According to the Gospel of John, Jesus demonstrated his love for his disciples through a symbolic action, when he washed their feet before their last shared meal (**3**). In the ancient Middle East, it was a necessity for the people to wash their feet due to walking barefoot or in sandals along dusty roads. This service was usually undertaken by slaves. By washing the feet of the 12 disciples, Jesus made it clear to them that he understood himself as a servant of humankind. He had given them an example and ideal for their behavior with one another. The washing of the feet also provides an introduction to the Passion: Jesus presented himself, in the vein of the Old Testament, as the servant of humanity, even those on the extremities of society, and died on the Cross for their salvation.

The Last Supper Before his death, Jesus called the 12 together for a final meal (**4**). By breaking bread with them and passing wine, he anticipated his sacrificial death. Just like the earlier meals with customs officials and sinners, this meal referred to the messianic meal at the end of days. Matthew and Luke state that Jesus announced to the 12 in a prophetic fashion that they would take part in his role as the doomsday Messiah. When the world will be created anew, they would sit on 12 thrones and judge the Tribes of Israel.

In the Garden of Gethsemane

After the Last Supper, Jesus went with his disciples to the Garden of Gethsemane on the Mount of Olives (p. 415). At the entrance, Jesus asked the disciples to wait for him, as he wanted to pray alone. Only Peter and Zebedee's sons James and John were allowed to go with him. At this spot, Jesus became gripped with fear and horror. He asked God to let the cup of his suffering pass from him. When he returned, he found the disciples sleeping (**5**). He told them to wake up and pray, but they could not stay awake. The hour of Jesus' deliverance was at hand (p. 416).

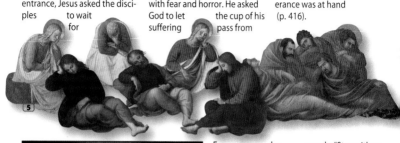

5

6

Emmaus, a nearby village. Deep in discussion, the disciples did not recognize Jesus as he approached them (**7**). Jesus began interpreting the Scriptures and showing how they applied to him as the Messiah. When they arrived at Emmaus, they invited Jesus to stay with them with the words: "Stay with us, because it is almost evening and the day is now nearly over." Jesus went with them, and when he broke bread with them, they recognized their teacher (**6**). Simultaneously, he vanished. They returned to Jerusalem and told the other disciples what they had seen.

Emmaus Disciples

According to the Gospel of Luke, soon after Jesus' Resurrection he appeared to two of his disciples, who were on their way from Jerusalem to

7

>> The Resurrection: pp. 424–425   Easter: pp. 426–427

Doubting Thomas The first three Gospels mention little more than Thomas' name. On the other hand, in the Gospel of John, Thomas, who was referred to as the "twin" (Hebrew: "tehoma") in three places, plays a central role in the Easter story, in which he acts as the archetypical role of the doubter and cynic. When Jesus appeared to the disciples at their first gathering after Easter, Thomas was not there. While the others had told him what had happened, Thomas was still not ready to believe in Jesus' Resurrection until he had laid his hands on his wounds (**8**). Eight days later, Jesus appeared to the disciples again. This encounter with Jesus ended all of Thomas' doubt and he said to Jesus: "My Lord and my God" (**9**).

Thomas Christians

In later texts (the Thomas files and the Gospel of Thomas), which were not incorporated into the New Testament, Thomas emerges as the receiver of additional, secret revelations. Along with this, there are old stories that Thomas spread the Christian faith in Persia and India after Jesus' Resurrection. Today's "Thomas Christians" in southern India trace their roots back to the Apostle. In spite of the old age of this tradition, this could still be fictitious.

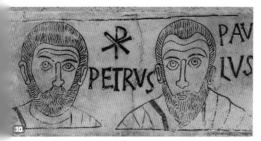

Peter and Paul Peter (pp. 450–451) and Paul (pp. 488–489) (**10**) are called the "Apostle princes." Both of them traveled to Rome, where it is said that they encountered Emperor Nero, and suffered a martyr's death. St. Peter's Cathedral was later built over his grave, whereas the relics of Paul are housed in the Basilica of Saint Paul Outside the Walls.

Death of Andrew According to the first three Gospels, Andrew—Peter's brother and a fisherman—was one of the first disciples to be called up by Jesus along with the sons of Zebedee. He played a role in the Gospel of John in the miraculous multiplication of the bread, as he pointed out a boy who had the five loaves and two fish (p. 406). Andrew was supposedly executed in Patras on a crucifix with diagonal beams (**11**), which is where the St. Andrew's Cross originates.

The Baptism of the Ethiopian
The first baptism of a gentile, which is detailed in the Book of Acts, was of an Ethiopian high official. Traveling home from Jerusalem, he had just read the writings of the prophet Isaiah when he met Phillip, a deacon (p. 500). He interpreted the words of the prophet for him and said that they indicated Jesus as the Messiah (p. 319). The Ethiopian thus found his faith and was baptized (**12**).

The Zealots

In the Gospel of Luke, a disciple appears by the name of Simon the Zealot. Before his vocation, he purportedly belonged to a group of Jewish freedom fighters, who were trying to incite an uprising against the Romans. The zealots—stemming from the Greek word "zelos"— refused to pay taxes, as they rejected coins depicting the emperor on religious grounds. The zealots held the cliff-top fortification of Masada by the Dead Sea during the Great Jewish Revolt from 66 C.E. When the fort was stormed, the zealots committed mass suicide.

>> Ethiopia: p. 245   Saints and Martyrs: pp. 484–485

Bartholomew Bartholomew was named as one of the 12 disciples called up by Jesus in the New Testament. Since the Bible contains no biographical information about him, only numerous legends exist. Bartholomew is purported to have met a martyr's death by being skinned alive (**13**) or through decapitation. Since the 11th century, he has been equated with Nathaneal, who is named as one of the first disciples in the Gospel of John. An apocryphal Gospel also carries his name.

Figures and Stories Relevant to the Apostles

Jesus of Nazareth, see pp. 402–409 and 414–419

The Evangelists, see pp. 430–433

Female Disciples, see Mary Magdalene, pp. 436–437

Judas Iscariot, see pp. 438–439

Peter, see pp. 450–453

Paul, see pp. 488–491

James Four people bear the name James in the New Testament. Jesus called James, son of Zebedee, and his brother the "sons of thunder," possibly as a play on their energetic temperament. James was probably the first of the 12 to suffer a martyr's death, when he was executed by sword under King Herod Agrippa in 44 C.E. His body supposedly made its way to Spain (**14**), where many legends (**15**) and a particular veneration of James developed.

The Way of St. James

A legend developed in the Middle Ages that James preached in Spain before his death. Another tale states that his body was subsequently brought to Santiago de Compostela by an unmanned ship. James was later alleged to have appeared to Charlemagne in a dream to ask him to liberate his grave from the Arabs. Santiago became one of the most important Christian pilgrimage sites. One of the symbols of the pilgrims on the way of St. James is the James scallop shell.

The Mission—The Transmission of the Gospel

Matthew 28:16–20

16 Now the eleven disciples went to Galilee, to the mountain to which Jesus had directed them. 17 When they saw him, they worshipped him; but some doubted. 18 And Jesus came and said to them, "All authority in heaven and on earth has been given to me. 19 Go therefore and make disciples of all nations, baptizing them in the name of the Father and of the Son and of the Holy Spirit, 20 and teaching them to obey everything that I have commanded you. And remember, I am with you always, to the end of the age."

■ Peter was the most important of Jesus' disciples

■ Peter is considered to be the founder of the Roman Church

■ His name was actually Simon, while Peter was a nickname meaning "rock"

Matthew 14:22–33 Peter tries to walk on water like Jesus

Matthew 16:13–20; Mark 8:27–30; Luke 9:18–21; John 6:67–69 Peter openly recognizes that Jesus is the Messiah

Matthew 16:17–20 Peter is labeled as the "rock" by Jesus and receives the keys to heaven

John 18: 10–11 While Jesus is being arrested, Peter cuts off a guard's ear

Matthew 26:69–75; Mark 14:66–72; Luke 22:54–62; John 18:12–27 After Jesus is taken prisoner, Peter denies him

Luke 24:12; John 20:1–10 Peter and John see Jesus' empty tomb

Acts 2:37–47 Peter establishes the first Christian community in Rome

And I tell you, you are Peter, and on this rock I will build my church, and the gates of Hades will not prevail against it. Matthew 16:18

Peter

In the Gospels and Acts, Peter is the most significant and frequently mentioned of Jesus' disciples. His birth name was Simon, but Jesus gave him the new name Peter (Greek: "rock").

The pope's coat of arms has keys, which reflect the symbolic transmission of leadership given to Peter by Jesus

Jesus met the fisherman Simon and his brother Andrew in Capernaum on the Sea of Galilee (**1**) (p. 442) and summoned them to be his disciples. The Gospels describe Peter as impulsive and committed, but sometimes scared and erratic. He was the first of the Apostles, but in the hour of the Crucifixion, he betrayed Jesus. On several occasions, Peter speaks for the disciples, most notably with the acknowledgment that Jesus was the Messiah: When Jesus asked the disciples who they thought he was, Peter answered: "You are the Christ!" But when Jesus told the disciples of his suffering and Peter protested against it, he was uncharacteristically sternly

①

Jesus as the Messiah: p. 404 **The Miracles of Jesus:** pp. 406–407

Jesus Walks on Water One night, the disciples were caught in a storm while on a boat in the middle of the Sea of Galilee. When Jesus walked on the water toward the boat, the disciples recognized him and Peter tried to meet him on the water (**2**). On the way, he became afraid and fell into the water. Jesus held out his hand to save him, then rebuked him for his lack of faith.

Keys to Heaven With a play on words, Jesus made clear the special position accorded to Peter: "You are Peter, and on this rock I will build my church" (**3**). It was in this way that Peter was assigned a leading role that was supplemented by the promise: "I will give you the keys of the kingdom of heaven" (**4**). Thus, Jesus put Peter in charge of his followers after his death and Resurrection. The powers associated with this calling, such as the absolution of sins, play an important role in the office of the pope today (p. 454). The pope is traditionally viewed as Peter's successor by Catholics. This is symbolized by the keys on the pope's coat of arms.

rebuked with: "Get behind me, Satan!"

After the women, Peter was the first male witness of the resurrected Christ on Easter morning (pp. 424–425). In Acts, Peter was the leading figure in management of the early Christian community in Jerusalem. After an intense debate between Peter and Paul, the Apostolic Council agreed with Paul's speech to make circumcision nonmandatory for Christians. After this, it was also decided that non-Jews be permitted to become Christians whereas before only Jewish people could convert (p. 489).

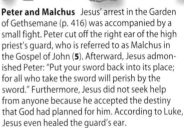

⑤

Peter and Malchus Jesus' arrest in the Garden of Gethsemane (p. 416) was accompanied by a small fight. Peter cut off the right ear of the high priest's guard, who is referred to as Malchus in the Gospel of John (**5**). Afterward, Jesus admonished Peter: "Put your sword back into its place; for all who take the sword will perish by the sword." Furthermore, Jesus did not seek help from anyone because he accepted the destiny that God had planned for him. According to Luke, Jesus even healed the guard's ear.

Peter Denies Jesus Soon after Peter had expressed his limitless loyalty to Jesus, his faith was tested, which ended in a great humiliation. As Jesus was arrested and brought before the high priest. Peter, meanwhile, ventured into the high priest's palace (**6**) to find out what was happening. When they heard his Galilee dialect, the people asked if he was one of Jesus' followers. Afraid, Peter denied knowing Jesus three times. After the third denial, a rooster (**7**) crowed, just as Jesus had foretold Peter felt ashamed of his betrayal and burst into tears. Like all of Jesus' followers, he did not understand the suffering of Jesus.

6

High Priests: p. 234   **Easter:** pp. 426–427

Peter's Works Acts reports that Peter and the rest of the Apostles performed many miracles in Jerusalem. The people took the sick out of their beds and brought them to the street on stretchers, hoping that Peter's shadow would fall on them and heal them (**8**). The stories of these miracles and the preaching of the Apostles enticed many people to join the early Christian community, which grew immensely. Emboldened by a vision, Peter performed the first baptism on a non-Jew, the Roman captain, Cornelius (**9**).

Peter's Death Sources outside of the Bible from the early second century recount Peter's legendary death during the Christian persecution under Emperor Nero in Rome. He was supposedly crucified upside down (**10**). According to the Acts of Peter—a writing not included in the New Testament—Peter was fleeing from Rome when he met the resurrected Christ (**11**). Peter asked him: "Quo vadis?" ("Where are you going?"), and Christ answered: "To Rome, to be crucified a second time." Thus, Peter returned and was crucified.

⏩ **Saints and Martyrs:** pp. 484–485

The Church

Today, people think the word "church" refers to an organization or a building. In the New Testament, the word represented the community of the followers of Jesus. "Church" was tantamount to the Jews and pagans, a bond similar to that between God and Israel (pp. 142–143). Contrary to Judaism, which bases one's inclusion upon birth, the Christian church based membership on baptism.

Jesus' followers, who met together after Easter, founded the first communities from bases in Galilee and Judea. These evolved into widespread networks of the early Christian church, partly due to Paul's missionary work (pp. 490–491).

The Church symbolized by the figure of a woman

The Pope Elements of today's Church structure can already be recognized in the New Testament, particularly within Timothy's first letter from around 100 C.E. For example, a differentiation is made between deacons (p. 500) and bishops. The Catholic Church went further and created the concept of the pope (**2**), the bishop of Rome (**3**). As Peter's successor (p. 451), the pope has a special position and authority over all Catholics.

The Protestants The reformer Martin Luther (p. 492) initiated a new denominational view of Christian beliefs and the Church (2, Protestant Church Congress) at the beginning of the 16th century. The Reformation movement disputed the pope's claim to infallibility and full legal authority. Their goal was to establish a "priesthood of all believers." The name "Protestants" comes from the protestation of the Protestant princes and cities against the Imperial Diet of Speyer in 1529.

Baptism: pp. 382–383   **Easter:** pp. 426–427   **The Early Christians:** pp. 480–481

3

■ Nicodemus was a Jewish Pharisee and follower of Jesus

■ In the Bible, Nicodemus is an ambivalent character who defended Jesus, but only met with him in private

John 3:1–21 Nicodemus and Jesus have theological discussions at night, mainly about death and rebirth

John 7:40–52 Nicodemus defends Jesus against the people

John 19:39–40 Nicodemus blesses Jesus' corpse with a mixture of costly myrrh and aloes, weighing 100 pounds

Nicodemus said to him, "How can anyone be born after having grown old?" John 3:4

Nicodemus

Nicodemus is only mentioned in the Gospel of John and plays a highly ambivalent role in the narration. He was a Pharisee and a member of the upper class. When Jesus referred to him as "the teacher of Israel", it was not entirely without irony.

Scribes attending a sermon in a synagogue

Because Nicodemus also referred to Jesus as "teacher," it appears that he was a follower of Jesus. However, he only came to see him in secret at night, obviously because he feared the reaction of other Jews. After Jesus' Crucifixion, he, along with Joseph of Arimathea, helped to prepare a kingly burial in which he blessed Jesus' body with precious spices (pp. 464–465). This may have been an expression of his appreciation, or perhaps he considered Jesus' death to be final. The figure of Nicodemus reflects the difficulties that the Jewish elite faced in trying to understand Jesus' message. Yet, an appeal to overcome these hardships lies within the Gospel of John (p. 433).

The Pharisees and the Rabbis

After the second destruction of the Temple around 70 C.E. (p. 368), the Pharisees ensured the survival of Judaism through a rabbinic movement. As the founder of Rabbinic Judaism, the scribe Yochanan ben Zakkai also created a school in Palestine for Jewish legal scholarship in Yavneh (Greek: "Jamnia"). There were also similar schools founded outside of Palestine in the diaspora (Greek: "dispersal") The rabbinic teachings were reproduced in the Talmud (Hebrew: "teachings") (p. 503) and the Midrash.

Longinus

In the apocryphal Acts of Pilate, which is attributed to Nicodemus, the Roman captain who pierced the dead Jesus' side with a lance was named Longinus. According to the Gospel of John, blood and water poured from Jesus' pierced body. Later, this was understood as a symbolic indication of Christ's two natures— the divine and the human.

Jesus and Nicodemus In the Gospel of John, Jesus and Nicodemus had nightly discussions about the Kingdom of God (**1**). Jesus said that it was impossible to see the Kingdom of God if you had not been reborn. When Nicodemus did not understand how rebirth was possible, Jesus explained that he meant the rebirth "through water and the Holy Spirit"— baptism. Thus in Christianity, baptism is a rebirth.

Nicodemus Buries Jesus After Jesus' Crucifixion, Joseph of Arimathea and Nicodemus were allowed to bury Jesus, since the people who were executed were not supposed to remain hanging overnight. The fact that they used a hundred pounds of myrrh and aloes creates an image of a lavish burial. Jesus' body was wrapped in linen cloths and placed in a grave (**2**) that was provided by Joseph of Arimathea.

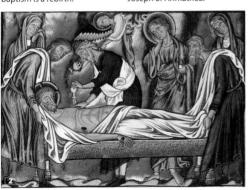

Figures and Stories Relevant to Nicodemus

God, see pp. 28–33

Jesus of Nazareth, see pp. 402–409 and 414–419

The Passion of Jesus, see pp. 420–421

The Resurrection, see pp. 424–425

John, see pp. 430–433

Joseph of Arimathea, see pp. 464–465

The Holy Spirit, see pp. 466–467

Baptism: pp. 382–383

The Pharisees

The Pharisees (Hebrew: "paruschim," or "separated ones"), who are referred to in the Gospels as both in dialogue with Jesus and in opposition to him, were a strict law-abiding group within Judaism. Although they were laymen, they followed the same purity laws that applied to the priests. For them, the oral tradition had the same authority as writings (**3**). They differed from the Sadducees (pp. 462–463), the priestly aristocracy, because of their belief in resurrection. In the Gospels, the Pharisees often appear as having self-righteous piety. However, it should not be overlooked that they often mirrored Jesus' teachings.

①

The Pharisees and Tax Collectors   Jesus typically criticized the Pharisees by comparing them to tax collectors (**1**). While both attended the services of the Temple to pray, the Pharisees were giving thanks for an opportunity to prove their piety, while the tax collectors came before God and saw that they were sinners.

Jesus and the Adulteress
In John 8:1–11, the Pharisees brought Jesus a woman who had been caught in the act of adultery, and who was supposed to be stoned (**2**). Setting a trap, they asked him to decide her fate based on the Jewish writings. However, Jesus did not answer directly; instead he stated: "Let anyone among you who is without sin be the first to throw a stone at her." Ashamed, the Pharisees left one after another. No one dared to condemn her anymore. When Jesus was left alone with the woman, he did not condemn her either.

②

≫ The Parables of Jesus: pp. 408–409

Then Pilate said to him, "Do you not hear how many accusations they make against you?" Matthew 27:13

Pontius Pilate

Pontius Pilate was the governor of the Roman province of Judea between about 27 and 37 C.E. He was given the official title of "praefectus Iudaeae" (Latin: prefect of Judea) on an inscription in the Caesarea Maritima (**1**). His time in office was marked by ruthlessness against the Jews. As the emperor gave him the office of governor as a reward for military accomplishments, it is possible that Pilate also carried the name of "friend of the emperor," with which he is cited in the Gospel of John in his story of the Passion. Although there is no clear portrait of Pilate from the Gospels, he has achieved significance in the history of theology, as he was one of the few historical figures, along with Jesus and Mary, in the Christian creed.

Pilate deflected the guilt from himself and washed his hands in innocence

■ Pontius Pilate was the governor of the province of Judea

■ Pilate is the only historical figure, along with Jesus and Mary, in the Christian creed

Matthew 27:1–14; Mark 15:1–5; Luke 23:1–5; John 18:28–38 Pilate judges Jesus

Matthew 27:24 Pilate washes his hands of guilt

Matthew 27:15–26; Mark 15:6–15; Luke 23:13–25; John 18:39–40 Pilate frees a prisoner

(1)

⟫ Roman Vassals Since Herod: pp. 362–365 and 370–371

Figures and Stories Relevant to Pontius Pilate

Passover, see pp. 118–119

Herod the Great, see pp. 362–365

The Romans, see pp. 372–373

Mary, Mother of Jesus, see pp. 386–389

Jesus of Nazareth, see pp. 402–409 and 414–419

The Passion of Jesus, see pp. 420–421

The Evangelists, see pp. 430–433

Jesus and Barabbas

Barabbas awaited a trial for high treason like Jesus. As the Romans customarily let one prisoner free at Passover, Pilate offered to release Jesus, according to the Bible (**2**). Nevertheless, the people demanded the release of Barabbas. The episode is probably unhistoric, as the amnesty was not necessarily restricted to one prisoner.

Pilate Washes His Hands

Typical of the ambivalent portrayal of Pilate in the New Testament is the episode, only described by Matthew, in which Pilate washes his hands of guilt (**3**). However, he gave the order for execution, which the crowd shouted for with increasing fervor. At the same time, he demonstrated that he considered Jesus to be innocent.

The Romans in Palestine

In 63 B.C.E., the Romans brought Palestine, which had been independent for decades, under their dominion. At first, they let independent kings and princes from the Hasmonean, or the Herodian dynasty, rule. Judea and Samaria were then incorporated into a province under direct Roman control in 6 C.E., and then the whole of Palestine in 44. The Great Jewish Revolt in 66 C.E. led to the destruction of Jerusalem by the Romans in 70. The last Jewish uprising was in 135 with the Bar-Kokhba Revolt.

Acts of Pilate: p. 457

■ Caiaphas and Annas were high priests in Jerusalem

■ Caiaphas was a clever religious politician

Matthew 26:1–5 Caiaphas is a high priest at the time of Jesus' conviction

John 18:13 Annas is Caiaphas' father-in-law

John 18:24 Annas sends the incarcerated Jesus to Caiaphas

Mark 14:60–64 Caiaphas tears his robes when Jesus claims that he is the Messiah

Then Annas sent him bound to Caiaphas the high priest. John 18:24

Caiaphas and Annas

At the time of Jesus' public ministry and execution, Caiaphas held the position of high priest. This office made him director of the priesthood for the Temple of Jerusalem, as well as the chairman of the Sanhedrin (the High Council), which made significant decisions about religious-political questions. According to the Gospel of Matthew, Caiaphas, as the acting high priest, led the proceedings against Jesus. According to the Gospel of John, Annas, Caiaphas' influential father-in-law, who had been a high priest, was also complicit. It was he who asked Jesus about his teachings and disciples. Caiaphas was a talented religious politician who understood throughout his 19-year-long term in office how to bring the wishes of the priestly aristocracy and the Roman claims to power into harmony. With the governorship of Pontius Pilate, both men collaborated for the satisfaction of both parties.

Christian Anti-Judaism

In the Passion tales of the Gospels, a great deal of the guilt for Jesus' death is placed upon his Jewish opponents. This accusation has been extended over time to Jews in general ("Jesus murderers") and provoked pogroms against Jewish communities. The partially negative portrayal of the Jews in the Gospels is a product of history and should be understood in terms of a background of gradual separation of Jews and Christians, which was in full flow during the creation of the Gospels.

Before Annas and Caiaphas

The roles that Caiaphas and Annas played in the trial and sentencing of Jesus are inconsistently described in the four Gospels. In the Passion account of the Gospel of John, Annas carried out the first interrogation and sent Jesus to Caiaphas (**1**). What then occurred was not discussed any further. The first three Gospels report on the interrogation by the high priests, but only Matthew mentions Caiaphas by name. When Jesus said "yes" when asked if he was the Messiah, Caiaphas tore his robes, according to Mark and Matthew, and accused Jesus of blasphemy. This scene demonstrates that Jesus' claim as the Messiah was viewed by the priestly aristocracy in political terms. Thus, Caiaphas and the High Council had reasons for the execution of Jesus, as they wanted to avoid any rupture in the balance of power between the Roman forces and the Jewish upper classes.

Sadducees and Sanhedrin

Centered at the Temple of Jerusalem, the Sadducees were a Jewish party recruited from the priesthood and affluent families. The Sanhedrin (the High Council), which was involved in the highest authority on religious questions and also the trial of Jesus, mainly consisted of Sadducees.

Figures and Stories Relevant to Caiaphas and Annas

The Romans, see pp. 372–373

Jesus of Nazareth, Questioned by Caiaphas and Annas, see pp. 402–409 and 414–419

The Passion of Jesus, see pp. 420–421

The Evangelists, see pp. 430–433

Pontius Pilate, see pp. 460–461

High Priests: p. 234   **Jesus as the Messiah:** p. 404

■ Joseph of Arimathea was one of Jesus' disciples

■ Joseph of Arimathea was a rich and respected man, who put his gravesite at the disposal of Jesus

Matthew 27:57–60; Mark 15:42–46; Luke 23:50–54; John 19:38–42 Joseph of Arimathea asks Pilate for Jesus' corpse and he wraps it in a linen cloth and entombs it

Joseph of Arimathea, a respected member of the council, who was also himself waiting expectantly for the kingdom of God, went boldly to Pilate and asked for the body of Jesus. Mark 15:43

Joseph of Arimathea

Joseph of Arimathea was an aristocratic alderman, who was possibly a member of the High Council in Jerusalem. His home city lay in Judea between Jerusalem and Joppa. He appears in the Bible exclusively in connection with the burial of Jesus. The statement in the New Testament that Joseph awaited the Kingdom of God places him in the circle of Jesus' disciples. After Jesus' death, Joseph took up the role of the other disciples, whose task it should have been to bury Jesus. Joseph thus became a contrasting figure, who presented a positive variation from the disciples who failed repeatedly. That he owned his own burial cave is proof of his wealth.

Right: Joseph's burial tomb, which is located today in Jerusalem within the Church of the Holy Sepulchre (below).

High Council: p. 463

Removal From the Cross According to the Gospel of John, Nicodemus and Joseph of Arimathea removed the body of Jesus from the Cross (**1**), anointed it, and buried it (p. 457). They did this in response to the religious rule that the condemned were not allowed to be left hanging on the cross during the Passover festival. According to the Gospel of Peter, which was not included in the New Testament, Joseph also washed Jesus' body, wrapped him in a linen cloth, and buried him in his grave. In the likewise apocryphal Acts of Pilate, he was persecuted for asking Pilate for the corpse. Joseph was locked up, but was liberated by Jesus. In the later legends of the Holy Grail, Joseph spent 40 years in jail before being freed upon the Roman destruction of Jerusalem. Supposedly, Joseph caught the blood of Christ in the wondrous Holy Grail.

Mourning for Christ The common artistic depiction of Jesus' body wrapped in linen (**2**) and lying on the ground, being mourned by women, Nicodemus, and Joseph of Arimathea has no foundation in the New Testament. It often links Jesus' removal from the Cross and his descent into hell, which is also not described in the Bible.

The Shroud of Turin

A piece of linen—14.3 x 3.6 ft or 4.36 x 1.10 m—from Turin has been venerated since the 14th century as Jesus' burial shroud. The body of a man, who has been flagellated and crucified, can be discerned on this shroud like a photonegative. The linen is disputed by scientists. Attempts to equate it with the shroud of Jesus, which went missing in 1204, remain hypotheses.

Figures and Stories Relevant to Joseph of Arimathea

» **Acta Pilati:** p. 457

■ The Holy Spirit is usually symbolized as a dove

■ The New Testament understands the Holy Spirit as a force of God

Matthew 3:13–17; Mark 1:9–11; Luke 3:21–22; John 1:32–34 The Holy Spirit descends upon Jesus

Matthew 1:18; Luke 1:35 When Mary conceives Jesus, the Holy Spirit descends upon her

Acts 2:1–13 The Holy Spirit descends upon the disciples during Pentecost

Acts 19:1–7; I Corinthians 14:14 Speaking in tongues is a sign of the Holy Spirit

And the Holy Spirit descended upon him in bodily form like a dove. And a voice came from heaven, "You are my Son, the Beloved; with you I am well pleased." Luke 3:22

The Holy Spirit

The New Testament depicts the Holy Spirit (Greek: "pneuma") as a driving force in the life of Jesus and the Church. In the first three Gospels, the Holy Spirit descended from heaven in the form of a dove during Jesus' baptism (p. 404). The dove had a long tradition as the messenger bird of ancient Middle Eastern goddesses of love. This symbol was possibly taken up as a symbol of the Holy Spirit because God called Jesus his "beloved" son during his baptism. In the Gospel of John, Jesus announced to his disciples that he would send the spirit after his Crucifixion and Resurrection, and that it would bring his works to fruition. In the communes founded by Paul, the phenomenon of speaking in tongues (pp. 500–501) was viewed as a manifestation of the Holy Spirit. Along with the Father and the Son, the Holy Spirit is the third aspect of the divine Trinity.

The Mercy Seat

In Christian art since the Middle Ages, the Mercy Seat has been the most popular way of portraying the Trinity. As a rule, it consists of three elements: The Father sits on a throne in heaven and holds his Son, the crucified Christ, in his hands. The Holy Spirit hovers over both of them in the form of a dove. This motif has been around since the 12th century, but the name "Mercy Seat" dates back to a translation by William Tyndale of Martin Luther's German term "Gnadenstuhl" from the Epistle to the Hebrews. Due to its connection with the Last Supper, the Mercy Seat is often integrated into great altar compositions.

⟫ The Holy Trinity: p. 32   **Animals in the Bible:** p. 140

Conception of Jesus According to the stories of Matthew and Luke, the Holy Spirit descended upon Mary at the conception of Jesus, while the angel Gabriel announced it to her (p. 387) (**1**). The concept of a virginal birth should be understood as a statement of faith. It asserts that the son of this virgin was the Son of God from the very beginning of his mortal existence.

Pentecost Pentecost is celebrated 50 days after Easter. It developed from the Jewish holiday of Shabuoth, which is celebrated on the 50th day after Passover in remembrance of the Covenant on Mount Sinai. According to the Books of Acts, the Holy Spirit came down upon the disciples on this day in the form of tongues of flame (**2**). This is supposed to have enabled the disciples to speak with the pilgrims, who came to Jerusalem from all over the world, in their own languages.

» **The Virgin Birth:** p. 388

The Pentecost Miracle—The Holy Spirit Descends Upon the Disciples of Jesus

Acts 2:1–12

1 *When the day of Pentecost had come, they were all together in one place.*
2 *And suddenly from heaven there came a sound like the rush of a violent wind, and it filled the entire house where they were sitting.*
3 *Divided tongues, as of fire, appeared among them, and a tongue rested on each of them.*
4 *All of them were filled with the Holy Spirit and began to speak in other languages, as the Spirit gave them ability.*
5 *Now there were devout Jews from every nation under heaven living in Jerusalem.*
6 *And at this sound the crowd gathered and was bewildered, because each one heard them speaking in the native language of each.*
7 *Amazed and astonished, they asked, "Are not all these who are speaking Galileans?*
8 *And how is it that we hear, each of us, in our own native language?*
9 *Parthians, Medes, Elamites, and residents of Mesopotamia, Judea and Cappadocia, Pontus and Asia,*
10 *Phrygia and Pamphylia, Egypt and the parts of Libya belonging to Cyrene, and visitors from Rome, both Jews and proselytes,*

11 *Cretans and Arabs—in our own languages we hear them speaking about God's deeds of power."*
12 *All were amazed and perplexed, saying to one another, "What does this mean?"*

The Holy Spirit descended upon the disciples of Jesus in the form of fiery tongues during Pentecost.

Pentecost

The Christian festival of Pentecost developed from the Jewish holiday week of Shabuoth. The festival celebrates the descent of the Holy Spirit (**1,3**), which was dated by Acts as taking place on Jewish Pentecost day, 50 days after the feast of Passover. For the disciples, the arrival of the Holy Spirit had been announced to them by Jesus before his Ascension. It is possible to consider the Pentecost as the beginning of the Christian Church, as well as the start of global missionary work. The first consequence of the emanation of the Holy Spirit was the Pentecost miracle, as the Holy Spirit overcame the divisional borders of different languages: The Apostles could speak in other peoples' languages and hear others speak in their own. There is a song in the Latin Pentecost liturgy in remembrance of the disciples who had assembled in Jerusalem, which asks for the continued support of the Holy Spirit with the words "Come, Holy Spirit" (Veni, Sancte Spiritus).

Pentecostal Churches

Christian "Pentecostal Churches" emphasize the importance of the Holy Spirit (**2**). The "gifts of the Spirit" (charismas) play a special role, as described by Paul. Charismatic phenomena such as speaking in tongues, prophetic discourses, and healings are typical of the Pentecostal movement. In some parts of the world, this movement has become popular in recent times.

>> The Ascension: pp. 428–429

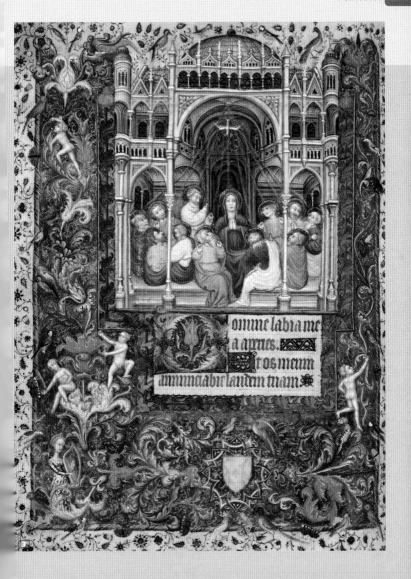

The Spreading of the Gospel

The Apostle Paul proclaims the Gospel in Athens

The Spreading

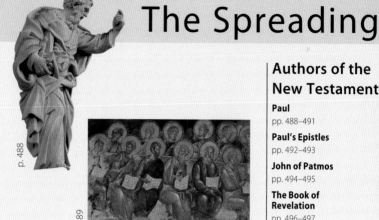

Authors of the New Testament

p. 488

p. 489

0   10   20   30   40   50

p. 484

p. 483

of the Gospel

p. 488

p. 497

p. 496

The Early Christians

p. 483

p. 480

The Spreading of the Gospel

Soon after the death of Jesus on the Cross (**2**), the Gospel (from the Old English: "god spell" and Greek: "Evangelion") of Jesus' Resurrection started to spread from the early Christian community in Jerusalem to the entire Syrian province. The large Christian community that originated in the Syrian city of Antioch was at first completely composed of non-Jewish parishioners. Although Jews were not traditionally allowed to eat with non-Jews, both Judeo-Christians and Pagan Christians shared communal meals.

The fact that pagans could now become Christian without having had to be Jewish beforehand opened the message of Christianity to the rest of the Greco-Roman world. This was confirmed in 48 C.E. by the Apostolic Council. At the same time, Peter and Paul (**1**) agreed that Peter would preach to the Jews and Paul would preach to the pagans. Paul kept in contact with the newly established congregations throughout the entire Mediterranean region with his Epistles (Greek: letters). Today, they are the oldest part of the New Testament and mark the transition from the oral to the written transmission of the Gospel.

Most of the New Testament writings originated between around 70 and 120 C.E. After Paul's Epistles, the four Gospels first appeared. The term "gospel" expanded to mean not only the good news of the death and Resurrection of Jesus, but also denote a literary genre in which Jesus' biography was told as a theologi- cal interpretation. Mark was the first one to write such a Gospel. While Matthew and Luke broadened Mark's model and added other influences that were drawn from extra oral traditions from the Q document, which is a postulat- ed lost source for the Gospel of Matthew and Gospel of Luke. John com- posed a theological biography of Jesus that was influenced by Mark, Matthew, and Luke, but in many aspects set its own course.

Half a century later, the four Gospels were formulated, but there was still plenty of oral tradition being circulated. Various collections of the preachings of Jesus and reports of his works originated from these, and they then served as a basis for religious education in the Christian community. These were com- piled into three groups of writings, which were not put in the New Testament: the Apocrypha (Greek: "hidden things"), the writings of the apostolic fathers, and the literature of the Christian gnostics (Greek: "knowledge"). The Apoc- rypha is a collection of the material that has not yet been deemed canonical and that has been handed down in various ways. The apostolic fathers were Christian writers from the time around and after 100 C.E., from whom, among other things, letters were handed down. The gnostics were a movement in which various religious and philosophical traditions were merged together, including elements from the philosophy of Plato. A stark comparison between the (good) spirit and the (evil) matter was typical for them. The gnostics' relationship with Christianity was tense. While there was influence shared on both sides, the gnostics were seen as opponents and were fought against by the early Church.

The Gospels and Paul's Epistles were read during the Christian services, as well as the Hebrew Bible, which was simply referred to as "the writings." As time went by, the question of which texts should be included in the parish's distributed writings brought into question the establishment of a canon (Greek: "standard"), which would streamline the Christian belief system. The selection of texts compiled to form today's New Testament is the result of a long process. In 140 C.E., there was an initiative in Rome, headed by the gnostic Markion, to only accept a short summary of Luke's Gospel and several of Paul's Epistles in the Christian canon. However, this proposal was not approved and it provoked more precise definitions. In 367 C.E., the bishop Athanasius of Alexandria compiled the 27 books that form today's New Testament. Since about 400 C.E., this compilation of the New Testament has been generally accepted. In contemporary times, it is considered to be an authoritative collection of the basic Christian belief system. Since Erasmus of Rotterdam, discussions regarding the canon have been opened, such as Martin Luther's creation of his own canon in German. On the other side of these historical differences, the Gospel of Jesus Christ (**3**) and the hope of his return are the creed that binds together all Christians around the world.

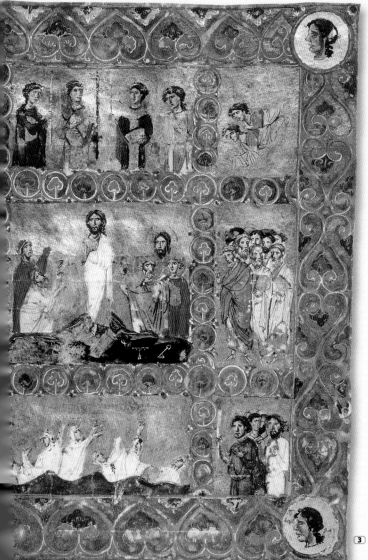

3

The Early Christians— Underground Church

After the Easter and Pentecost experiences, a Christian community emerged from the circle of Jesus' followers in Jerusalem. They awaited the return of Christ, which would initiate the Last Judgment. Paul and other missionaries quickly spread the Gospel in Palestine and beyond through their missionary work. As Christianity began to emerge as its own autonomous religion, it attracted Rome's suspicion. They considered the Christians' monotheistic belief to be politically dangerous. As it eliminated the practice of sacrifices to the Roman gods, it was dangerous to the state, according to the Roman point of view. When Rome was devastated by fire in 64 C.E. under Emperor Nero, he blamed the Christians and had many of them executed (**3**). The persecution of Christians continued in the Roman Empire until the Edict of Milan under Constantine in 313 C.E.

Symbol of Christ The fish served as an identification mark for the first Christians (**1**). During the time of persecution in the Roman Empire, the Christians would trace two lines in the sand in the form of a fish to identify fellow Christians. When the other person recognized the symbol, it meant that they were also a Christian. The Greek word for fish is *ikhthus*, and it was used as an acronym in which each letter (in Greek it is five) represents the first letter of a description of Jesus. In English, this translates as "Jesus—Anointed—God—Son—Savior."

Catacombs Since the Roman Christians were not allowed to have their own cemetery, they began to bury their dead in underground chambers located on the outskirts of the city. This was the origin of the catacombs; a narrow system of underground passageways with hollowed grooves in which to place bodies (**2**). The numerous inscriptions and wall paintings in the catacombs grant insight into the lives and beliefs of the early Christian communities.

⏩ **From the Descendants of Adam and Eve to David:** pp. 208–209

■ Stephen was one of Jerusalem's early Christian deacons

■ Stephen was stoned to death and is considered a martyr

Acts 6:1–6 The Jerusalem community elects seven people to care for the poor; one is Stephen

Acts 6:8–10 Stephen performs a miracle

Acts 7:54–60 Stephen is stoned to death

Stephen, full of grace and power, did great wonders and signs among the people. Acts 6:8

Stephen

According to Acts, the immense growth of the early Christian community in Jerusalem led to a large number of issues that required more leadership than the 12 Apostles alone.

St. Stephen reliquary

Therefore, the office of the deacons was created, and they were given the responsibility of taking care of the widows and the poor in the community. Along with Stephen, there were six other men who were called to this office. They all took on Greek names, since they represented the Greek-speaking group (the "Hellenists" differing from the Aramaic-speaking "Hebrews") in the community. With his sermons (**1**) and miracles, Stephen provoked the anger of the Jewish High Council.

①

» **High Council / Sanhedrin :** p. 463   **Saints and Martyrs :** pp. 484–485

Stephen Is Blessed Together with Philip, Prochorus, Nicanor, Timon, Parmenas, and Nicholas, Stephen worked with the Apostles of the early Christian community in Jerusalem (**2**). With prayers and blessings, they were given the office of deacon so that they could spread the teachings of the Gospel.

Stephen Is Stoned Speaking before the High Council, Stephen tried to show that the Israelites had been in opposition to God and the Holy Spirit since the start. He argued that they had not followed the laws given to Moses, and had persecuted the prophets sent by God—including Jesus. This outraged the High Council so much that they condemned him to be stoned to death for blasphemy (**3**).

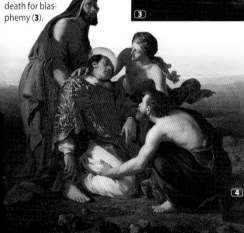

Stephen Is Buried Acts portrays the martyrdom of Stephen with strong similarities to the suffering of Jesus during the Crucifixion. Like Jesus, Stephen prayed for his persecutors in the hour of his death. Just as Jesus had laid his own spirit back in the hands of his Father, the dying Stephen laid his spirit in Jesus' hands. After the cruel stoning, his death was described as peaceful. Stephen was the first martyr who died for his belief in Jesus (**4**).

Saints and Martyrs— A Model of Belief

In the Bible, saintliness is a characteristic of God. However, in Paul's letters or in Peter's first letter, the Christians were also generally addressed as "saint." In the early Church, people soon began to honor particular Christians who in some way had modeled Christian beliefs and life. During the persecution of Christians in the Roman Empire, martyrs were often branded as saints as they had died for their beliefs, such as St. Sebastian (**4**). Later, saints were named for their actions in life, including Augustine, Elizabeth of Thüringen, Francis of Assisi, and Teresa of Ávila. A popular saint is also Christopher (**1**), who was supposed to have carried the child Jesus on his shoulders across a river.

Edith Stein Born in 1891 to a Jewish family (**2**), Edith Stein was named a saint by Pope John Paul II in 1988. As a philosopher, she became a Christian through reading the writings of the Spanish mystic Teresa of Ávila. In 1933, she entered the Carmelite cloister in Cologne. In vain, she appealed to Pope Pius XI to intervene in the Nazi persecution of the Jews. In 1942, she was killed in the gas chambers of Auschwitz for her Jewish ancestry.

Halloween Halloween (from "All Hallows Eve") is a celebration on the eve of All Saint's Day (November 1st). Originating from Ireland, Halloween has diffused to the United States and the world. Dressing up in costumes and carving pumpkins has become popular with adults and children (**3**).

⟫ The Carmelites: p. 309

4

The Damascus Experience— The Conversion of Saul

Acts 9:1–8, 10–11, 15–18

¹ *Meanwhile Saul, still breathing threats and murder against the disciples of the Lord, went to the high priest* ² *and asked him for letters to the synagogues at Damascus, so that if he found any who belonged to the Way, men or women, he might bring them bound to Jerusalem.* ³ *Now as he was going along and approaching Damascus, suddenly a light from heaven flashed around him.* ⁴ *He fell to the ground and heard a voice saying to him, "Saul, Saul, why do you persecute me?"* ⁵ *He asked, "Who are you, Lord?" The reply came, "I am Jesus, whom you are persecuting.* ⁶ *But get up and enter the city, and you will be told what you are to do."* ⁷ *The men who were traveling with him stood speechless because they heard the voice but saw no one.* ⁸ *Saul got up from the ground, and though his eyes were open, he could see nothing; so they led him by the hand and brought him into Damascus.* ¹⁰ *Now there was a disciple in Damascus named Ananias. The Lord said to him ...* ¹¹ *"Get up and go to the street called Straight, and at the house of Judas look for a man of Tarsus named Saul. At this moment he is praying ...* ¹⁵ *Go, for he is an instrument whom I have chosen to bring my name before Gentiles and kings and before the people of Israel;* ¹⁶ *I myself will show him how much he must suffer for the sake of my name."*

17 So Ananias ... laid his hands on Saul and said, "Brother Saul, the Lord Jesus, who appeared to you on your way here, has sent me so that you may regain your sight and be filled with the Holy Spirit." 18 And immediately something like scales fell from his eyes, and his sight was restored. Then he got up and was baptized.

■ Paul is thought to be the writer of numerous New Testament letters

■ Paul is considered one of the most significant Apostles

Circumcised on the eighth day, a member of the people of Israel, of the tribe of Benjamin, a Hebrew born of Hebrews. Philippians 3:5

Paul

Although he was not one of the original 12 disciples summoned by Jesus, Paul was the most important Apostle, as well as the writer of numerous letters. As a member of the Jewish diaspora (p. 500), he bore the Jewish name Saul along with his Latin name Paul; he also had Roman citizenship. He came from the city of Tarsus in Asia Minor, where he had learned the tent-making trade. In Jerusalem, he had a Pharisaic upbringing and in the beginning persecuted the Christians. After the Damascus experience (**1**), he ▷▷

①

Paul Flees From Damascus When Paul began to preach in the synagogues that Jesus was the son of God, the Jews of Damascus tried to arrest him. Unable to leave without being detected, Paul was lowered down from the city wall at night in a basket (**2**). Thus, he was able to escape for Jerusalem. Once there, the people of the Christian community were afraid of him because he had been a persecutor of the Jews. Barnabas, an important member of the community, was the first one who put aside his distrust.

Paul and Timothy Timothy, the son of a Jewish mother and a heathen father was designated by Paul as his "beloved child" (**3**). He accompanied Paul on his second mission to Greece, where both of them established communities in Philippi, Thessalonica, and Corinth. When Paul was absent Timothy took care of these communities in his place.

The Apostolic Council As more and more non-Jews joined the Christian community, there were conflicts. Many Judeo-Christians thought that the Pagan-Christians should also be circumcised. The Apostolic Council in Jerusalem (**4**) confirmed Paul's opinion: The non-Jews must not become Jews in order to be able to be Christian.

Paul's Epistles: pp. 492–493

became a passionate preacher of the Gospel. He proved to be a great mediator between the Jews and the non-Jews (pagans). His missions, during which he created numerous church communities, took him to Asia Minor and Greece (**7**, Corinth). He was the first great Christian theologian. The influence of his theology, in which the Crucifixion and the Resurrection were central, cannot be overestimated. Without him, Christianity would probably have remained a Jewish reform group instead of an entire alternative religion.

Paul and Barnabas in Lystra In Lystra, located in Asia Minor, a cripple was listening to Paul. When Paul healed him (**5**), the people thought that Barnabas, Paul's companion, was Zeus and that Paul was Hermes. With much effort, they were able to stop the people from making a sacrifice (**6**).

Paul in Ephesus

Ephesus was the center of Paul's missionary work in Asia Minor. In Acts, Paul performed great miracles there. When he removed a demon from a young man, the indigenous people were so impressed that they burned their spell books (**8**). However, a more serious conflict emerged when the silversmiths, who created statues of the god Artemis, saw Paul as a danger to their business. A mass of rioters gathered, but at the last moment the town administrator was able to calm everyone down with a clever speech.

Paul's Execution

During a visit to Jerusalem, Paul was taken prisoner. Since his opponents' accusations had not been cleared, even after two years of prison in Caesarea, he made an appeal to the Emperor and was taken to Rome. Acts ends with him being held in a low-security prison so that he was still able to preach the Gospel. According to legend, Paul was later executed by sword in Rome (**10**).

Figures and Stories Relevant to Paul

Jesus of Nazareth, see pp. 402–409 and 414–419

Luke, Author of the Acts of the Apostles, see the Evangelists, pp. 430–433

The Apostles, see pp. 442–447

Peter, Fellow in the Apostolic Council, see pp. 450–453

Saints and Martyrs, see pp. 484–485

The Damascus Experience, see pp. 486–487

Paul's Shipwreck

Toward the end of Acts, Luke tells the story of how Paul was shipwrecked by a storm while he was on the way to Rome. Shortly after the landing in Malta, he started collecting small sticks for a fire and was bitten by a snake (**9**). The indigenous people thought that the goddess of vengeance wanted to kill the people who had just been saved. When nothing happened, they thought that he was a god. Paul stayed in Malta for three months before he continued his trip to Rome.

Paul's Epistles and Missions

Paul (**1**) stayed in contact with the communities that he had established on his missions by writing letters. These Epistles, written between 50 and 55 C.E., are the oldest writings of the New Testament and were sent to communities (**4**) in the cities of Thessalonica, Rome, Corinth, Philippi, and in Galatia. They mirror Paul's worries for the community. According to most scholars, other Epistles in his name were composed by his students.

Paul and Women Unlike the pastoral Epistles written by Paul's students (for example, both Epistles from Timothy and the Titus Epistle), Paul was not a misogynist. In Paul's commune, women such as Phoebe and Priska held leading positions. They performed offices at the same level as men, as equality was a specific characteristic of the early Christians. In contrast, the letter to the Corinthians (14:34–36) contains the much cited quote that women should be silent and subordinate within the community. In many churches, this statement is a fundamental argument used to deny women the possibility of being ordained as priests (**3**). However, many scholars consider this passage to be a later addition. Both the supporters and opponents of female priests base their arguments on Paul's Epistles.

Luther and Paul
Paul's thoughts played a central role in the Reformation. Through his theological studies, the young Martin Luther (**2**) found an answer to a pressing question about the absolution of sin before God. Based on the first chapter of Paul's Epistle to the Romans, he created the main theme of his theology: Absolution was made possible through faith (Latin: "sola fide") and not through works.

›› **Jesus and Women:** p. 436   **The Church:** pp. 454–455

⌈ CRIOS ·II·

Incipit prologus in ſcdm epiſtolam
Poſt actam ad ꝛoꝛinthi.
corinthios penitentiam
conſolatoꝛiam ſcribit eis epiſtolam apoſtol⁹ a troade
per ꝃhitū: et collaudēs eos hoꝛtās ad
meliora: triſtatos quidē eos ſed emē-
datos oſtendēs. Explicit ꝓlogus.
Incipit epla ſcdm ad corinthios.

Paulus apoſtolus
criſti iheſu per volū-
tatem dei et thimo-
teus frater: eccleſie
dei que eſt corinthi
cū omnibus ſanctis qui
ſunt in univſa achaia. Gratia vobꝭ
et pax a deo patre noſtro ⁊ dūo noſtro
iheſu criſto. Benedict⁹ deus et pater dūi nri
iheſu criſti pater miſericordiaꝛ: ⁊ deus
totius ꝛſolationis: qui cōſolat⁹ nos
in omni tribulatione noſtra: ut poſſi-
mus et ipſi conſolari eos qui in omni
preſſura ſunt per exhortationē qua exhortamur et ipi a deo: quoniā ſicut ha-
bundant paſſiones criſti in nobis: ita
et per criſtū habūdat ſolatio noſtra.
Siue autē tribulamur pro veſtra exhoꝛ-
tatione et ſalute: ſiue cōſolamur pro
veſtra conſolatione: ſiue exhortamur
pro veſtra exhortatione ⁊ ſalute: que oꝑa-
ratur tolleratiā earūdem paſſionum
quas et nos patimur: ut ſpes noſtra
firma ſit pro vobis: ſcientes quoniā
ſicut ſocij paſſionū eſtis: ſic eritis
⁊ cōſolationis. Nō eni volum⁹ igno-
rare vos fratres de tribulatione nra
que facta eſt i aſia: quoniā ſupra mo-
dū grauati ſum⁹ ſupra virtute: ita ut
tederet nos etiā viuere. Sed ipi in no-
biſmetipſis reſpōſum moꝛtis habui-
mus: ut nō ſim⁹ fidentes in nobis ſed
in deo qui ſuſcitat moꝛtuos: qui de tātis

periculis nos eripuit et eruit: in quem
ſperam⁹ quoniā et adhuc eripiet ad-
iuuātibꝰ et vobis in oratione pro nobis: ut ex multaꝛ perſonis facieꝛ eius
que in nobis eſt dōnationis per multas
gratie agant pro nobis. Nam glori-
a noſtra hec eſt teſtimoniū cōſcientie
noſtre: qp in ſimplicitate coꝛdis et ſin-
ceritate dei et non in ſapiētia carnali
ſed in gratia dei cōuerſati ſum⁹ in hoc
mūdo: habundantius autē ad vos.
Nō eni alia ſcribimus vobis qp que
legiſtis et cognouiſtis. Spero autem
qp uſqꝫ i finē agnoſcetis: ſicut ⁊ cognouiſtis nos ex parte: qa gloria veſtra
ſum⁹ ſicut et vos noſtra i die dūi nri
iheſu criſti. Et hac confidētia volui pri⁹
us venire ad vos ut ſecūdam gratiā
haberetis: et per vos tranſire in mace-
doniam et iteꝛu a macedonia venire
ad vos et a vobis deduci in iudeam.
Cū ergo hoc voluiſſen: nūquid leui-
tate uſus ſum? Aut que cogito ſcdm
carnē cogito ut ſit apud me eſt et nō?
Fidelis autē deus quia ſermo noſter
qui fuit apud vos nō fuit in illo eſt ⁊ nō
ſed eſt in illo eſt. Dei eni fili⁹ iheſus cri-
ſtus qui in vobis per nos pdicat⁹ eſt
per me ⁊ ſiluanū ⁊ ꝺhimotheū nō fuit
in illo eſt et nō: ſed eſt i illo fuit. Quot-
quot eni promiſſiones ꝺei ſunt i illo ē.
Ideo et per ipſm amen deo ad gloriā
nrām. Qui autē ꝺfirmat nos vobiſcū
i criſto: ⁊ qui unxit nos deꝰ: et qui ſigna-
uit nos ⁊ dedit pign⁹ ſpirit⁹ in coꝛdi-
bus nris. Ego aut teſte ꝺei inuoco in
animā meam qp parcens vobis non
veni ultꝛa corinthum: non quia do-
minamur fidei veſtre ſed adiutores ſu-
mus gaudij veſtri: nā fide ſtatis.

II

Statui autē hoc ipſum apud mene iterum in triſtitia venire ad

■ John of Patmos was probably the writer of the Book of Revelation

■ John of Patmos described himself as a seer

Revelation 1:1-3 John writes the Book of Revelation

Revelation 1:9–20 John is filled with the spirit of God and is told to write a book and send it to the seven communities of Asia Minor

Revelation 2–3 John wants to encourage the Christians in Asia Minor to keep faith

Revelation 20:11–15 The telling of Doomsday

Revelation 21 John talks about the new Jerusalem

John to the seven churches that are in Asia: Grace to you and peace from him who is and who was and who is to come. Revelation 1:4

John of Patmos

The last book of the New Testament, the "Revelation" (Greek: "apokalypsis," or "apocalypse") of John, was written on the Greek Aegean island of Patmos (**1**). The "seer," as John called himself, was not the same John that wrote the Gospel of John nor the three letters by John in the New Testament. This is made clear by numerous stylistic and theological differences. It is more likely that John the Seer was a person of great importance in Asia Minor and to whom the seven missives at the beginning of the book are addressed. The Doomsday visions that make up a large part of the book were written to encourage the Christians of this community to hold on to their faith in God and Christ during a time of great hardship.

▶▶ The Early Christians: pp. 480–481

The Apocalypse The term "apocalypse" refers to a literary classification that originated in Judaism. The best example was the Book of Daniel, which dates back to the Jewish persecution by the Seleucid rulers in the second century B.C.E. A similar situation during the reign of Emperor Domitian (81–96 C.E.) created the historical background of the Apocalypse. When he decreed that he be addressed as "Emperor and God," the Christians refused because of their belief in monotheism and were persecuted, especially in Asia Minor. The Apocalypse was meant to strengthen them (**3**, apocalyptic riders).

The Last Judgment At the end of John's Revelation, he envisions the Last Judgment (**2**). With this, God acts as the judge who measures the acts of people. The conclusion of the Book of Revelation creates a vision of a new heavenly Jerusalem. Thus, instead of a menacing message, a positive message about God's salvation ends the Book.

Numeric Symbolism

Throughout John's Revelation, it is typical to find numeric symbolism, which originated from the use of numbers for many letters in Hebrew. Thus, the number 666, which designated a beast bringing doom, in Hebrew transcription means "Emperor Nero." This might have represented Domitian, who considered himself to be "Nero Returned" (Latin: Nero redivivus).

New Jerusalem: pp. 498–499

The Book of Revelation

In the Book of Revelation, which is often referred to as a "picture book at the end of the Bible," one can read about the expectations of the early Christians, namely the return of Jesus. At the end of the book, Jesus says: "Yes, I am coming soon." Revelation ends with the promise by Jesus that he will return, a message of hope in the face of the hardships endured by the populations of Asia Minor. The nightmarish pictures of the Doomsday plagues that abound (**3**) in Revelation, mirror the conditions that the Christians in Asia Minor were living under during the persecution by the Romans. The hardships they were facing was never so clearly represented in the New Testament as in the book of Revelation. The final message is that God will prevail against all opponents and that salvation awaits the faithful.

Perceptions of the Afterlife The idea that a person's actions will be judged at the end of their life is a theme that goes back to ancient Egypt (**2**). In the Bible and post-biblical tradition, the archangel Michael not only guards the entry to paradise, but also the path that people take to return to God. If sin had blocked this path beforehand, Michael conquers the dragon as a symbol of sin and opens the path to God. The soul-weighing scale (**1**) and sword in Michael's hands point to God's righteousness that judges without distinction but which is also not bereft of compassion.

➤➤ **Archangels:** p. 43

The Early Christians: pp. 480–481

New Jerusalem

Revelation 21:1–8

1 Then I saw a new heaven and a new earth; for the first heaven and the first earth had passed away, and the sea was no more.

2 And I saw the holy city, the new Jerusalem, coming down out of heaven from God, prepared as a bride adorned for her husband.

3 And I heard a loud voice from the throne saying, "See, the home of God is among mortals. He will dwell with them; they will be his peoples, and God himself will be with them;

4 he will wipe every tear from their eyes. Death will be no more; mourning and crying and pain will be no more, for the first things have passed away."

5 And the one who was seated on the throne said, "See, I am making all things new." Also he said, "Write this, for these words are trustworthy and true."

6 Then he said to me, "It is done! I am the Alpha and the Omega, the beginning and the end. To the thirsty I will give water as a gift from the spring of the water of life.

7 Those who conquer will inherit these

» **From the Descendants of Adam and Eve to David:** pp. 208–209

things, and I will be their God and they will be my children.

8 But as for the cowardly, the faithless, the polluted, the murderers, the fornica-tors, the sorcerers, the idolaters, and all liars, their place will be in the lake that burns with fire and sulphur, which is the second death."

Glossary

The following entries explain selected theological expressions and basic terms related to the Bible and its development.

Apocalypse (Greek: "revelation") A genre of literature that describes the end of the world as we know it—which is often viewed negatively—and awakens hope for a new world.

Apocrypha (Greek: "hidden") Texts that have not been accepted into the biblical canon. In a narrower sense, the Apocrypha are the 14 books that are not included in today's Jewish and Protestant Bibles, but formed part of the Septuagint, the Greek translation of the Old Testament. These books are included in the Old Testament canon for the Roman Catholic and Greek Orthodox Bibles.

Apostles (Greek: "envoys") In contrast to the general term "disciples," the Apostles are considered to be the 12 successors directly called on by Jesus to spread his message. However, Paul, who was not in Jesus' circle of disciples, is also considered an Apostle.

Canon (Greek: "standard") Term for a guideline, standard or norm of belief. Later, the term was primarily used for the list of biblical texts formally recognized by the Church. Each of the various religions and denominations has its own canon.

Church (Greek: "kyriaké," "belonging to the Lord") Term for the community of believers established after the time of Jesus. The term is also used for regional religious communities, such as the "Syrian Church." The English word "church" also refers to a building in which religious services are held.

Contemplation (Latin: "observation") Thinking about and immersing oneself into spiritual questions; similar to meditation but is more related to the sphere of religion.

Deacon (Greek: "servant") A church official who carries out specific liturgical and pastoral activities. Deacons were first selected in the early Christian community in Jerusalem as helpers for the Apostles. While the deacons in the Catholic Church play an official role in worship services, they are mainly involved in social ministries within the Protestant churches.

Denomination / Religious Denomination A subgroup of a religion, such as Catholic or Lutheran as subgroups of the Christian faith.

Diaspora (Greek: "dispersal") Communities of belief which have left their homelands and now live elsewhere as religious minorities.

Disciples People who join a religious master as students and followers. In the New Testament, Jesus of Nazareth and John the Baptist both have disciples.

Dogma (Greek: "theorem") A collection of the basic beliefs of a church. In Protestant thought, dogma is known as systematic theology, because it attempts to systematize the content of belief.

Early Christian Community The first Christian community, based in Jerusalem, which arose directly after Jesus' Crucifixion under the leadership of the Apostles.

Exegesis (Greek "explanation") The interpretation and explanation of holy scriptures. In all religions, the aim of exegesis is to help make religious texts more comprehensible for believers.

Feminist Theology A recent field of research based on feminism, represented by Christian and Jewish theologians since the 1960s. Feminist theology inerprets religion within a female perspective.

Glossolalia Speaking in a manner incomprehensible to others while in an ecstatic state. Also called speaking in tongues. The ability to speak in tongues is considered a gift from the Holy Spirit.

Hebrews A term for the Israelites and the Aramaic-speaking Jews in Palestine.

High Priest Title of the leading priest of the Temple in Jerusalem. The high priest had authority over all affairs of the Temple, worship services, and the priesthood. The position was generally hereditary. With the destruction of the Temple in 70 C.E., the office of the high priest was abolished.

Historical-Critical Exegesis A special direction of research within the practice of exegesis, using a clearly defined methodology. This type of exegesis is historical because it views the Bible's existing textual form as having developed over time, and it attempts to reconstruct this historical development process. It is critical because it uses general criteria to examine texts in a scientific manner, regardless of their faith-based content.

History of Salvation God's actions that result in positive effects for humanity. The idea of the History of Salvation is linked to the Old Testament's understanding of history. History is not viewed as a series of random events, but a setting in which people experience the positive works of God. These works include the creation, God's covenant with humankind, and the Resurrection of Jesus. The History of Salvation aims toward a goal set by God.

Holy Spirit In most Christian denominations, the Holy Spirit is viewed as a form of being within the Trinitarian God. It includes God's positive, life-affirming power and can provide people with gifts such as a deeper understanding of biblical texts.

Israel According to the biblical account, the ancestry of the people of Israel trace back to the 12 sons of Jacob. After wrestling with an angel, Jacob received the name Israel (Hebrew "God's warrior") from God. The people of Israel are also called the Hebrews.

Jews The word "Jew" derives from the term for members of the tribe of Judah (Hebrew: "jehudi." After the Israelites' return from Babylonian exile, inhabitants of the earlier northern empire of Israel were also referred to as Jews. Today, all those who are born to a Jewish mother or who have converted to Judaism are considered Jews.

Judeo-Christians In biblical times, Jews who converted to Christianity were known as Judeo-Christians in contrast to "Pagan Christians."

Judgment Day The idea of Judgment Day goes back to the Jewish apocalyptic texts. The concept was further developed in Christianity and Islam to a great court in the hereafter presided over by God. Human lives are evaluated, and the decision is made to save or condemn the person. According to the New Testament account, Jesus will be the ultimate judge, dividing the righteous from the unrighteous.

Kingdom of God The Kingdom of God does not refer to a specific place, but God's reign of justice during the Last Days. In the New Testament, the Kingdom of God represents the new life offered through God's promise of salvation. The Kingdom of God is said to come with Jesus, and it will culminate on Judgment Day.

Martyrs (Greek: "witnesses") Individuals who are persecuted, suffer and die for their religion. According to early Christian thought, martyrs enter directly into heaven.

Mercy God's unconditional love for people in spite of their behavior.

Messiah (Hebrew: "anointed one") A title of honor for a person chosen by God to fulfill a specific mission to benefit humanity, for instance as a prophet or king. The Greek term is "christos," which became part of the name of Jesus of Nazareth.

Monolatry The worship of a single god, without denying the existence of other gods.

Monotheism The worship of, and belief in the existence of, only one God. Contemporary examples of monotheistic religions include Judaism, Christianity, and Islam.

Pagan-Christians In biblical times, those who were not Jews or Christians were referred to as pagans or heathens. Early Christians of non-Jewish lineage were known as "Pagan Christians" in contrast to "Judeo-Christians."

Panentheism The view that God is a personal being, present in every manifestation of the universe but also transcending it.

Pantheism In pantheism, God is viewed as being present within everything in the universe. He is considered equivalent to the idea of the universe itself and can be found everywhere in nature.

Parable A form of storytelling in which a religious or moral principle is illustrated using metaphoric language. Jesus often uses this narrative form to clarify his teachings.

Pharisees (Hebrew: "those who are set apart") A group within ancient Judaism which followed a specific theological direction. The Pharisees were mostly laypeople who highly valued the knowledge of biblical texts. Although they interpreted the Torah in a relatively pragmatic and liberal manner, they were accused in some New Testament accounts of combining superficial strictness with internal laxity.

Polytheism The worship of multiple gods.

Prophet (Greek: "speaker") Prophets, who can be men or women, have a special relationship with God, who gives them assignments and messages to convey to the people.

Qur'an The holy scripture of Islam. According to Islamic tradition, the Qur'an was received word for word by the Prophet Muhammad from the archangel Gabriel. The Qur'an is divided into 114 sections, known as Surahs.

Rabbi (Hebrew: "master" or "teacher") The position of religious teacher within the Jewish community. Rabbis are primarily concerned with the duties of preaching, teaching, pastoral counseling, and providing answers on issues of religious law.

Rapture Without experiencing death, a person is taken up to God in heaven with both body and soul, as with the prophet Elijah or Enoch in Genesis 5:24.

Sacrament (Latin: "religious secret") Acts within the church which allow people to partake of God's mercy. The acts considered sacraments vary among different religious denominations. The establishment of the sacraments can be traced back to Jesus. By participating in a sacrament, an individual can directly experience God's love.

Seder Evening The first evening and initiation of the Feast of Passover. A clearly regulated sequence of events is established for this evening—thus the term "Seder," Hebrew for "order." They include a shared meal with symbolic foods commemorating the Israelites' flight out of Egypt. In addition, religious texts are read and songs are sung.

Septuagint Greek translation of the Old Testament. The name (Latin for the number 70) refers to the 72 scholars who are said to have translated the Old Testament texts in 72 days.

Seraphim Angels with six wings. In Isaiah 6:2, they are described as covering their faces with two wings and their feet with another two, while flying with a third pair.

Setting in Life A theological term that refers to the sociological background and other contextual aspects of a particular writing. Most important to researchers is revealing the text's original function.

Sin Human behavior which harms and disturbs the relationship between the person and God. In Judaism and Christianity, sin traces back to the expulsion of Adam and Eve from the Garden of Eden: Humans damaged their relationship with God by attempting to be like God themselves. In contrast to Protestant thought, Catholic teachings differentiate the nature and degree of sins. Protestant theology emphasizes the redemption of sinners through God's mercy.

Synagogue (Greek: "gather together") The term for the Jewish place of worship, religious teaching and social gatherings.

Synoptic Gospels (Greek: "next to each other") The first three books of the New Testament—Matthew, Mark, and Luke—are known as the Synoptic Gospels. These texts show significant areas of agreement in content and construction. The fourth Gospel, the Book of John, clearly deviates from the Synoptic Gospels in both of these aspects.

Talmud (Hebrew: "teaching") After the Jewish Bible (Tanach), the Talmud is the most important text of Judaism. There are two versions of the Talmud, named after the places in which they arose: the Palestinian and the Babylonian Talmuds. The Babylonian Talmud is longer and more significant; it became the most important

foundation for decisions in matters of religious law.

Theodicy (French: "théodicée" from Greek "theós," "God," and "díke," "justice") The question of God's justice: how can a good and all-powerful God permit suffering in the world? This problem is addressed, for example, in the Old Testament's Book of Job.

Theophany A theophany (Greek: "appearance of God") occurs when God shows himself visibly to a human being, such as with Moses.

Tongues, Speaking in
See Glossolalia

Torah (Hebrew: "teaching," "law") The first five books of the Old Testament (the Hebrew Bible) are known as the Torah. In a broader sense, the term refers to the entire body of Jewish religious teachings and religious law.

Trinity The unity of God in three different persons: the Father, the Son, and the Holy Spirit.

Vulgata (Latin: "widespread") The Latin translation of the Bible, initiated by the religious teacher Jerome in the late fourth century C.E.

Zealots (Greek: "enthusiasts") The Zealots were a radical Jewish resistance movement against the Roman occupation of Judah in Jesus' time.

Motivated by religion, they viewed themselves as defenders of God's sovereignty in Israel.

Index

Bold-faced page numbers indicate the main pages of the entry. *Italicized* entries indicate biblical, literary, and musical titles.

This edition was originated by Peter Delius Verlag

Authors: Dr. Christian Cebulj (pp. 352–499),
Frauke Dobek (pp. 200–259, 296–351, 500–503),
Prof. Dr. Ursula Rudnick (pp. 14–199, 260–295)

Editors: Detlef Berghorn, Michele Greer, Udo Richter
Editorial Assistants: Olivia De Santos, Alma Fathi
Translators: Charles Booth, Patricia Linderman
Layout Assistant: Angela Aumann
Graphic Design: Burga Fillery

The publishers would like to express their gratitude to akg-images Berlin/London/Paris, dpa Deutsche Presse Agentur, Hamburg, fotolia, iStockphoto, NASA – National Aeeronautics and Space, and Bill Adler, Ahuvah Berger, David Bjorgen, BJ Bolender, Karen Brinkman Rogers, Dale C. Carr, Simson Garfinkel, Fairouz Hammache, Heatkernel, Philipp Hohage, Evan Lewis, Libär, Stanislao Loffreda, Alexandru Macarii, Parkerman & Christie, Tim Read, Helen Savill, Oren Shavit, Richard Shotton, Mark Twells and Benjamin E. Wood for the permission of image reproduction in this book. For detailed credits, links and picture captions please visit our website www.theKnowledgePage.com

National Geographic
Essential Visual History of the Bible

Published by the National Geographic Society
John M. Fahey, Jr., President and Chief Executive Officer
Gilbert M. Grosvenor, Chairman of the Board
Nina D. Hoffman, Executive Vice President; President, Book Publishing Group

Kevin Mulroy, Senior Vice President and Publisher
Marianne R. Koszorus, Director of Design
Barbara Brownell Grogan, Executive Editor
Carl Mehler, Director of Maps
Judith Klein, Project Manager
Gary Colbert, Production Director

Founded in 1888, the National Geographic Society is one of the largest nonprofit scientific and educational organizations in the world. It reaches more than 285 million people worldwide each month through its official journal, NATIONAL GEOGRAPHIC, and its four other magazines; the National Geographic Channel; television documentaries; radio programs; films; books; videos and DVDs; maps; and interactive media. National Geographic has funded more than 8,000 scientific research projects and supports an education program combating geographic illiteracy.

For more information, please call
1-800-NGS LINE (647-5463)
or write to the following address:

National Geographic Society
1145 17th Street N.W.
Washington, D.C. 20036-4688 U.S.A.

Visit us online at www.nationalgeographic.com/books

Library of Congress Cataloging-in-Publication Data available upon request.

ISBN: 978-1-4262-0217-9
Printed in China